Practical Nutrition
A Quick Reference for the Health Care Practitioner

Margaret D. Simko, Ph.D., R.D.

Professor Emerita
Director, Center for Food and Hotel Management
Consultant, Department of Home Economics and Nutrition
New York University
New York, New York

Catherine Cowell, M.S., Ph.D.

Director, Bureau of Nutrition
New York City Department of Health
Adjunct Professor, Department of Home Economics and Nutrition
New York University
New York, New York

Maureen S. Hreha, M.S.N., P.N.P., R.N.

Assistant Professor of Nursing
Raritan Valley Community College
Somerville, New Jersey
Director, American Nanny Academy, Inc.
Edison, New Jersey
Consultant, Child Care and Child Health Care
Edison, New Jersey

AN ASPEN PUBLICATION®
Aspen Publishers, Inc.   1989

Rockville, Maryland
Royal Tunbridge Wells

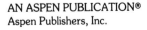

Library of Congress Cataloging-in-Publication Data

Practical nutrition.
"An Aspen publication."
Includes bibliographies and index.
1. Diet therapy. 2. Nutrition. I. Simko, Margaret D.
II. Cowell, Catherine. III. Hreha, Maureen S.
[DNLM: 1. Diet. 2. Nutrition. QU 145 P896]
RM217.2.P73   1989   615.8′54   88-35105
ISBN: 0-8342-0048-1

The authors have made every effort to ensure the accuracy of the information herein,
particularly with regard to drug selection and dose. However, appropriate information
sources should be consulted, especially for new or unfamiliar procedures. It is the
responsibility of every practitioner to evaluate the appropriateness of a particular
opinion in the context of actual clinical situations and with due consideration to new
developments. Authors, editors, and the publisher cannot be held responsible for any
typographical or other errors found in this book.

Editorial Services: Mary Beth Roesser

Library of Congress Catalog Card Number: 88-35105
ISBN: 0-8342-0048-1

Printed in the United States of America

1 2 3 4 5

To Michael, my husband, for his help and encouragement.

M.D.S.

To Vernon and Virginia for their loyal support.

C.C.

To Mike, Adam, and Eric.

M.S.H.

Table of Contents

Contributors

Irene R. Alton, M.S., R.D.
Chief Nutritionist
Health Start/St. Paul Ramsey Medical
  Center
St. Paul, Minnesota

Garland D. Anderson, M.D.
Professor and Chief
Maternal/Fetal Division
Department of Obstetrics and Gynecology
University of Tennessee
Memphis, Tennessee

Adriana G. Austin, Ph.D., R.N.
Assistant Professor
College of Nursing
Rutgers–The State University of New
  Jersey
Newark, New Jersey

Claudette Austin, M.A., R.D.
Clinical Pediatric Nutritionist
University of Medicine and Dentistry of
  New Jersey
Newark, New Jersey

**Rosemary Barber-Madden, Ed.D.,
  R.N.**
Associate Clinical Professor of Public
  Health
Director

Maternal and Child Health Program
Center for Population and Family Health
Columbia University School of Public
  Health
New York, New York

Ronni Chernoff, Ph.D., R.D.
Associate Director
Geriatric Research Education and Clinical
  Center (GRECC)
Veterans Administration
John L. McClellan Memorial Medical
  Center
Little Rock, Arkansas

George Christakis, M.D., M.P.H.
Adjunct Professor
Department of Epidemiology and Public
  Health
University of Miami School of Medicine
Miami, Florida

Johanna T. Dwyer, D.Sc., R.D.
Professor of Medicine
Department of Medicine
Tufts University School of Medicine
Director
Frances Stern Nutrition Center
New England Medical Center Hospital
Boston, Massachusetts

Jeannette Endres, Ph.D., M.P.H., R.D.
Professor, Food and Nutrition
Southern Illinois University
Carbondale, Illinois

Veronica D. Feeg, Ph.D., R.N.
Associate Professor of Nursing
George Mason University
Fairfax, Virginia
Editor, *Pediatric Nursing*

Cheryl A. Fisher, M.S.N., R.N.
Clinical Staff Nurse
National Institutes of Health
Bethesda, Maryland
Cardiovascular Education Consultant
American Heart Association

Samuel J. Fomon, M.D.
Professor
Department of Pediatrics
College of Medicine
University of Iowa
Iowa City, Iowa

Georgia L. Heiberger, M.S., R.N.
Research Associate
School of Nursing
University of Colorado Health Science
    Center
Denver, Colorado

Dorothy Hyde, M.S., C.P.N.A., R.N.
Pediatric Nurse Associate
Health Start/St. Paul Ramsey Medical
    Center
St. Paul, Minnesota

Judith B. Igoe, M.S., R.N.
Associate Professor/Director
School Health Programs
University of Colorado Health Science
    Center
Denver, Colorado
Parry Chair
Health Promotion

College of Nursing
Texas Woman's University
Houston, Texas

Howard N. Jacobson, M.D.
Professor
Department of Community and Family
    Health
College of Public Health
Tampa, Florida

Lucille A. Joel, Ed.D., R.N., F.A.A.N.
Professor and Chair
Department of Adults and the Aged
Director-Teaching Nursing Home Project
College of Nursing
Rutgers-The State University of New
    Jersey
Newark, New Jersey

James G. Jones, M.D., D.A.B.F.P.
Chairman
Department of Family Medicine
East Carolina University School of
    Medicine
Greenville, North Carolina
President, American Academy of Family
    Physicians

Janet C. King, Ph.D., R.D.
Professor
Department of Nutritional Sciences
University of California
Berkeley, California

**Rosemary Liguori, M.S.N., C.P.N.A.,
    R.N.**
Assistant Professor
Tulsa University
Tulsa, Oklahoma

Kathleen A. Mammel, M.D.
Assistant Professor of Pediatrics
Section of Adolescent Medicine
University of Colorado
    Health Science Center
Denver, Colorado

Carolyn McKay, M.D., M.P.H.
Director
Maternal and Child Health
Minnesota Department of Health
University of Minnesota
Minneapolis, Minnesota

Celia Z. Padron, M.D.
Junior Fellow
Department of Pediatrics
Robert Wood Johnson University Hospital
    School
New Brunswick, New Jersey

Mary-Elizabeth A. Petschek, M.P.H.
Senior Staff Associate
Assistant Director
Academic Programs
Center for Population and Family Health
Columbia University School of Public
    Health
New York, New York

Dena Rakower, M.S., R.D.
AIDS Nutrition Specialist
Bellevue Hospital Center
New York, New York

Daphne A. Roe, M.D.
Professor of Nutrition
Division of Nutritional Sciences
Cornell University
Ithaca, New York

Susan R. Rosenthal, M.D., M.S.
Associate Professor
University of Medicine and Dentistry of
    New Jersey
Robert Wood Johnson University Hospital
New Brunswick, New Jersey

**Deborah Thomas-Dobersen, M.S.,
    R.D.**
Senior Clinical Dietitian
Barbara Davis Center for Childhood
    Diabetes
University of Colorado Health Sciences
    Center
Denver, Colorado

**Joan Howe Walsh, Ph.D., M.P.H.,
    R.D.**
Clinical Nutritionist
Department of Family Practice
San Joaquin General Hospital
Stockton, California

Donna Wong, M.N., P.N.P., R.N.
Nurse Counselor in Private Practice
Consultant
Department of Education
St. Francis Hospital
Tulsa, Oklahoma

Foreword

As a practitioner and teacher of family medicine, I am pleased that the authors have provided a practical guide for nutritional problems encountered almost daily in the family physician's office. Beginning with nutrition during pregnancy and lactation and concluding with the special considerations of the elderly, this book covers common nutritional problems of each stage of the life cycle. It provides assessment guidelines and therapeutic recommendations for early detection of patients at risk for the sequela of poor nutrition.

Biomedical science continues to provide solutions to the problems of infectious diseases and other more direct causes of death. However, we still have a long way to go in resolving health problems that are influenced primarily by lifestyle. Poor nutrition has been identified as a contributor to heart disease, hypertension, and even some types of cancer.

This volume is a well-organized reference for the family physician to help assess nutritional status and to direct effective intervention where it is needed for patients of any age. I am certain you will find it useful to help you work in partnership with your patients to overcome the barriers to good nutrition.

James G. Jones, M.D., D.A.B.F.P.

Forew

Interdisciplinary collaboration requires high-level professional functioning. *Practical Nutrition: A Quick Reference for the Health Care Practitioner* provides such a forum. The physician, nurse, and nutritionist contributors of this book have shared their professional expertise, with nutrition being the common ground and health promotion being the common goal.

Medicine's discussion of nutrition assessment, nursing's appraisal of the environment, and nutrition's recommended intervention orchestrate to a usable format for clinical practice. This collaborative organization is applied to each of the seven developmental sections.

The outcome of this collaboration is a unique contribution in health care. The beneficiary of this professional sharing and communication is the client.

Lucille A. Joel, R.N., Ed.D., F.A.A.N.

Foreword

Appropriate nutrition care begins with screening and assessment to identify problems. It progresses to nutrition intervention based on a soundly conceived nutrition care plan that builds on the problem identification phase. Nutrition intervention consists of counseling, help with home and money management, and food assistance and education. It concludes with evaluation, documentation, and successive iterations as realities for the patient change.

This book gives the health care practitioner convenient and usable guidelines when confronted with various nutrition-related problems in different types of patients. It is innovative in several ways. First, with a unique problem-solving format, it emphasizes a team approach and referral. In addition to direct care, it suggests specific mechanisms for referral to registered dietitians and other specialized health care practitioners when the realities of patients require it.

Second, this book builds health promotion and risk reduction through dietary means into routine health care encounters, and integrates them with disease treatment when appropriate.

Finally, the book provides us with useful perspectives of national experts in health care. It will be a valuable tool for health care practitioners.

Johanna T. Dwyer, D.Sc., R.D.

Preface

This book was written for physicians, nurses, and entry level nutritionists and dietitians. It contains practical, easily accessible guidelines for incorporating basic nutrition principles into routine clinical practice.

Integrating nutrition into health care is often perceived as time-consuming and not given priority status. *Practical Nutrition: A Quick Reference for the Health Care Practitioner* provides concise basic information to readily utilize nutrition theory in health maintenance and promotion.

The text is organized in a developmental format so that access to a particular age group is convenient. Each part discusses nutrition in an orderly presentation: nutrition assessment, environmental management, and dietary management. The expertise of the disciplines of medicine, nursing, and nutrition provide an inter-disciplinary approach for promoting health through nutrition. Each author has contributed a personal hallmark derived from experience in practice. Common nutritional problems of each age group are presented with the problem-solving approach of assessment, action, and evaluation.

The text offers a practical tool for incorporating nutrition into health care for all clients. It actualizes the reality that nutrition is basic to health.

Acknowledgments

We wish to thank Kathleen S. Babich for graciously sharing materials and ideas. We are appreciative to Anne Goldstein for her diligence, care, and promptness in word-processing the manuscript. From New York University, Mary Tai was most helpful in reviewing selected technical data, and Lena Singh gave us her continuing support. We extend our gratitude to the Nurse Practitioner Forum of the New Jersey Nurses Association for responding to the needs assessment survey. To Ann O'Sullivan and Joan Lynaugh from the University of Pennsylvania, School of Nursing, thank you for encouragement in the development of the idea for this book. We are grateful to Chris Jackson and Kathleen Nottage for identifying the need for this type of book in practice settings. We thank New Jersey Congressman Bernard J. Dwyer and his staff who provided reference materials. Most importantly, we recognize and acknowledge the efforts of all of the contributors who made this book a reality.

Part I

Overview of Practical Nutrition

Chapter 1

Nutrition and the Health Care Practitioner

Catherine Cowell, Maureen S. Hreha, and Margaret D. Simko

It is the time and the season for America's next health care revolution, for the dawn of a society in which health promotion and disease prevention characterize our health care culture and add a new dimension of quality to the life of each of our citizens. . . . Nutrition is central to America's health.

Joseph A. Califano, Jr., 1987

INTRODUCTION

A new era in the history of diet and disease was ushered in upon the release of the first *Surgeon General's Report on Nutrition and Health* in July 1988.[1] This unprecedented report presented evidence that in the United States diet plays a prominent role in five of the top ten causes of death; another three are associated with excessive alcohol intake. The message of the report is to give priority for dietary change and to reduce intake of total fats, especially saturated fat, because of their relationship to several chronic diseases. A major concern for Americans is the overconsumption of certain dietary components at the expense of other desirable foods, such as those high in complex carbohydrates and dietary fiber that may be more conducive to health.

At the other end of the spectrum are those who have an inadequate income for purchasing the basic essentials of food, shelter, and clothing. Being poor leads to hunger, a poor diet, and undernutrition, which if prolonged results in problems of malnutrition commonly associated with third-world countries. Those in this subgroup of the population who are hungry and homeless are at higher risk for a variety of nutritional problems that require comprehensive, sustained, social-economic-health intervention strategies. Nutritional care for those lacking access to food and other support systems requires substantial effort by health care practitioners, who may be the first, and all too frequently the only, providers able to address their specific dietary needs. The difference between the poor and those with excessive dietary intakes is reflected in the magnitude of the poor's nutritional problems, which are further complicated by poor living conditions.

The 1988 *Surgeon General's Report on Nutrition and Health* extends the health-promotion initiative started in the early 1980s.[2] That report stimulated health care providers and the public to become aware of the need to reduce risks of disease and preventable deaths. The 226 health objectives addressed in the report

3

were designed to improve the health status of the population and increase the public's knowledge about behavior related to health. Among the objectives was nutrition, especially as it relates to risk reduction and health behavior (see Exhibit 1-1).

Exhibit 1-1 The 1990 Nutrition Objectives for the Nation

1. By 1990, the proportion of pregnant women with iron deficiency anemia should be reduced to 3.5 percent.
2. By 1990, growth retardation of infants and children caused by inadequate diets should have been eliminated in the United States as a Public Health Problem.
3. By 1990, the prevalence of significant overweight among the U.S. population should be decreased to 10 percent of men and 17 percent of women, without nutritional impairment.
4. By 1990, 50 percent of the overweight population should have adopted weight loss regimens, combining an appropriate balance of diet and physical activity.
5. By 1990, the mean serum cholesterol level in the adult population 18 to 74 years of age should be at or below 200 milligrams per deciliter.
6. By 1990, the mean serum cholesterol level in children aged 1 to 14 should be at or below 150 milligrams per deciliter.
7. By 1990, the average daily sodium ingestion for adults should be reduced to at least the three- to six-gram range.
8. By 1990, the proportion of women who breastfeed their babies should be increased to 75 percent at hospital discharge and to 35 percent at six months of age.
9. By 1990, the proportion of the population which is able to correctly associate the principal dietary factors known or strongly suspected to be related to disease should exceed 75 percent for each of the following diseases: heart disease, high blood pressure, dental caries, and cancer.
10. By 1990, 70 percent of adults should be able to identify the major foods which are low in fat content, low in sodium content, high in calories, high in sugars, and good sources of fiber.
11. By 1990, 90 percent of adults should understand that to lose weight people must either consume foods that contain fewer calories or increase physical activity, or both.
12. By 1990, the labels of all packaged foods should contain useful calorie and nutrient information to enable consumers to select diets that promote and protect good health. Similar information should be displayed where nonpackaged foods are obtained or purchased.
13. By 1990, sodium levels in processed food should be reduced by 20 percent from present levels.
14. By 1990, the proportion of employees and school cafeteria managers who are aware of and actively promoting USDA/DHHS dietary guidelines should be greater than 50 percent.
15. By 1990, all states should include nutrition education as part of required comprehensive school health education at the elementary and secondary levels.
16. By 1990, virtually all routine health contact with health professionals should include some element of nutrition education and nutrition counseling.
17. By 1990, a comprehensive national nutrition status monitoring system should have the capability for detecting nutritional problems in special population groups, as well as for obtaining baseline data for decisions on national nutrition policy.

Source: Reprinted from *Promoting Health/Preventing Disease,* U.S. Department of Health and Human Services, Public Health Service, Washington, D.C., 1980.

At about the same time, the U.S. Department of Agriculture and the Department of Health and Human Services issued a set of Dietary Guidelines for Americans (see Figure 1-1). Based on existing scientific and epidemiological evidence, seven specific recommendations were made for application to most Americans. Given the increased life expectancy at birth, a good diet, early identification of health problems, and intervention are important factors that can enhance and potentially contribute to a quality of life in later years.

FROM PUBLIC HEALTH TO PERSONAL HEALTH

The recognition of nutrition as an essential factor in health promotion has never been more widespread. Increasingly, there have been shifts in the eating habits and behaviors of consumers. The dramatic surge in the number of fast food restaurants and the proliferation of convenience foods in the marketplace have influenced the kinds of foods individuals and families are eating, the frequency of their eating, and where they are eating. There is more eating away from home than ever before.

Individual eating habits have also been affected by the food supply. Meats with less fat, one-percent and two-percent milks, sodium-reduced canned vegetables and soups, and fortified products like frozen orange juice with calcium and fruit drinks with vitamin C have become available and are being promoted in the marketplace. Food manufacturers have responded to a more health-conscious consumer. Food consumption patterns have also changed. Though calories from total fat for individuals and cholesterol levels have been above suggested levels,[3] there has been a decline in the intake of saturated fatty acids and an increase in the intake of polyunsaturated fatty acids.

On the other hand, the consumer has been subjected to volumes of media information and marketing strategies regarding food and diet. Often the conflicting information has caused confusion or misunderstanding. For instance, consumers are told that vitamins are good for them. The result is that they serve their children vitamin-fortified, sugary, and artifically flavored and colored cereals, believing that such products are nutritious. Though such behavior is certainly well intended, it is unfortunately also misinformed. The consumer clearly needs further clarification about the nutritive value of the food supply.

THE CHALLENGE TO THE PRIMARY HEALTH CARE PRACTITIONER

All of these events and circumstances have generated interest in diet and nutrition. In some instances, health providers have been bombarded by clients seeking help and answers to their questions. To respond appropriately, health care practitioners need easily accessible, sound nutrition information to integrate into

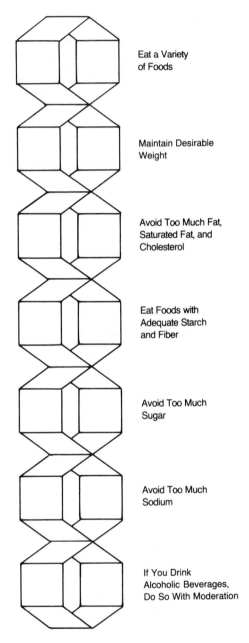

Figure 1-1 Dietary Guidelines for Americans. *Source:* Reprinted from *Nutrition and Your Health, Dietary Guidelines for Americans*, revised, U.S. Department of Agriculture and U.S. Department of Health and Human Services, Washington, D.C., August 1985.

their delivery of health care. The physician's office, the school health office, and a wide range of community-based health clinics and other neighborhood health sites that offer alternative health services are locations where captive audiences are available for health care and nutrition information. Health care practitioners working in these environments can coordinate, communicate, and maximize the continuity of care they provide. Using their base of knowledge about nutrition theory, the integration of practical and relevant nutritional care can help these practitioners fulfill their mode of delivering primary health care.

Clearly, helping clients understand and follow the dietary guidelines listed in Figure 1-1 is a challenging mandate for health care practitioners. Califano reminds us that "we can certainly take a host of actions to encourage Americans to choose wisely, and the evidence is accumulating that when people have the right kind of encouragement, they choose healthier habits."[4]

The right kind of encouragement requires the practice of nutritional interventions with all clients. The 1988 *Surgeon General's Report on Nutrition and Health* provides recommendations that are broadly focused for the entire U.S. population (see Exhibit 1-2). These recommendations should assist the health care practitioner to encourage clients to select diets that promote and protect good health. However, practitioners must individualize and apply this information with each of their clients. Planned, routinely implemented nutrition information and counseling are a necessary part of every health visit; indeed, they are perhaps the best way to keep healthy people healthy. The recognized health care provider is the source of accurate and relevant nutrition information.

The National Nutrition Objectives for 1990 cannot be realized without the concerted effort of all health care practitioners—family physicians, nurse practitioners, school nurses, pediatricians, and health care professionals in clinics and Health Maintenance Organizations (HMOs). The issue now is to make nutrition education a high priority. Clients will begin to accept nutrition information as an important issue if it becomes part of routine care. Individualizing the dietary guidelines and helping people incorporate them into their lifestyles should become a part of reasonable and expected care.

The guidelines provided in the following chapters are designed to assist primary health care practitioners in utilizing and integrating their nutrition knowledge in the care of their clients. As explained in chapter 2, the format is deliberately organized to facilitate practical nutrition interventions in health promotion. The book thus becomes a tool to aid in keeping healthy clients healthy.

THE TEAM APPROACH

The text is organized in a developmental format of seven parts focusing sequentially on various age groups, from pregnancy and lactation to the elderly.

Each part focuses on three factors: nutrition assessment, environmental management, and dietary assessment management. In each part, respected professionals from medicine, nursing, and nutrition contribute their particular expertise, with the primary focus on the particular age group.

Exhibit 1-2 Key Recommendations Based on the Surgeon General's 1988 Report

---

Issues for Most People:

- *Fats and cholesterol:* Reduce consumption of fat (especially saturated fat) and cholesterol. Choose foods relatively low in these substances, such as vegetables, fruits, whole grain foods, fish, poultry, lean meats, and low-fat dairy products. Use food preparation methods that add little or no fat.

- *Energy and weight control:* Achieve and maintain a desirable body weight. To do so, choose a dietary pattern in which energy (caloric) intake is consistent with energy expenditure. To reduce energy intake, limit consumption of foods relatively high in calories, fats, and sugars, and minimize alcohol consumption. Increase energy expenditure through regular and sustained physical activity.

- *Complex carbohydrates and fiber:* Increase consumption of whole grain foods and cereal products, vegetables (including dried beans and peas), and fruits.

- *Sodium:* Reduce intake of sodium by choosing foods relatively low in sodium and limiting the amount of salt added in food preparation and at the table.

- *Alcohol:* To reduce the risk for chronic disease, take alcohol only in moderation (no more than two drinks a day), if at all. Avoid drinking any alcohol before or while driving, operating machinery, taking medications, or engaging in any other activity requiring judgment. Avoid drinking alcohol while pregnant.

Other Issues for Some People:

- *Fluoride:* Community water systems should contain fluoride at optimal levels for prevention of tooth decay. If such water is not available, use other appropriate sources of fluoride.

- *Sugars:* Those who are particularly vulnerable to dental caries (cavities), especially children, should limit their consumption and frequency of use of foods high in sugars.

- *Calcium:* Adolescent girls and adult women should increase consumption of foods high in calcium, including low-fat dairy products.

- *Iron:* Children, adolescents, and women of childbearing age should be sure to consume foods that are good sources of iron, such as lean red meats, fish, certain beans, and iron-enriched cereals and whole grain products. This issue is of special concern for low-income families.

Source: Reprinted from *The Surgeon General's Report on Nutrition and Health*, p. 3, U.S. Department of Health and Human Services, Public Health Service, Washington, D.C., 1988.

Nutrition Assessment

The chapters on nutrition assessment were developed by physicians. This area includes history, physical assessment, anthropometry, and biochemical data relevant to the client's actual nutritional status. While the same format is used consistently, the contributing physicians have added information based on their particular clinical strengths. For example, in chapter 6, "Nutrition Assessment of the Infant," accurate measurements and incremental growth are emphasized in the anthropometry section.

Environmental Management

Nursing professionals were invited to evaluate the client's environment with regard to access to sound nutrition. Both the existence of barriers to good nutrition and the factors that foster it are addressed. Because the relationship between environment and nutrition is often overlooked, the result is a series of very creative responses. The nursing authors were able to look at nutrition as more than just the right food; they were also concerned with the right situations. Thus, issues such as the media and the client's knowledge, mobility, socialization, and family are examined. In this context, by looking at age groups and life styles, nursing makes a unique contribution in the area of nutrition.

Dietary Assessment and Management

Nutritionists focused their professional expertise on common nutrition problems of particular age groups. Here, a problem-solving approach is applied. Dietary assessment and analysis are established and additional assessments that relate to the client's nutritional problems are suggested. A plan of action is recommended, and a method of evaluation is presented. A unique feature of the text, the table format, is specifically designed to be quickly accessed and easily utilized.

SUMMARY

Multidisciplinary collaboration combines the best of each profession. Nutrition is a common denominator among all members of the health care team. The unique sharing and combining of nutrition information among the team members thus provides the client with the optimum motivation to achieve improved health through sound nutrition practices.

NOTES

1. *The Surgeon General's Report on Nutrition and Health* (Washington, D.C.: U.S. Department of Health and Human Services, Public Health Service, 1988).

2. U.S. Department of Health and Human Services, Public Health Service, *Promoting Health/ Preventing Disease* (Washington, D.C.: U.S. Department of Health and Human Services, Public Health Service, 1980).

3. U.S. Department of Health and Human Services, U.S. Department of Agriculture, *Nutrition Monitoring in the United States* (Rockville, Md.: U.S. Department of Health and Human Services and U.S. Department of Agriculture, July 1986), 35–54.

4. J.A. Califano, Jr., ''America's Health Care Revolution: Health Promotion and Disease Prevention,'' *Journal of the American Dietetic Association* 84 (1987): 437.

Chapter 2

How to Use This Reference

Margaret D. Simko, Maureen S. Hreha, and Catherine Cowell

PURPOSE OF THE BOOK

Undernutrition has long-term consequences that negatively affect growth, behavior, and health. But these consequences are preventable. The health care practitioner should be prepared to recognize actual and impending nutritional problems and to recommend preventive measures.[1] The purpose of this book is to provide a quick reference offering practical, readily available nutrition information that will give direction in treating and preventing selected common nutrition problems throughout the life span. Its hallmark is its usability and clinical application.

The text is intended to be used by health care practitioners as a guide in promoting health care through basic nutrition intervention. It is particularly applicable for practicing physicians, nurses, and entry level nutritionists, but its nutritional guidelines can also be used by graduate students in schools of medicine, nursing, nutrition, and dietetics. Its basic philosophy is that each practitioner should respect and seek out the knowledge of other health care disciplines (see chapter 1). The client can only benefit from such collaboration.

Nutrition intervention and counseling thus become essential and ongoing aspects of health care. Health care practitioners often must necessarily respond to the nutritional needs of the client in outpatient, clinic, community, and, in some cases, inpatient settings. This requires the planned, practical application of basic nutrition theory as an integral part of health care.

Busy practitioners may overlook or may not feel skilled in nutrition intervention. There may not always be a nutritionist on hand, or a nutritionist may be available only on a consultation basis. Also, questions may arise regarding the nutritional needs of specific age groups. An informal survey among primary health care providers has indicated that many practitioners are relying on basic courses or publications written for the public for nutrition information. Furthermore, many providers view nutrition as their "weakest area" of practice.

This situation is disheartening, yet the remedy is available. This book can serve as a handy reference to help accurately and more thoroughly assess the client's nutritional status and to make recommendations that, through early detection and intervention, may offset more serious health problems. Nutrition intervention is a cost-effective means of keeping people healthy.

The text addresses how to assess each client's nutritional status, suggests appropriate intervention and evaluation of actions, and offers guidance on referral to a nutrition specialist and/or physician. It is not a reordering of nutrition theory, but rather a tool for integrating nutrition into daily practice. Supportive references are provided to promote a better understanding of the rationale for specific dietary recommendations.

WHAT THE BOOK CAN DO FOR THE READER

The reader is provided with a practical, quick reference to help solve common nutritional problems prevalent throughout the life cycle. Each stage of the life cycle is addressed with age-specific nutrition assessments for early detection and identification of actual and potential problems. Practical dietary recommendations are made to recommend appropriate nutrition support. Guidelines for evaluating the effectiveness of the suggested treatments are included with parameters to measure progress, with alternative approaches and with criteria for referral for specialized evaluation. The reader will find that cross-references from section to section are useful and uniform.

UNIQUE FEATURES

The book offers the reader the following unique features:

1. It is a quick reference that is easy to read and provides ready access to relevant information.
2. Its developmental format encompasses pregnancy through gerontology.
3. Each section covers a specific stage of the life cycle, including:
   a. recommendations for physical, anthropometric, and biochemical assessment
   b. recommendations for environmental assessment and management, including discussion of the barriers and facilitators of optimal nutrition
   c. recommendations for management of common nutritional problems during each stage of the life cycle, addressing in table form (1) nutrition

assessment of the client (what to look for), (2) action (what to do with the assessment information), and (3) evaluation (how to judge if the action was successful, and to make referral if further action is warranted)
4. It provides tools that are simple and ready to use.
5. It contains selected, useful references for the practitioner.
6. Its uniformity of format makes it easy for the reader to go from one chapter to another and to find needed information.
7. It provides Appendixes containing generic forms that can be adapted for each age group.
8. It includes age-appropriate anthropometric charts for accurate evaluation of heights and weights.

A WORD ABOUT ANTHROPOMETRIC MEASUREMENT

The book was designed to be particularly useful for the busy health care practitioner who is often involved in high case load settings. The decision was made to focus on height and weight measurements to obtain anthropometric assessment data. The importance of accurate instruments and techniques in obtaining such data has been pointed out by Fomon (see chapter 6) and others. The use of more technical and time-consuming assessment measures, such as use of skinfold calipers, is not covered. Roe states that "when information is being obtained on changes in the nutritional status . . . over time, a record of mid-arm circumference measurements provides a gauge from which to assess changes in body mass. Measurement of triceps skinfold thickness requires greater skill, and measurement error is common when those making the measurement are inexperienced" (see chapter 21). (For in-depth discussion of other anthropometric techniques, see Robbins and Trowbridge.[2])

DIETARY ASSESSMENT AND TOOLS

The complete nutrition assessment includes an examination of clinical, biochemical, and anthropometric data in addition to dietary data. Thus, the dietary assessment becomes part of the overall nutrition assessment.

All dietary assessment tools have both strengths and weaknesses. (For a more complete discussion of this subject, see Smiciklas-Wright and Guthrie.[3]) Yet such tools are critical instruments for dietary assessment and should be used consistently to make dietary assessments, plan intervention, and evaluate progress.

The following dietary assessment tools can be universally applied and can be adapted for each specific age group. Using the samples provided in appendixes A and B, modify each one to meet the specific needs of each health care setting. Two or more tools may be used to provide additional information about the dietary intake of the client.

The *Generic Nutrition Questionnaire* (see appendix A-1) was developed by adapting information provided by several contributors. It is a generic or general questionnaire that avoids repetitive applications of a different form specific to each age group. Practitioners can select those questions that are appropriate for each situation, then add others to elicit specific information required in their particular health care setting. In settings for infants and young children, and in some geriatric settings, the questions can be phrased for the caregiver to answer; in other settings, the questions can be answered by the client.

The *24-Hour Recall* (see appendix A-2) is a dietary assessment tool that provides a "pulse" on food behaviors. It is based on the premise that information about foods and beverages that were consumed during the previous 24-hour period represents a broad picture of the client's food intake and habits. The 24-hour recall can be used for any age group. It is especially useful during follow-up visits to determine if the client is adapting to dietary recommendations. The sample form can be adapted to specific needs. The recall may be obtained by an interviewer or it may be self-administered.

The *Food Frequency Form* (see appendix A-3) is a checklist that elicits data regarding the kinds of food eaten and the frequency of intake. It can help to confirm the adequacy or deficiency of the client's diet.

The *Food Diary* (see appendix A-4) describes a client's intake over a period of days (usually three). It is recorded by the client or caregiver and returned in a follow-up visit. Similarly, the *Food and Activity Record* (see appendix A-5) describes food intake, activity, and mood. Each of these tools may be used as they appear or they may be adapted to specific situations.

The *Food Group Guide and Suggested Portions* (see appendix B-1) provides a framework for the evaluation of a client's food intake. Seven food groups are used to classify foods similar in nutrient content. This grouping of foods with recommended portions provides general guidelines. It assumes that the individual is eating a variety of foods within each group; once the recommended amounts are consumed, other foods can be added to the total nutrient intake. The suggested number of servings to consume daily is calculated on the calorie requirements for the average weight and height of the specified age group. Actual calorie requirements may differ, depending on individual weights, heights, and activity levels.

Development of a more accurate, yet simple, system to evaluate diets continues to be explored.[4] Many assumptions regarding portion size, food habits, classification of foods into groups by the client, and individual food and nutrient needs must be made in using a food-grouping system to evaluate dietary intakes.[5] Still, the authors believe that such a tool must be provided, with the understanding that it can assist clients in selecting and consuming more adequate diets.

Recommended Daily Dietary Allowances (RDA) (see appendix B-2) are the levels of intake of nutrients considered essential by the Committee on Dietary Allowances of the National Research Council to be, on the basis of scientific knowledge, adequate to meet the known nutritional needs of practically all healthy persons.[6] The RDAs are recommended intakes, not requirements, and are suggested for the evaluation of diets of groups rather than individuals. Detailed analysis of diets is not suggested for the users of this book; this table has been included for referencing specific nutrient requirements of various age groups.

APPENDIX MATERIALS

In addition to dietary assessment tools, the appendixes contain tables and exhibits that can aid in routine nutrition interventions. Tools for clinical assessment and anthropometric measurement, energy information, major food sources of selected nutrients, and food selection and preparation tips are provided. Organizations that can provide additional information and teaching materials are also listed (see appendix I).

SUMMARY

The primary goal of this text is to make basic nutrition practical in the clinical arena. Clients should not simply be considered for nutrition interventions only when there is underlying pathology.

Clients look to health care practitioners for information on health. Good nutritional practices are basic to good health. Thus, providers need to incorporate planned nutritional strategies into their commitment to health care promotion with their clients. This book provides guidelines to this end.

NOTES

1. J.R. Galler, "Examining the Long-Term Consequences of Undernutrition," in *Pediatric Basics*, no. 47 (Fremont, Mich.: Gerber Products Company, 1987), 2–4.

2. G.E. Robbins and F.L. Trowbridge, "Anthropometric Techniques and Their Application," in *Nutrition Assessment: A Comprehensive Guide for Planning Intervention*, ed. M.D. Simko, C. Cowell, and J.A. Gilbride (Rockville, Md.: Aspen Publishers, Inc., 1984), 69–92.

3. H.W. Smiciklas-Wright and H.A. Guthrie, "Dietary Methodologies: Their Uses, Analyses, Interpretations, and Implications," in *Nutrition Assessment: A Comprehensive Guide for Planning Intervention*, ed. M.D. Simko, C. Cowell, and J.A. Gilbride (Rockville, Md.: Aspen Publishers, Inc., 1984), 119–137.

4. F.J. Cronin et al., "Developing a Food Guidance System to Implement the Dietary Guidelines," *Journal of Nutrition Education* 19 (1987): 281–302.

5. B. Haughton, J.D. Gussow, and J.M. Dodds, ''An Historical Study of the Underlying Assumptions for United States Food Guides from 1917 through the Basic Four Food Groups Guide,'' *Journal of Nutrition Education* 19 (1987): 168–176.

6. Committee on Dietary Allowances, Food and Nutrition Board, *Recommended Dietary Allowances*, 9th rev. ed. (Washington, D.C.: National Academy of Sciences, 1980), 1.

Part II

Pregnancy and Lactation

Chapter 3

Nutrition Assessment of Pregnant and Lactating Women

Garland D. Anderson and Howard N. Jacobson

OVERVIEW

In the last decade, concern about the role of diet in pregnancy has stemmed from the persistently high neonatal and infant mortality in the United States. Most infant deaths occur within the first four weeks of life. Low birthweight is a major contributing factor in two-thirds of all infant deaths. As a result, reducing the number of low-birthweight infants has become a national goal.[1]

Low birthweight, or delivery of an infant 2,500 grams (about 5.5 pounds) or less, may be due to prematurity or inadequate fetal growth (intrauterine growth retardation), or both. The risk of morbidity and mortality increases as the birthweight decreases. Low birthweight infants who do not die may be handicapped with mental or motor problems, which adds to the emotional and economic burden of the family and to the cost of the already strained health care budget of the nation.[2]

In 1962, attention was focused on diet in pregnancy by the President's Panel on Mental Retardation, which presented a report that linked birthweight and mental retardation. This led, in turn, to a number of programs and initiatives that have, over the years, laid a heavy emphasis on maternal nutrition.[3]

Nutrition intervention requires that a complete assessment be taken before establishing a care plan. A pregnant woman's total life situation must be reflected in this assessment. Quality assurance requires that the results of the nutrition intervention also be monitored.

The state of our current knowledge of nutrition and pregnancy, therefore, is best understood when it is set against this background: the need for better understanding of the many factors influencing maternal nutrition, on the one hand; and the outcome criteria of good maternal health, fewer complications of pregnancy, and the weight, vigor, and development of the infant, on the other.

Great progress on key issues in maternal nutrition has been made in the past few years, mainly because of the legislative requirements of the U.S. Department of Agriculture's Special Supplemental Food Program for Women, Infants, and Children (WIC Program). The advances are particularly timely because of the general recognition that in this period of finite resources we will need to make optimal use of such resources as the food package, nutrition education, and health services that together make up the WIC Program benefits.

Major progress has been made in the following critical areas: (1) agreement on nutritional risk criteria; (2) identification of dietary risk factors; (3) increased availability of a variety of computer-assisted techniques for collecting, managing, and analyzing dietary intakes on large numbers of patients; and (4) recognition of the need for and the availability of a variety of alternative dietary standards in the provision of overall services to pregnant women.[4]

Of even greater importance is the recognition in practice that we can no longer treat nutrition as a single variable, independent of the many other forces that together influence the course and outcome of a pregnancy. Rather, we must recognize the seamless web of influences, all of which need to be taken into account in attempts to provide for the needs of pregnant women at risk of poor pregnancy outcomes.

The 1985 recommendations and guidelines of the American College of Obstetricians and Gynecologists assert that:

> every woman should have a comprehensive program of obstetric care that begins as early as possible in the first trimester of pregnancy, and preferably before conception and extends through the postpartum period. Early diagnosis of pregnancy and risk assessment are important to establish the management plan appropriate to the individual. The concept of family-centered care, emphasizing family involvement in the childbirth experience, is an important aspect of obstetrics. Considera- tion of each patient's special needs—medical, emotional, and educa- tional—can help promote quality obstetric care.[5]

HEALTH HISTORY

Preconceptional History

The preconceptional period can be a most opportune time to concentrate on nutri- tion intervention. For example, the couple anticipating their first child may be unusually receptive to dietary and health guidance. Women who have been taking oral contraceptives for prolonged periods may derive particular benefits from a planned nutritional support program.

Focusing on this period offers the hope of reducing the risk for underweight women who would otherwise present severe management problems during pregnancy. Women with a history of poor prior outcomes of pregnancy should be assessed to determine whether a nutritional component might be identified and corrected.

The preconception inventory should include:

- present height-weight status
- weight-control activities and physical fitness programs currently and previously utilized
- use of dietary supplements
- alternative or unusual dietary practices; for example, vegetarianism (see chapter 17)
- medical risk factors that might affect nutritional status, especially diabetes, anemia, colitis, and any surgery on the gastrointestinal (GI) tract such as gastroplasty or intestinal bypass

Initial and periodic evaluations with special attention to risk factors are key elements in the provision of quality care in pregnancy and childbirth. In addition to the monitoring aspects, such occasions provide opportunities for additional education and positive reinforcements.

Along with the preconceptional information, a health history of both the patient and the patient's family is important. A nutritional database should be established for each woman as part of the initial evaluation. This should include:

- pregravid weight
- medical risk factors, including diabetes; anemia; hypertension; cardiac, pulmonary, kidney, and thyroid disease; allergies; gall stones; pancreatitis; colitis; and any previous surgery on the gastrointestinal tract
- methods of family planning, since oral contraceptives can affect the level of various nutrients in the blood; for example, by decreasing vitamins B_6 and B_{12}, folacin, and the minerals calcium, phosphorus, magnesium, and zinc; plasma albumin may also be decreased in some women
- a detailed record of all past pregnancies, including prematurity, multiple births, low birthweight, macrosomia, fetal or neonatal deaths, abortions, miscarriages, and the interval between pregnancies

Current Pregnancies

Data collection for health history of current pregnancy should cover the following three areas:

1. medical risks affecting nutritional status, such as years from menarche if adolescent, percentage of ideal body weight for gestational age, infections, gestational diabetes, elevated blood pressure, generalized edema, hyperemesis, ptyalism, severe heartburn, active gallstone, chronic diarrhea, and an inability to consume an adequate diet due to previous gastroplasty or intestinal bypass surgery
2. substance abuse such as use of drugs, alcoholism, and smoking (see Table 3-1)
3. family and social history, including information on:
   - metabolic disorders
   - mental retardation

Table 3-1 Drug Use During Pregnancy

Drug	Effect on Fetus	Safe Use of Drug
Nicotine	Heavy smoking may lead to low-birthweight babies, which means that the babies may have more health problems. Especially harmful during second half of pregnancy.	Should be avoided.
Alcohol	Daily drinking of more than two glasses of wine, or a mixed drink, may cause "fetal alcohol syndrome." Babies tend to have low birthweights, mental retardation, physical deformities, and behavioral problems, including hyperactivity, restlessness, and poor attention spans.	Should be avoided.
Aspirin	During last three months of pregnancy, frequent use may cause excessive bleeding at delivery and may prolong pregnancy and labor.	Use only under doctor's supervision.
Tranquilizers	Use during the first three months of pregnancy may cause cleft lip or palate or other congenital malformation.	Avoid if you might become pregnant and during early pregnancy. Use only under doctor's supervision.
Barbiturates	Mothers who have taken large doses may have babies who are addicted. Babies may have tremors, restlessness, and irritability.	Use only under doctor's supervision.
Amphetamines	May cause birth defects.	Use only under doctor's supervision.

Source: Reprinted from *Deciding about Drugs*, Alcohol, Drug Abuse and Mental Health Administration, Public Health Service, Department of Health and Human Services, U.S. Government Printing Office, Washington, D.C., 1979.

- cardiovascular disease
- multiple births
- congenital abnormalities
- genetic risk (The history should be sufficiently detailed to identify possible genetic disorders, such as family history of birth defects, mental retardation, and known or suspected inherited metabolic disorders.)

PHYSICAL ASSESSMENT

Physical assessment of the pregnant woman, focusing on nutritional status, includes assessment of the health and well-being of the growing fetus. The issue of sufficient calorie intake is reviewed in the anthropometry section. Significant findings reflecting nutrient deficits are shown in Table 3-2 (see also appendix C-1).

ANTHROPOMETRIC ASSESSMENT

Patterns of healthy fetal growth and development are measurable by the quantity and rate of maternal weight gain. Figure 3-1 demonstrates weight gain during pregnancy for average, overweight, and underweight women. Subgroups, such as the adolescent and multiple fetus, are noted. Incremental weight gains should be

---

Table 3-2 Significant Findings Reflecting Nutrient Deficits During Pregnancy

Nutrient Deficit	Maternal	Fetal
Protein	Edema Hair loss Change in hair color or texture	Prematurity
Iron	Pallor	Low birthweight
B_{12}	Glossitis, pallor	
Folic acid	Glossitis	Neural tube defects
Calcium	Acceleration of osteoporosis	Decreased bone density
Zinc	Seborrheic dermatitis Alopecia Diarrhea	Fetal malformation Neural tube defects

Source: Adapted by permission from *Pocket Guide to Nutrition and Diet Therapy* by M.C. Moore, p. 24, The C.V. Mosby Company, St. Louis, © 1988.

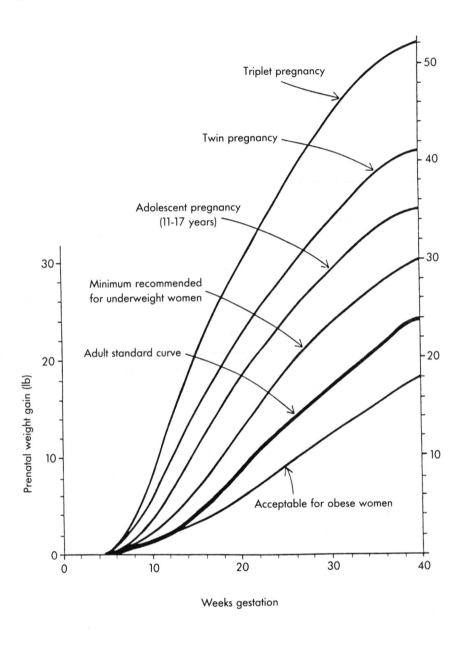

Figure 3-1 Weight Gain During Pregnancy for Selected Subgroups of Women. *Source:* Reprinted by permission from *Nutrition through the Life Cycle* by S.R. Williams and B. Worthington-Roberts (Eds.), p. 121, The C.V. Mosby Company, St. Louis, © 1988.

plotted on a weight-gain grid as part of the regular record (see chapter 5, Figure 5-1). Weight and height status can be estimated from chapter 5, Table 5-2 and weight gain can be evaluated accordingly. Nutrition assessment is summarized in Table 3-3, which lists recommended tools to be used and includes a timeframe for obtaining the data.

RISK ASSESSMENT

Based on the findings of the history and physical examination, the risk factors can be identified and a care plan can be developed. As Table 3-4 illustrates, however, nutrition intervention only in those patients who are at medical risk will miss many women who are at nutritional risk. Frequently, nutritionists are placed only in high-risk clinics. Yet some of the most significant risks for low-birthweight infants include underweight status and poor weight gain. In addition, GI problems, such as gastroplasty, are not listed as medical risks in obstetrics; neither are psychological problems that predispose a woman to risk of low birthweight, such as anorexia, bulimia, or hyperemesis.[6]

It should be noted that the customary nutritional risk factor identifications do not make systematic use of dietary intake data (see chapter 5). It should be emphasized that only when suitable dietary risk factors are identified should appropriate interventions be employed for women at nutritional risk.

Table 3-3 Assessing Nutritional Status During Pregnancy

Tool	Timing
Anthropometric	
Prenatal weight graph (Figure 5-1 and Table 5-2)	Initial visit and all subsequent visits
Laboratory	
Hemoglobin or Hct	Initial visit and each trimester
Blood glucose determinations	Initial visit for women at risk for diabetes
	At 24 to 28 weeks for all women
Urinalysis	Every visit for protein and glucose
Dietary	
Nutrition questionnaire (appendix A-1)	Initial visit
24-hour dietary recall (appendix A-2)	Initial visit and whenever indicated
Ongoing nutrition risk guide (Tables 3-4, 5-1, and 17-1)	At each visit whenever a risk is identified

Table 3-4 Maternal Risk Factors

A. Risk factors at the onset of pregnancy
  • Adolescence: less than three years postmenarche
  • Three or more pregnancies within two years
  • Past reproductive performance characterized by abortions, pregnancy complications, low-birthweight infants, or perinatal loss
  • Economic deprivation
  • Unusual dietary practices
  • Heavy smoker (more than 20 cigarettes per day)
  • Excessive alcohol intake (chronic use of more than five ounces of whiskey per day or its equivalent in beer, wine, or wine coolers or a history of binge drinking
  • Drug addiction
  • Chronic systemic diseases
  • Prepregnant weight below 85 percent of standard height and weight (less than 60 inches in height and 100 pounds in weight) or obesity above 120 percent of standard weight for height
B. Risk factors during pregnancy
  • Hemoglobin below 11 g/dl or hematocrit below 33 percent
  • Inadequate weight gain (less than 1 kg/month)
  • Excessive weight gain (3 kg/month), possibly associated with fluid retention
C. Risk factors following pregnancy
  • Nutritional demands of lactation

Source: Reprinted from *Nutrition Services in Perinatal Care* by Committee on Nutrition of the Mother and Preschool Child, with permission of National Academy Press, © 1981.

LACTATION

In 1984, the incidence of breastfeeding was 60 percent of all women giving birth. By three months of age only 38 percent continued to breastfeed. In our experience, the women least likely to breastfeed are those less than 20 years of age, those with only a grade-school education, and lower-income black women. The role of the health care practitioner is one of support and instruction.[7] Known contraindications to breastfeeding include certain medications or severe illness. Table 3-5 lists contraindicated medications.

THE HEALTH CARE TEAM

Recommendations for the management of any nutritional problem should be formulated and discussed with all the members of the health care team, including

Table 3-5 Drugs That Are Contraindicated During Breastfeeding

Drug	Reported Sign or Symptom in Infant or Effect on Lactation
Amethopterin*	Possible immune suppression; unknown effect on growth or association with carcinogenesis
Bromocriptine	Suppresses lactation
Cimetidine**	May suppress gastric acidity in infant, inhibit drug metabolism, and cause CNS stimulation
Clemastine	Drowsiness, irritability, refusal to feed, high-pitched cry, neck stiffness
Cyclophosphamide*	Possible immune suppression; unknown effect on growth or association with carcinogenesis
Ergotamine	Vomiting, diarrhea, convulsions (doses used in migraine medications)
Gold salts	Rash, inflammation of kidney and liver
Methimazole	Potential for interfering with thyroid function
Phenenindone	Hemorrhage
Thioracil	Decreased thyroid function; does not apply to prophylthioracil

*Data not available for other cytotoxic agents.
**Drug is concentrated in breast milk.

Sources: From *Nutrition through the Life Cycle* by S.R. Williams and B.S. Worthington-Roberts (Eds.), p. 174, The C.V. Mosby Company, St. Louis, © 1988; and *Pediatrics*, Vol. 72, p. 375, American Academy of Pediatrics, © 1983.

the patient. The team should include a physician, an obstetric nurse, and a nutritionist who is a registered dietitian, preferably with a masters degree and experience in obstetric nutrition. If a registered dietitian is not available, one should be enlisted on a consulting basis. Other team members may include social workers and health educators. Team discussions should include explanations of ambulatory care, laboratory studies, expected course of the pregnancy, signs and symptoms to be expected, timing of subsequent visits, educational programs, hospital admission, labor and delivery, and postpartum care. The discussion should also include an explanation of policies, including those for emergencies, and the roles of the various members of the health care team. Specific information about costs should also be provided so that the patient can make suitable arrangements.

NOTES

1. H.N. Jacobson, "Progress on Key Issues in Maternal Nutrition," *Public Health Reports Supplement*, July–August 1987:50.

2. Committee to Study the Prevention of Low Birthweight, *Preventing Low Birthweight* (Washington, D.C.: National Academy Press, 1985), 17.

3. H.N. Jacobson, "Nutrition and Pregnancy," in *Nutrition in Pediatrics*, ed. W.A. Walker and J.B. Watkins (Boston: Little, Brown & Company, 1985), 373.

4. Jacobson, "Progress on Key Issues," 50.

5. American College of Obstetricians and Gynecologists, *Standards for Obstetric-Gynecologic Services*, 6th ed. (Washington, D.C.: American College of Obstetricians and Gynecologists, 1985), 109.

6. Committee on Nutrition of the Mother and Preschool Child, *Nutrition Services in Perinatal Care* (Washington, D.C.: Food and Nutrition Board, National Academy Press, 1981), 72.

7. B. Worthington-Roberts, J. Vermeersch, and S.R. Williams, *Nutrition in Pregnancy and Lactation* (St. Louis: C.V. Mosby Co., 1985), 199.

Chapter 4

Environmental Management for Pregnant and Lactating Women in the Work Place

Rosemary Barber-Madden and Mary-Elizabeth A. Petschek

OVERVIEW

Current labor statistics show that more American women than ever before are entering and remaining in the labor force. Over the past 40 years, the number of women participating in the labor force has nearly doubled, from 28 percent in 1940 to 53 percent in the 1980s.[1] An estimated 65 percent of these women are of prime childbearing age, that is, between the ages of 18 and 44. According to Kamerman, 85 percent of these women are likely to become pregnant at some point in their working lives.[2]

In 1980, 62 percent of the nearly 3 million married women who gave birth were employed at some time during the year prior to delivery.[3] An even more telling increase has occurred in the labor force participation rates of mothers with children. The percentage of working mothers has increased from a mere 8.6 percent in 1940 to over 59 percent in 1980. The category of mothers with very young children has also been increasing; according to the 1982 Current Population Survey, mothers in the labor force with children less than one year of age reached 41 percent, as compared with 32 percent in 1977.[4]

ENVIRONMENTAL INFLUENCES

Work, Pregnancy, and Breastfeeding

In examining the employment trends of women today, it is clear that their health and nutritional needs require special attention. Recently, a medical endorsement of this requirement has been made by the Council on Scientific Affairs of the American Medical Association. The council stated that "pregnant employees should be able, in most cases, to continue productive work until the onset of labor."[5]

Research has revealed that the proportion of mothers who obtained early prenatal care was greater among employed women (87.7 percent) than among unemployed women (80.7 percent). Over 17 percent of employed mothers who experienced fetal deaths had late or no prenatal care. These data also show that among employed, married women having low-birthweight infants, 37 percent smoked during pregnancy. Nearly 50 percent of these women reported drinking alcohol during pregnancy, and 65 percent reported drinking coffee or tea.[6] (See Table 3-1, Drug Use During Pregnancy.)

Another issue is the influence of certain work activities on pregnancy outcome. Studies related to employment during pregnancy indicate that there may be some association between low birthweight and activities that require long periods of substantial amounts of physical stress.[7,8] However, it cannot be concluded that maternal employment increases the risk of low birthweight and other negative pregnancy outcomes.

Prenatal Services

Prenatal care is clearly related to positive pregnancy outcome.[9] The American College of Obstetricians and Gynecologists has established the components of prenatal care in the *Standards of Obstetrics and Gynecologic Services* (see chapter 3). These standards recommend 13 prenatal care visits beginning in the first trimester, including the provision of specific services and laboratory tests. In a report released in 1985, the Committee to Study the Prevention of Low Birthweight of the Institute of Medicine outlined seven components of prenatal care that merit stronger emphasis. Of these seven components, two are particularly relevant to working women: detection of behavior risks (including nutrition, personal health habits, and stress) and prenatal education.[10] It should be noted, however, that arranging to attend public or privately sponsored prenatal services and educational classes may for many be nearly impossible, due to time constraints, incompatible work schedules, or the lack of such services and classes where the woman resides.

Workplace Influences

Growing attention to the issue of breastfeeding and employment can also be attributed to the growing number of women in the work force. In 1976, the American Academy of Pediatrics issued a policy statement calling for "changes in employment policies and working conditions to make breastfeeding practical for working mothers."[11] Little is known about the experience of employed women who choose to breastfeed as they attempt to balance work and feeding schedules and family responsibilities. One survey of 567 women who breastfed while employed outside of the home showed that the most significant difficulty was role overload, a result of the multiple demands to which they were responding. Other major obstacles cited were worry about milk supply, lack of time to eat properly, pressure from others, and finding a place at work to pump.[12]

The 1984 Surgeon General's Workshop Report on Breastfeeding and Human Lactation identifies several barriers to breastfeeding while working, such as lack of time, a place to nurse the baby or pump the breasts while working, and the lack of information on the part of employers and health providers regarding effective breastfeeding promotion for employed women. Yet Touger-Decker provides a very encouraging, first-hand report on working while breastfeeding, storing milk, and diet for lactating mothers.[13]

MATERNAL NUTRITION PROMOTION STRATEGIES

One of the most important influences on the course and outcome of pregnancy is maternal nutrition.[14] Similarly, the significant nutritional and immunological benefits of breastfeeding for the infant are influenced by maternal diet during lactation.[15] It is by no means a coincidence that nutrition assessment, diet counseling, and follow-up evaluation are essential components of both pre- and postnatal care.

The most commonly used nutrition guidelines for pregnant and lactating women are the Recommended Dietary Allowances (RDA) established by the Food and Nutrition Board of the National Academy of Sciences, National Research Council (see appendix B-2). Nearly all nutrients are recommended in increased amounts during pregnancy and lactation, with variations from nutrient to nutrient (see appendix B-1). Smoking and alcohol consumption during pregnancy, which are associated with low birthweight, should not be overlooked when considering nutrition-related concerns in pregnancy. Furthermore, there is some indication that the use of illicit drugs and some prescriptive drugs may affect breast milk (see Table 3-5, Drugs That Are Contraindicated During Breastfeeding).

A review of the literature calls attention to the need for special consideration of the nutrition concerns of employed pregnant and lactating women and for the design of nutrition promotion and education programs specifically geared to this population. Strategies to promote nutrition among pregnant and lactating employed women need not be complex.

There are several issues to consider in designing effective strategies to promote nutrition for this population. First, efforts should be part of a prenatal program, whether offered by private/public health care providers or at the worksite, and should be guided by knowledgeable professionals. Second, health professionals, especially those who provide prenatal, postnatal, and pediatric services (such as obstetricians, midwives, nutritionists, pediatricians, and nurses) and occupational health professionals should have a basic knowledge and understanding of the special health and nutrition concerns of pregnant and lactating women (see Table 5-1, Common Nutrition Problems During Pregnancy and Lactation). Third, any attempt to promote healthy pregnancy and lactation for working women will be partially lost if the employer and the work environment are not supportive in either policy or physical structure.

Maternal nutrition promotion programs for employed women may include a range of activities, depending upon the setting when they are provided, the individual needs, and the resources available. The following nutrition promotion interventions are suggested:[16]

- Maternal nutrition education should emphasize the importance of early confirmation of pregnancy and initiation of prenatal care; the nutritive requirements during pregnancy and lactation; food selection and eating behaviors; and the implications of tobacco, alcohol, drug, and caffeine use during pregnancy and lactation.
- The importance of infant feeding choices—with an emphasis on the known immunological, biological, and psychological benefits of breastfeeding—should be emphasized in prenatal education.
- Individual and group dietary counseling can address special nutritional needs identified by the maternal nutrition assessment. Periodic weight and blood pressure checks provide indicators for counseling needs as the pregnancy progresses.
- Preparation of and/or use of existing nutrition education materials—including nutrition charts, posters, pamphlets, and films designed for this population—are essential.
- Cafeterias and vending machines can help to reinforce nutrition education. For example, food selection in vending machines might include choices of milk, fruit, and nuts. Social support for modifications in food consumption patterns is possible if group dynamics at the lunch table or coffee break are carefully developed.
- The availability of exercise and stress reduction and smoking cessation classes—on- or offsite—can further reinforce nutrition education, particularly for this population.
- A supportive environment for breastfeeding mothers who have returned to work requires
  a. some flexibility in time schedules to allow mothers to pump their breasts or, depending on the availability of child care, to breastfeed their infants while at work

b. a clean area or room where a mother can breastfeed or pump her breasts in privacy

c. refrigeration to store pumped breast milk that can be fed to the infant at home

- An employer health policy congruent with the concepts of nutrition education provides a firm foundation for the program. Employer awareness and support for measures to promote nutrition for pregnant and lactating employees on- or offsite are essential. These measures should include personnel policies concerning vending machines, availability of and eligibility for using exercise facilities, education regarding smoking, periodic physical exams, and insurance coverage for maternity care.

SUMMARY

In recent years, family workstyles and lifestyles have been changing as a result of the necessary influx of women into the labor force and the increased numbers of dual career households. It is apparent that effective approaches to meet the resulting challenges must be developed. Health professionals in all settings will play a pivotal role in addressing the newly emerging health and nutrition needs. Their responsibilities will range from determining the needs of working women, to developing appropriate health and nutrition promotion strategies, to working with employers to achieve common goals.

Pregnancy, lactation, and work are no longer considered socially or medically incompatible. Health professionals in the community or at the worksite need to develop innovative approaches that support pregnant and lactating workers. Maternal nutrition promotion strategies that stress the importance of proper nutrition during pregnancy and lactation and assist workers to understand their nutritional and health needs will contribute to healthy pregnancy outcome and successful breastfeeding.

NOTES

1. U.S. Department of Labor, Women's Bureau, Employment Standards Administration, *Working Mothers and Their Children* (Washington, D.C.: U.S. Department of Labor, August 1982), 1.

2. S.B. Kamerman, A. Kahn, and P. Kingston, *Maternity Policies and Working Women* (New York: Columbia University Press, 1983), 25.

3. S. Shilling and N. Lalich, "Maternal Occupation and Industry and the Pregnancy Outcome of U.S. Married Women, 1980," *Public Health Reports* 99 (March–April 1984): 154.

4. Department of Commerce, Bureau of the Census, *Current Population Survey* (Washington, D.C.: U.S. Department of Commerce, 1982), 1.

5. "Effects of Pregnancy on Work Performance," Report of the Council on Scientific Affairs, *Journal of the American Medical Association* 251 (1984): 1996.

6. Shilling and Lalich, "Maternal Occupation and Industry," 156.

7. R.L. Naeye and E.C. Peters, "Working During Pregnancy: Effects on the Fetus," *Pediatrics* 69 (1982): 724–727.

8. N. Marmelle, B. Lauman, and P. Lazar, "Prematurity and Occupational Activity during Pregnancy," *American Journal of Epidemiology* 119 (1984): 309–322.

9. Institute of Medicine, Committee to Study the Prevention of Low Birthweight, *Preventing Low Birthweight* (Washington, D.C.: National Academy Press, 1985), 146.

10. Ibid., 176–180.

11. "The Promotion of Breastfeeding," A policy statement based on a task force report of the American Academy of Pediatrics, *Pediatrics* 69 (May 1982): 656.

12. K.G. Auerback, "Employed Breastfeeding Mothers: Problems They Encounter," *Birth* 11 (Spring 1984): 17–20.

13. R. Touger-Decker, "The Working Mother: Nursing and Nutrition," *Women's Wellness* 2 (1988): 9.

14. A. Leader, K.H. Wong, and M. Deitel, "Maternal Nutrition in Pregnancy. Part I: A Review," *CMA Journal* 125 (1981): 545–547.

15. B. Winikoff and E. Baer, "The Obstetrician's Opportunity: Translating 'Breast Is Best' from Theory to Practice" (New York: The Population Council, July 1980), 1–3.

16. R. Barber-Madden et al., "Nutrition for Pregnant and Lactating Women: Implications for Worksite Health Promotion," *Journal of Nutrition Education* 18 (April 1986): S72–S75.

Chapter 5

Dietary Assessment and Management of Pregnant and Lactating Women

Janet C. King

- Is the pregnant client eating unusual foods?
- Is she trying to lose weight while pregnant?
- Is her weight gain sufficient?
- Is the pregnant client vomiting more than three times a day?

DIETARY ASSESSMENT

Overview

Diet and nutrition are factors that if controlled may reduce risk during the course of pregnancy as well as the pregnancy outcome. Prepregnancy diet and diet during pregnancy influence the adequacy of nutritional support for the developing fetus. Therefore, if at all possible, for optimal health of the mother and newborn, attention should focus on diet both before and during pregnancy.

Assessing the Diet of the Pregnant Woman

The overall purpose of the dietary assessment is to determine the quality and quantity of nutrients consumed by the mother. A dietary assessment should be completed at the first prenatal visit of the mother. Areas of concern should be evaluated at subsequent visits.

The prenatal nutrition questionnaire provides personal background data about factors that may influence food habits and attitudes. This information is useful for

---

The information in the first section of this chapter is adapted from *Nutrition During Pregnancy and Lactation*, published by the California Department of Health, 1975.

developing a personal plan of care that considers the mother's lifestyle, cultural background, and economic resources.

A prenatal nutrition questionnaire can be prepared for use specifically with pregnant clients (see appendix A-1). A column headed "Follow-Up Required" can be added in the right-hand margin so that the evaluator can highlight easily those areas needing further attention. It may be helpful to supplement the questions to get more specific information from the client.

The Prenatal Nutrition Questionnaire should include these dietary assessments:

- *Weight and weight gain history*. This may identify potential problems for the pregnancy, for example, an underweight or overweight woman, a woman who failed to gain a good weight in a previous pregnancy, a woman who does not want to gain a desirable weight during the present pregnancy, or a woman who recently had a change in her weight that may have influenced her nutritional stores. At each visit, the weight should be recorded on the Prenatal Weight Gain Grid (see Figure 5-1). A total weight gain of 24 pounds with a range from 22 to 30 pounds for normal-weight women is recommended[1,2,3] (see Figure 3-1).

- *Appetite*. Poor appetite in early pregnancy may be related to nausea and/or vomiting. The client's appetite should be considered in subsequent counseling.

- *Eating pattern and attitudes about food*. A client's current eating pattern and her beliefs about the relationship between diet and health will influence how receptive she is to nutrition counseling.

- *Food choices*. Many factors may influence the food choices of a client. It is necessary to ascertain the woman's commitment to these factors.

- *Household information*. Information about food budgeting, cooking facilities, and meal planning and preparation must be considered when counseling a client regarding her diet.

- *Supplements and pills*. Taking certain unprescribed pharmaceutical preparations may influence nutritional status. The use of appetite suppressants or diuretics in pregnancy and lactation is potentially dangerous.

- *Alcohol and smoking*. These may adversely affect the client's nutrient intake and utilization.

- *Food programs*. Information about food assistance programs will aid in understanding of the client's food availability.

- *Infant feeding*. How the mother plans to feed her baby after delivery should be determined. Information and tips regarding the preparation of infant feeding can be included in prenatal counseling.

PRENATAL WEIGHT GAIN GRID

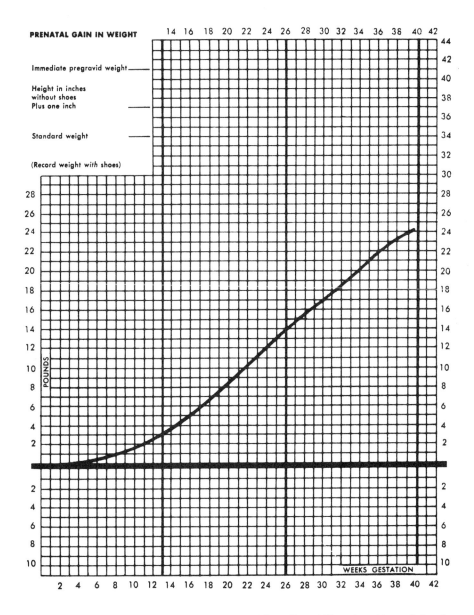

Figure 5-1 Prenatal Weight Gain Grid *Source*: Reprinted from *Clinical Obstetrics*, with permission of J.B. Lippincott and Company, © 1983.

The usual pattern of food intake is determined by an interviewer, using the 24-Hour Recall Form (see appendix A-2). This is designed to identify a client's diet pattern and to evaluate its nutritional adequacy for pregnancy or lactation. The diet intake form should be completed after the prenatal nutrition questionnaire. This provides an opportunity to stress the importance of nutrition and to begin counseling the client about aspects of her diet that need improvement.

The Food Frequency Form (see appendix A-3) can be used to further evaluate the adequacy of a client's diet and to identify omissions of groups of foods. For example, a client may indicate that she does not consume any milk or milk products. This would point out a suboptimal intake of calcium, riboflavin, vitamin D, and possibly protein.

Diet Analysis

After obtaining information about the client's food intake, using the 24-Hour Recall Form and/or the Food Frequency Form, the practitioner should evaluate the diet in terms of the nutritional needs for pregnancy or lactation. Two methods of diet analysis may be used: nutrient check by food groups or nutrient calculation.

After completing the diet intake record, the interviewer converts the amounts of food into serving(s) of the food group (see appendix B-1). After converting the amounts eaten to serving sizes, the number of servings for each food group are totaled. It is thus possible to compare what the woman has eaten with the servings suggested and to note any desired changes.

When more specific nutrient intake data are needed, the amount of protein, kilocalories, vitamins, and minerals may be calculated from data in a food composition table or by computer, using a number of available nutrient data bases. Nutrient composition tables are frequently included in the appendixes of nutrition textbooks. The adequacy of the nutrient intake may be determined by comparing it with the Recommended Dietary Allowances (RDA) as published by the National Research Council (see appendix B-2).

COMMON NUTRITIONAL PROBLEMS DURING PREGNANCY AND LACTATION

Detailed information about common nutritional problems during pregnancy and lactation of the pregnant and lactating woman is provided in Table 5-1. Also included in the table are suggestions for further assessment questions, recommended actions, and evaluation of outcomes. A method for estimating pregnancy weight status is provided in Table 5-2.

Table 5-1 Common Nutrition   Problems During Pregnancy and Lactation

I. CHRONIC NAUSEA AND/OR VOMITING

Difficulty with nausea and vomiting, or "morning sickness," is common during early pregnancy.

If nausea or vomiting is identified, the condition usually responds to further counseling for a modified dietary intake.

Assessment	Action
When did your nausea begin in your pregnancy? How often are you nauseous?	Recommend small, frequent meals that are fairly dry, drinking liquids between meals, and avoiding cooking odors.
Is the nausea associated with vomiting? How often do you vomit and at what times of the day?	Recommend eating easily digested foods such as toast or crackers when nauseous, and having some food at the bedside to take in the morning, which may offset "morning sickness."
Did you have nausea or vomiting in a previous pregnancy? How long did it last?	Questioning may disclose use of some acceptable food or practice that may be encouraged.
Have you changed your diet as a result of the nausea or vomiting?	Emphasize the importance of eating meals as recommended.
What are you eating each day?	Using the 24-Hour Recall Form (see appendix A-2), if necessary, review foods suggested during pregnancy with the client (see appendix B-1).

Evaluation

Have client keep a three-day food record (see appendix A-4), noting periods of nausea and/or vomiting and bring it to the next visit. Review intake to determine adequacy of diet.

If the diet remedies do not alleviate or correct the problem of nausea and/or vomiting and the overall food intake of the client is affected by the condition, refer to a physician for evaluation.

II. UNDERWEIGHT

Underweight is the reported pregravid weight-for-height of less than 90% of standard (see Table 5-2, "Estimating Pregnancy Weight Status").

Assessment	Action
Is the reported pregravid weight-for-height less than 90% of standard (Table 5-2)?	Determine the food intake of the client by the 24-hour recall. Compare with food groups and amounts suggested during pregnancy (see appendix B-1).
Is the food intake less than the amounts recommended?	Review food groups and amounts recommended. If intake is insufficient, counsel her to increase her intake. Stress the importance of good food during pregnancy, pointing out that underweight

Table 5-1 continued

	women tend to have smaller babies who may have more health problems.
Is she willing to consume 300–500 additional kcal/day to increase her weight?	Suggest examples of foods that provide about 300 kcal such as a cup of chili, a peanut butter sandwich with two slices of bread, a hamburger, or a milkshake (about 8 oz.)

Evaluation

Have client keep a three-day food record and bring it to next visit. If weight gain falls below 1 kg/month in second and third trimester, re-evaluate her diet to ensure that her food intake is adequate.

If her intake continues to be less than recommended, try to determine the cause. Is her appetite poor? Has she been ill? Is food not available because of economic problems?

If she cannot obtain sufficient food because of economic problems, recommend her to a federal food assistance program, e.g., Food Stamps or Supplementary Foods for Women, Infants and Children (WIC).

If there is a possible medical problem, refer her for evaluation.

III. INSUFFICIENT WEIGHT GAIN

Calculate change in body weight per month from weights made at each visit. Be sure that all weights are made without shoes, purse, or coat.

A woman should gain at least 1 kg (2.2 pounds) per month in the second and third trimesters.

Plot body weight changes on the prenatal weight gain grid (Figure 5-1) to determine if the client's weight gain follows a normal pattern for pregnancy.

Assessment	Action
Is the weight gain inadequate?	Determine the food intake of the client by repeating the 24-hour recall. Compare with the reported intake at the initial visit and the food groups and amounts suggested during pregnancy (see appendix B-1).
What is the cause of the insufficient weight gain?	
Has she been ill?	If it persists, consider referral for illness.
Has her appetite decreased?	Stress the importance of a good weight gain during pregnancy by pointing out that non-obese women with low weight gains during pregnancy tend to have smaller babies who may have more health problems following birth.

Table 5-1 continued

	Suggest that the client consume 300-500 kcal/day more than she did before she became pregnant (see Table 5-1, Underweight, for suggestions).
Is she unable to buy the food she needs?	Refer the client to a federal food assistance program if she is not able to buy the foods she needs.

Evaluation

Schedule a follow-up visit in two weeks to evaluate the client's response to dietary counseling. A weight gain of at least 1 lb or 0.5 kg should be seen in two weeks.

If the gain is insufficient, the importance of good weight gain should be re-emphasized and the client's food intake should be re-evaluated, using the 24-Hour Recall Form.

If social problems are possibly contributing to the poor weight gain pattern, refer the client to a social worker or family counselor.

IV. OBESITY

Obesity is defined as greater than 30 percent of standard weight for height (see Table 5-2).

Obese pregnant women are at increased risk for hypertension, toxemia, and gestational diabetes.

There is evidence that obese women tend to have large babies although their weight gains are below normal.

NEVER ADVISE AN OBESE PREGNANT OR LACTATING WOMAN TO FOLLOW A LOW CALORIE DIET.

Assessment	Action
Compare the reported pregravid weight-for-height to the published standard for that height to determine if the woman is more than 30% of the standard.	Referring to the Nutrition Questionnaire (see appendix A-1), determine the weight history of the woman.
How long has she been overweight? Is the weight gain recent? Was it associated with a previous pregnancy? Has she dieted previously? Was she successful? Did she regain any weight after dieting?	Determine the food intake of the client by completing the 24-hour recall.
Is the food intake in excess of the amount recommended during pregnancy?	Compare the 24-hour recall with the number of servings consumed from each food group with the amount suggested to evaluate the quality of the diet (see appendix B-1).
Is the caloric intake too high?	Make specific suggestions on how the woman can reduce her caloric intake.

Table 5-1 continued

What is the amount of soft drinks and snack foods consumed?	Make specific suggestions for substituting more nutritious foods for snack foods, such as fruit juice for soft drinks, fiber-rich crackers or bread for potato chips.
Is the total quality of the diet poor?	Make specific suggestions for substituting low-nutrient dense foods for foods that are suggested from the food group (see appendix B-1). NEVER ADVISE AN OBESE PREGNANT OR LACTATING WOMAN TO FOLLOW A LOW CALORIE DIET. Focus on improving diet quality while maintaining an adequate caloric intake. Obese pregnant women should consume at least 2,000 k/cal per day to ensure an adequate intake of vitamins and minerals.
Is there any evidence of binge eating?	The health of obese pregnant women, especially those reporting bizarre eating behavior, should be monitored closely by a physician during gestation.
Is the weight gain due to lack of exercise?	Suggest routine exercise, such as brisk walking.

Evaluation

Schedule a follow-up visit in no more than four weeks to evaluate the client's response to dietary counseling. Calculate the amount of weight gained during the interval.

If excessive weight gain continues, refer to a registered dietitian (R.D.) for in-depth counseling.

V. EXCESS CAFFEINE CONSUMPTION

Massive doses of caffeine in experimental animals appear to be teratogenic.

Data from human populations do not provide convincing evidence that caffeine affects pregnancy outcome.

However, it seems prudent to use caffeine in moderation during pregnancy, since large intakes of caffeine-containing beverages may displace other nutrient sources in the diet.

Based on birth defects produced by caffeine in experimental animals, the Surgeon General in 1981 advised pregnant women to avoid unnecessary caffeine consumption.

Assessment	Action
Is the pregnant woman consuming excessive (greater than four servings) amounts of caffeine-containing beverages (e.g., coffee, tea, colas)?	From the information obtained in the 24-hour recall, determine the sources of caffeine in the diet and the number of servings consumed each day.

Table 5-1 continued

What is the nutrient quality of the diet?	Assess the overall quality of the diet. Ascertain if caffeine-containing beverages are displacing other more nutritious beverages, such as milk or fruit juice.
	Discuss with the client the importance of reducing the intake of caffeine-containing beverages in the diet, pointing out that it may increase the risk of birth defects.
	Suggest ways to reduce caffeine: (1) replace regular coffee with a caffeinated/decaffeinated blend or decaffeinated coffee, (2) replace black or green tea with herbal tea, or (3) substitute water or fruit juice for caffeinated beverages.

Evaluation

At the next visit determine the amount of caffeine-containing beverages consumed by completing the 24-hour recall.

If the amount is greater than four servings, repeat information about possible risk factors. If she continues to report excessive consumption of caffeine-containing beverages at subsequent visits, refer her to a registered dietitian (R.D.) for in-depth counseling.

If the client eliminates caffeine from her diet abruptly, she may experience headaches and malaise for several days to a week.

VI. POOR-QUALITY DIET (a diet high in fat, sugar, and/or sodium)

Diets that contain a high amount of energy from foods high in fat or sugar may satisfy the woman's energy needs before her protein, vitamin, and mineral needs have been met. This is a low nutrient-dense diet.

Assessment	**Action**
What is the quality of the pregnant woman's diet?	Determine the usual food intake by completing the 24-hour recall. Use the Food Frequency Form (appendix A-3) for assessment of snack intake.
	Recommend alternative snack foods, such as raw fruits and vegetables, high-fiber crackers and cheese, dried fruit, frozen fruit juice bars, and yogurt.

Evaluation

An abrupt reduction in foods that have been the major source of energy in the diet may cause a fall in total energy intake and a decline in the rate of weight gain.

To prevent this, it is important to recommend alternative energy sources.

Table 5-1 continued

A decrease in the intake of sodium and simple carbohydrates may cause a loss of total body water and, therefore, weight.

At the next visit determine the quality of the diet by repeating the 24-hour recall and the food frequency forms. If the diet has not improved sufficiently, repeat counseling about the need for nutrient-dense foods.

If the diet continues to be of poor quality, refer the client to a registered dietitian (R.D.) for in-depth counseling.

VII. FOOD CRAVINGS OR PICA

Cravings for certain foods, such as sweets or dairy products, are common during pregnancy.

The mechanism leading to food cravings during pregnancy is unknown.

These cravings may result in an increased intake of energy- and calcium-containing foods.

The nutritional significance of food cravings during pregnancy cannot be assessed without knowing the total food intake of the woman.

A few women experience a compulsion to ingest nonfood substances, such as clay, dirt, or laundry starch, during pregnancy.

The displacement effect of pica substances could result in a reduced intake of nutritious foods.

Substances, such as laundry starch, that provide calories could lead to excessive weight gain if ingested in amounts above the usual dietary need.

Some pica substances may interfere with the absorption of certain minerals, e.g., iron.

Assessment	Action
Does the pregnant woman have changes in food preferences or cravings?	Identify changes in food preferences, cravings, and pica from the Pregnancy Nutrition Questionnaire (see appendix A-1).
Are the changes in food preferences or cravings potentially harmful, or will they reduce the overall nutrient quality of the diet?	If any of the changes in food preferences are potentially harmful, discuss with the client the possible problems resulting from these food habits.
	Recommend alternative food choices that will improve the diet quality.

Evaluation

Schedule a follow-up visit in two to four weeks and repeat the 24-hour recall, stressing that the client must report all substances ingested, both food and nonfood items.

Follow the weight gain pattern to ensure that energy intake is adequate to support smooth, progressive weight gain.

For clients consuming dirt, clay, or laundry starch, recommend laboratory assessment of the minerals for possibility of risk.

If continued pica practice that may be potentially harmful is reported, refer the client to a registered dietitian (R.D.) for in-depth counseling.

Table 5-1 continued

VIII. FOOD FADS AND MYTHS

Elimination of entire groups of food, e.g., the dairy group, from the diet because of beliefs in food fads or myths will increase the pregnant woman's risk of a nutrient deficiency.

Assessment	Action
Does the client state that there are certain foods she does not eat for health or religious reasons?	Identify beliefs in food fads or myths from the Nutrition Questionnaire (appendix A-1).
How long has she followed these practices?	Ask follow-up questions to determine how long she has been following the practices and, specifically, what foods she eliminates.
What is the overall nutrient quality of her diet?	Evaluate the nutrient quality of her diet from the 24-hour recall.
Are the beliefs in food fads or myths reducing the diet quality?	If the food beliefs are having a deleterious effect on the overall diet quality, discuss the risk to the health of the mother and baby. Recommend modifications in her food practices to improve the quality of the diet.
Is the mother likely to be at risk for any nutrient deficiencies because of the quality of her diet?	Refer the client for laboratory tests to evaluate the status of any nutrients likely to be deficient, e.g., iron status.

Evaluation

If the deleterious food habits continue, refer the client for evaluation of potential nutritional problems, such as anemia or insufficient weight gain.

If the food habits continue and are affecting the overall quality of the diet, refer the client to a registered dietitian (R.D.) for in-depth counseling.

Table 5-2 Estimating Pregnancy Weight Status

Height (without shoes)		Weight* (without clothes)			
Feet	Inches	Underweight	Normal Weight	Overweight	Obese
4	8	< 89	89–109	110–129	>129
4	9	< 91	91–111	112–131	>131
4	10	< 94	94–114	115–135	>135
4	11	< 96	96–117	118–139	>139
5		< 99	99–121	122–143	>143
5	1	<102	102–124	125–147	>147
5	2	<105	105–128	129–152	>152
5	3	<109	109–133	134–157	>157
5	4	<112	112–137	138–162	>162
5	5	<116	116–142	143–167	>167
5	6	<120	120–146	147–173	>173
5	7	<123	123–151	152–176	>178
5	8	<127	127–155	156–183	>183
5	9	<130	130–159	160–188	>188
5	10	<134	134–163	164–193	>193
5	11	<137	137–167	168–197	>197
6		<140	140–171	172–202	>202
6	1	<143	143–175	176–207	>207

*Calculations of relative weight are based on the midpoint values by height for women with a "medium" frame at age 25, as given in the 1959 Metropolitan Life Insurance Table. Underweight is defined as a weight-for-height of <90 percent of the midpoint, normal weight as 90–110 percent, overweight as 110–130 percent, and obese as >130 percent of standard weight.

Source: Adapted from Metropolitan Life Insurance Company, Statistical Bulletin No. 40, 1949, by J.E. Brown, University of Minnesota, October 1987. Used with permission of Metropolitan Life Insurance Company, and J.E. Brown.

NOTES

1. B. Worthington-Roberts, "Nutritional Support of Successful Reproduction: An Update," *Journal of Nutrition Education* 1 (February 1987): 1.

2. J.E. Brown, *Nutrition and Your Pregnancy* (Minneapolis: University of Minnesota Press, 1983), 39–46.

3. P. Rosso, "A New Chart to Monitor Weight Gain During Pregnancy," *American Journal of Clinical Nutrition* 41 (1985): 644–652.

Part III

The Infant

Chapter 6

Nutrition Assessment of the Infant
(Birth Through Two Years)

Samuel J. Fomon

OVERVIEW

Nutrition assessment by health care practitioners is a subcategory of general health assessment. As such, one cannot be satisfied merely by detection of nutritional disorders. Equally important is the identification of individuals who are at increased risk of nutritional deficiencies or excesses.

Approaches to nutrition assessment must be adapted to the setting. In developing countries, where protein-energy malnutrition and vitamin A and other vitamin deficiencies are common, nutrition assessment is focused on detection of advanced nutritional deficiencies and can be based primarily on the health history, physical examination, and measurement of body weight; whereas in industrialized countries, nutrition assessment is focused on early detection and prevention. The discussion in this chapter concerns nutrition assessment of infants in the United States and is oriented toward the individual. A somewhat different approach would be more appropriate if the goal were to identify nutritional disorders most prevalent in a specified community.

HEALTH HISTORY

The health history is a primary tool in individual infant nutrition assessment. A satisfactory history will include information about the family and environment, the period of intrauterine development, and the events surrounding birth. A detailed dietary history is needed (see chapter 8 and appendix A-1). Details of illnesses and abnormalities should be recorded, and as much information as possible should be obtained about the infant's growth.

Family

The ages of the parents and their educational backgrounds, occupations, medical histories, and dietary practices should be reviewed. One should note any cultural, religious, or other considerations that result in avoidance of certain classes of foods. If either parent is reported to experience adverse reactions to various foods or inhalants, an attempt should be made to determine the reliability of the reports: type of adverse reaction, timing of reaction in relation to exposure, severity of reaction, and response to treatment. The medical histories of siblings should be explored in a similar manner.

Intrauterine and Immediate Postnatal Period

In industrialized countries, the maternal diet during pregnancy is rarely responsible for abnormal nutritional status of the newborn. An exception concerns vitamin B_{12} status of infants born to strict vegetarian mothers. If the woman has been a strict vegetarian for several years and has received no supplements of vitamin B_{12}, the infant will be born with low vitamin B_{12} stores and, if breastfed by the vitamin B_{12}-deficient mother, may soon develop hematologic and/or neurologic manifestations of vitamin B_{12} deficiency.[1]

The possibility of blood loss from the infant at the time of birth should be explored. The infant will be at increased risk of iron deficiency if iron stores have been decreased by blood loss.

The history of neonatal vitamin K supplementation is important, especially for breastfed infants in the first few months of life. Breastfed infants who have not received a vitamin K supplement are at risk of serious bleeding because of vitamin K deficiency.[2]

Infants with a history of neonatal disease or abnormality, especially those requiring surgical intervention or extended hospital care, must be considered at increased risk of subsequent nutritional deficiency. Details of the illness should be obtained. The largest group of such infants are those of low birthweight.

Illnesses and Abnormalities

Disease or abnormality of any system is likely to interfere with nutrient intake and place the infant at increased risk of nutritional deficiency. Hypertonia, athetosis, and chronic respiratory disease may result in increased energy requirements that aggravate the problem of unusually low intake. Disorders that result in malabsorption are likely to be associated with deficiencies of fat-soluble vitamins.

Anemia resulting from sickle cell disease or thalassemia should not be mistaken for iron-deficiency anemia.

Presumed adverse reactions to foods need to be explored in detail. Many reports of such adverse reactions cannot be confirmed by challenge with the food in question.[3] When the possible reactions are serious or life-threatening (for example, laryngeal edema, anaphylaxis), challenge should be undertaken only under the supervision of qualified medical specialists. Thus, it is necessary to obtain information about the type of reaction as well as information about foods that have been excluded from the diet. An infant erroneously believed to be allergic to milk, soy, and several other foods may be fed an unnecessarily restricted diet that increases the likelihood of developing a nutritional deficiency disorder.

PHYSICAL ASSESSMENT

Clinical signs of specific nutritional deficiencies are sometimes detectable in the hair, eyes, tongue, skin, neck, and skeleton; but even trained examiners rarely demonstrate firm agreement on the presence or absence of such signs.[4] A physical finding suggesting nutritional abnormality should be looked upon as a clue rather than as major evidence favoring a diagnosis (see appendix C-1). Costochondral beading or enlarged joints should not be accepted as evidence of rickets without roentgenographic confirmation. Abnormal hair should not be accepted as evidence of protein malnutrition without laboratory confirmation of serum protein.

Most helpful in the physical examination will be evidence of chronic illness or detection of diseases that interfere with growth and general health. Special attention should be paid to such general features as pallor, apathy, and irritability and the presence of petechiae, ecchymosis, dermatitis, or edema. The condition of the gums and teeth should be recorded. The possibility of cardiovascular, pulmonary, hepatic, or renal disease should be considered.

ANTHROPOMETRIC ASSESSMENT

Growth

In nutrition assessment, changes in weight and length are much more sensitive indexes than are current weight and length. Data from prior measurements of length and weight should be obtained. The precise dates of the measurements should be recorded. Under most circumstances of measurement, data on length will be inaccurate; therefore, major effort should be directed toward obtaining data on weight.

Publication of "growth charts" by the National Center for Health Statistics in 1976 was a major advance because, for the first time, charts on weight for length became available.[5] Nevertheless, to refer to size charts as growth charts is somewhat misleading. Growth is dynamic and must be expressed as gain per unit of time. Weight for age, length for age, and weight for length permit comparison of an individual's size at a specified age with that of peers. Still, these indexes are of limited value in detecting any but gross deviations from normal. Obesity, a state in which the ratio of fat to fat-free tissue is excessive, is often indicated by excessive weight for length. However, in the use of decreased growth rate as an index of nutritional deficiency, measurements of size (weight for age, length for

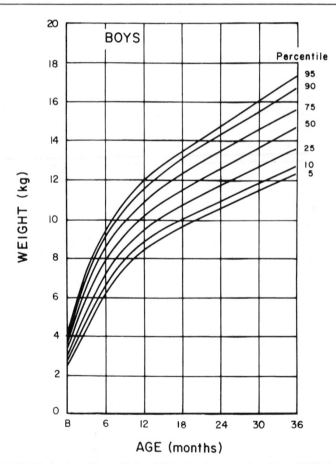

Figure 6-1 Weight for Age of Boys, Birth to 36 Months. *Source:* Adapted from *NCHS Growth Curves for Children: Birth-18 Years, United States* by P.V. Hamill et al, National Center for Health Statistics, U.S. Government Printing Office, 1977.

age, and weight for length) are insensitive. Even when repeated measurements have been made, interpretation of the data is usually difficult.

Body Weight, Length, and Weight for Length

Body weight should be measured with the infant unclothed, using beam scales with nondetachable weights or direct-reading electronic scales. The scales should permit reading to the nearest 10 g and should be calibrated at intervals of three to four months. The relation of weight to age is indicated in Figure 6-1 for males and in Figure 6-2 for females. As already mentioned, this relation is of limited value in assessing nutritional status.

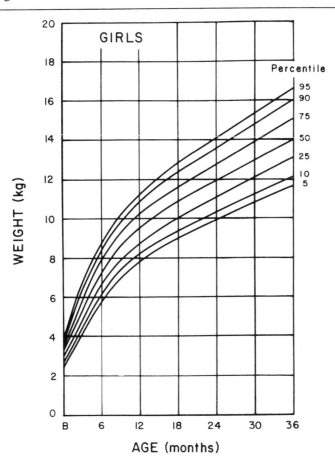

Figure 6-2 Weight for Age of Girls, Birth to 36 Months. *Source:* Adapted from *NCHS Growth Curves for Children: Birth-18 Years, United States* by P.V. Hamill et al, National Center for Health Statistics, U.S. Government Printing Office, 1977.

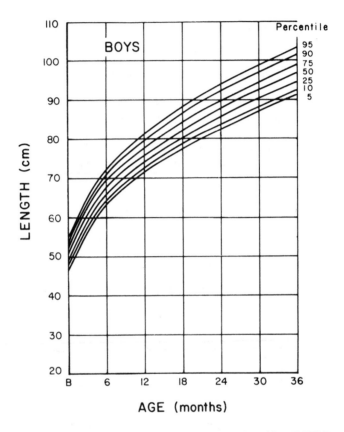

Figure 6-3 Length for Age of Boys, Birth to 36 Months. *Source:* Adapted from *NCHS Growth Curves for Children: Birth-18 Years, United States* by P.V. Hamill et al, National Center for Health Statistics, U.S. Government Printing Office, 1977.

The relation of length to age is presented for males in Figure 6-3 and for females in Figure 6-4. The relation of weight to length is presented for males in Figure 6-5 and for females in Figure 6-6.

Accurate measurements of body length require suitable equipment, standardized procedures, and well-trained personnel. The equipment and procedures have been described in detail elsewhere.[6] Under the best conditions, measurement error is usually 0.4 cm or less. However, such reproducibility is not possible with untrained personnel (mothers are not good head-holders).

It is probable that under usual circumstances in offices, clinics, and hospitals, measurement errors not infrequently exceed 0.5 cm and may at times exceed 1 cm. As may be seen from Figure 6-3, for an 18-month-old male with a body length of 79 cm (10th centile), underestimation by 1 cm would result in body

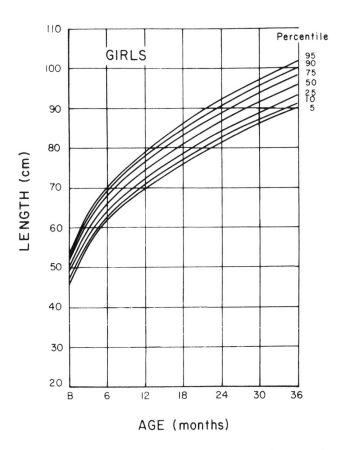

Figure 6-4 Length for Age of Girls, Birth to 36 Months. *Source:* Adapted from *NCHS Growth Curves for Children: Birth-18 Years, United States* by P.V. Hamill et al, National Center for Health Statistics, U.S. Government Printing Office, 1977.

length at about the 5th centile; whereas overestimation by 1 cm would result in body length at about the 25th centile. A 1 cm error in length will introduce a generally similar problem in interpreting data on weight for length.

In nutrition assessment, one seeks clues to indicate which individuals merit greater scrutiny than the general population. Infants with length for age below the 10th centile and infants with weight for length above the 90th or below the 10th centile should receive particular attention. If measurement errors are as great as 1 cm, substantial numbers of subjects with lengths between the 10th and 25th centiles will mistakenly be assumed to fall in the group meriting special attention. Conversely, subjects with lengths less than the 10th centile will be mistakenly thought to require no special attention.

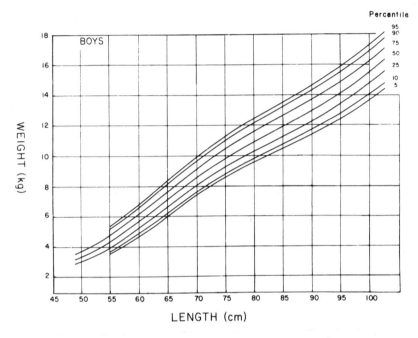

Percentile

Figure 6-5 Weight for Length of Boys, Birth to 36 Months. *Source:* Adapted from *NCHS Growth Curves for Children: Birth-18 Years, United States* by P.V. Hamill et al, National Center for Health Statistics, U.S. Government Printing Office, 1977.

Change in Weight and Change in Length

Data on change in weight and change in length per unit of time are more useful for clinical assessment than the size relationships presented in the figures. For the early months of life, such data are presented in Tables 6-1 and 6-2 for boys and Tables 6-3 and 6-4 for girls. Corresponding data for three-month or six-month age intervals from 6 to 24 months of age are presented in Table 6-5. However, these tables must be used with caution because the various centiles apply not only to the specified age but to the duration of the interval between measurements. For example, in Table 6-1, the 10th centile gains in weight of boys are 9.6, 9.0, and 5.2 g/day, respectively, for the age intervals 112 to 140 days, 140 to 168 days, and 168 to 196 days. However, for the same infants for the interval 112 to 196 days, the 10th centile gain is 11.9 g/day. Infants who gain least rapidly during one age interval are generally not the infants who gain least rapidly during the next age interval.

Although change in length is a valuable index of nutritional state, measurement errors are exceedingly serious. Data indicate that the 10th, 50th, and 90th centile

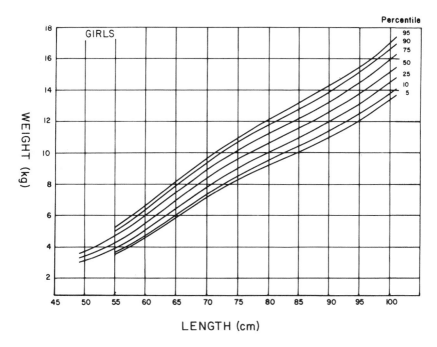

Figure 6-6 Weight for Length of Girls, Birth to 36 Months. *Source:* Adapted from *NCHS Growth Curves for Children: Birth-18 Years, United States* by P.V. Hamill et al, National Center for Health Statistics, U.S. Government Printing Office, 1977.

gains in length of males (Table 6-5) from 9 to 12 months of age are 3.2, 4.0, and 5.1 cm, respectively.[7] Thus, in the case of an infant who gained 4 cm in length during this age interval, if length measurement had an error of 0.6 cm in a positive direction at age 9 months and an error of 0.6 cm in a negative direction at age 12 months, the apparent gain would be only 2.8 cm—a value below the 10th centile. The need for a high degree of quality control of the measurement procedures is therefore apparent. Inaccurate data on body length are worse than no data, and in many circumstances it may be best to avoid measurements of length.

Head Circumference

In normal and malnourished infants, gain in head circumference closely parallels growth in length and adds little to assessment of nutrition status.[8] Measurement of head circumference is, of course, important in documenting the presence of microcephaly of nonnutritional origin and macrocephaly.

Table 6-1 Gains in Weight of Male Infants (g/day)

Age at First Measurement (days)	Centile	Age at Second Measurement (days)								
		14	28	42	56	84	112	140	168	196
8	10	13.4	26.8	28.9	28.4	25.9	24.1	22.3	21.5	20.2
	50	34.5	39.9	39.7	37.4	34.1	31.4	28.8	26.8	24.3
	90	53.8	53.8	50.1	47.8	42.7	39.3	33.7	38.9	28.5
14	10		28.8	29.1	28.2	25.5	23.8	21.6	20.9	19.6
	50		42.7	41.0	38.2	34.0	31.2	28.0	26.0	23.8
	90		57.3	51.3	48.8	42.6	39.2	34.0	38.9	28.4
28	10			26.6	26.0	23.3	21.4	19.3	18.9	17.7
	50			38.6	35.6	31.9	29.0	25.3	24.1	21.9
	90			51.6	47.9	40.9	37.7	31.9	29.0	27.0
42	10				20.4	20.3	19.3	16.9	17.7	15.7
	50				33.6	29.7	26.8	23.5	22.2	20.6
	90				48.5	39.7	35.8	30.6	27.8	25.4
56	10					18.4	18.1	15.7	15.8	14.7
	50					27.5	25.4	21.9	21.2	19.4
	90					38.4	34.7	28.4	26.7	24.0
84	10						14.5	12.9	12.9	12.6
	50						23.3	19.4	19.3	17.7
	90						33.8	27.4	25.0	22.5
112	10							9.6	11.9	11.9
	50							17.7	17.7	16.4
	90							25.9	23.9	21.5
140	10								9.0	10.7
	50								17.9	15.7
	90								25.4	21.9
168	10									5.2
	50									14.2
	90									21.7

583 subjects 8-112 days; 104 subjects 112-196 days; 65 subjects 8-196 days.

LABORATORY ASSESSMENT: IRON DEFICIENCY

Laboratory tests are essential for confirming suspicions about the existence of various deficiency disorders (see appendix C-2). Methods are available for detecting abnormalities in nutritional status with respect to protein, essential fatty acids, vitamins, and a number of minerals. A discussion of such tests is beyond the scope

Table 6-2 Gains in Length of Male Infants (mm/day)

Age at First Measurement (days)	Centile	Age at Second Measurement (days)						
		42	56	84	112	140	168	196
8	10	1.04	1.04	1.01	0.97	0.91	0.84	0.79
	50	1.32	1.26	1.17	1.10	1.02	0.95	0.89
	90	1.58	1.47	1.34	1.25	1.15	1.04	0.99
14	10		1.00	0.98	0.94	0.90	0.83	0.78
	50		1.23	1.15	1.08	0.99	0.94	0.87
	90		1.44	1.31	1.22	1.11	1.02	0.97
28	10			0.91	0.88	0.85	0.77	0.73
	50			1.10	1.04	0.95	0.89	0.83
	90			1.29	1.19	1.06	0.98	0.93
42	10			0.84	0.85	0.80	0.74	0.70
	50			1.06	1.00	0.92	0.85	0.80
	90			1.28	1.16	1.05	0.96	0.92
56	10				0.79	0.78	0.69	0.67
	50				0.98	0.87	0.82	0.76
	90				1.17	1.01	0.92	0.86
84	10					0.64	0.58	0.57
	50					0.81	0.75	0.69
	90					1.00	0.89	0.82
112	10						0.46	0.50
	50						0.70	0.63
	90						0.87	0.79
140	10							0.43
	50							0.59
	90							0.77

583 subjects 8-112 days; 104 subjects 112-196 days; 65 subjects 8-196 days.

of this chapter. However, some comments about iron deficiency—the most prevalent nutritional deficiency disorder—seem appropriate.

When iron deficiency has progressed to a severity in which anemia is present, iron stores are depleted, inadequate quantities of iron are available for erythropoiesis, and abnormal erythrocytes are formed. Laboratory tests useful in documenting the presence of iron deficiency are serum concentration of ferritin (less than 10 ng/ml), saturation of transferrin (less than 12 percent), concentration of protoporphyrin in erythrocytes (more than 70 μg/dl of packed erythrocytes), and mean corpuscular volume (MCV) of erythrocytes (less than 74 fl). It is generally recommended that at least two, and preferably three, of these tests be

Table 6-3 Gains in Weight of Female Infants (g/day)

Age at First Measurement (days)	Centile	Age at Second Measurement (days)								
		14	28	42	56	84	112	140	168	196
8	10	12.5	22.9	23.5	23.4	22.0	20.5	19.8	18.7	17.9
	50	30.8	33.9	33.6	32.0	28.6	26.8	24.4	22.8	21.5
	90	48.0	47.3	45.0	41.2	36.7	33.6	30.7	27.8	25.7
14	10		23.7	24.0	23.7	21.6	20.2	19.8	18.3	17.8
	50		36.2	33.7	32.2	28.7	26.5	24.4	22.5	21.2
	90		49.8	45.4	41.7	36.8	33.7	30.6	27.7	25.3
28	10			19.7	20.4	19.2	18.6	18.9	17.2	16.2
	50			31.6	29.9	27.0	25.2	22.8	21.1	19.7
	90			45.7	40.9	35.8	32.3	29.4	26.2	24.0
42	10				16.7	17.0	16.9	17.5	16.1	14.9
	50				27.7	25.5	23.5	21.8	20.0	19.0
	90				40.0	34.3	30.8	27.7	25.4	23.3
56	10					14.6	15.9	16.4	15.2	14.0
	50					24.4	22.6	20.2	18.9	17.9
	90					33.2	30.1	26.4	24.5	22.3
84	10						13.0	14.9	12.7	12.4
	50						21.0	18.8	17.4	16.5
	90						30.4	25.4	22.5	20.9
112	10							9.6	9.6	10.9
	50							16.6	15.9	15.0
	90							26.0	22.5	20.0
140	10								8.1	8.9
	50								14.5	14.2
	90								22.8	18.9
168	10									5.6
	50									13.0
	90									20.2

556 subjects 8-112 days; 115 subjects 112-196 days; 75 subjects 8-196 days.

performed because a normal value for any one of the tests may be obtained in the presence of iron deficiency and abnormal values may be obtained in subjects in good iron nutritional status.[9] The major problems in interpreting the laboratory tests are laboratory errors; fluctuations in transferrin saturation in an individual, even on the same day; lead intoxication, which results in elevated values for erythrocyte protoporphyrin concentration; and the effects of infection or inflammation: decreased transferrin saturation, increased serum ferritin concentration,

Table 6-4 Gains in Length of Female Infants (mm/day)

Age at First Measurement (days)	Centile	Age at Second Measurement (days)						
		42	56	84	112	140	168	196
8	10	1.00	0.99	0.95	0.90	0.86	0.80	0.76
	50	1.24	1.19	1.11	1.03	0.97	0.90	0.84
	90	1.49	1.40	1.22	1.15	1.00	1.02	0.93
14	10		0.93	0.91	0.87	0.83	0.77	0.74
	50		1.14	1.07	1.00	0.93	0.87	0.80
	90		1.35	1.21	1.13	1.05	1.00	0.90
28	10			0.85	0.82	0.76	0.73	0.70
	50			1.01	0.96	0.91	0.84	0.78
	90			1.18	1.10	1.01	0.95	0.87
42	10			0.78	0.77	0.74	0.69	0.63
	50			0.98	0.93	0.86	0.81	0.75
	90			1.17	1.08	1.02	0.94	0.85
56	10				0.72	0.68	0.65	0.60
	50				0.89	0.83	0.78	0.73
	90				1.07	0.98	0.91	0.82
84	10					0.56	0.58	0.53
	50					0.77	0.73	0.67
	90					0.94	0.87	0.78
112	10						0.49	0.47
	50						0.66	0.60
	90						0.79	0.70
140	10							0.36
	50							0.55
	90							0.74

556 subjects 8-112 days; 115 subjects 112-196 days; 75 subjects 8-196 days.

and, in chronic infection or inflammation, increased erythrocyte protoporphyrin concentration.

In many situations it will be feasible to determine hemoglobin concentration or hematocrit routinely, but it will not be feasible to determine the presence of iron deficiency by using several of the laboratory tests just mentioned. Hemoglobin concentration or hematocrit should generally be determined between 9 and 12 months of age in term infants and between 6 and 9 months of age in preterm infants. Between 9 months and three years of age, most anemia is the result of iron deficiency. Thus, there is no objection to proceeding with a therapeutic trial without confirming the presence of iron deficiency. Two conditions should be met:

Table 6-5 Daily Changes in Weight and Length Between Selected Ages

Age Interval (Months)	Percentiles	SD	Gain in Weight (gm/day)		Gain in Length (mm/day)	
			Males	Females	Males	Females
3-6		−2	8.9	9.3	0.4	0.4
	10		14.1	15.4	0.5	0.5
	25		16.6	18.1	0.6	0.6
	50		19.5	20.7	0.7	0.7
	75		24.4	23.6	0.8	0.8
	90		28.2	25.8	1.0	0.9
		−2	32.5	31.7	1.1	1.0
6-9		−2	5.4	4.6	0.2	0.3
	10		9.0	10.3	0.4	0.4
	25		11.3	12.3	0.4	0.5
	50		14.7	14.7	0.5	0.5
	75		18.3	17.9	0.5	0.6
	90		21.3	21.0	0.6	0.7
		−2	24.6	27.0	0.8	0.8
9-12		−2	−0.2	3.1	0.2	0.2
	10		5.7	5.9	0.3	0.3
	25		8.3	8.6	0.4	0.4
	50		11.7	10.9	0.4	0.4
	75		14.9	13.7	0.5	0.5
	90		18.6	15.6	0.6	0.6
		−2	24.3	18.8	0.7	0.7
12-18		−2	2.2	2.1	0.2	0.3
	10		4.9	5.0	0.3	0.3
	25		6.4	5.8	0.3	0.4
	50		8.2	7.2	0.4	0.4
	75		10.4	8.8	0.4	0.4
	90		12.0	10.4	0.5	0.5
		−2	14.9	13.1	0.6	0.5
18-24		−2	0.1	1.0	0.2	0.2
	10		2.2	2.9	0.2	0.2
	25		3.7	4.0	0.3	0.3
	50		6.0	6.5	0.3	0.3
	75		8.1	8.3	0.4	0.4
	90		10.1	10.6	0.4	0.4
		−2	12.3	12.0	0.4	0.5
24-36		−2	1.8	2.1	0.2	0.2
	10		3.6	3.6	0.2	0.2
	25		4.2	4.3	0.2	0.2
	50		3.4	3.8	0.2	0.2
	75		6.0	6.9	0.3	0.3
	90		7.3	7.9	0.3	0.3
		−2	9.0	9.7	0.3	0.3

Source: Reprinted from *Infant Nutrition*, 2nd ed., by S.J. Fomon, p. 52, with permission of W.B. Saunders Company, © 1974.

(1) the value for hemoglobin concentration or hematocrit should be verified by repeating the determination, and (2) a fail-proof follow-up mechanism should be in place.

Medicinal iron, 1 mg/kg twice daily in the form of ferrous sulfate or other well-absorbed preparation, should be given for four to six weeks. If the hemoglobin concentration has increased less than 1 g/dl or the hematocrit has increased less than 2 percent, other causes of anemia should be investigated. In any case, the child should remain under observation until the hemoglobin or hematocrit has returned to normal.

SUMMARY

As with older individuals, assessment of the nutritional status of infants must begin with a well-taken medical and nutritional history. It is the history that provides the clues about which possibilities of disorders should be explored. The nutritional history is generally easier to obtain in infants than in older individuals because the variety of foods consumed is less, especially in the case of young infants, and the caretakers often have more reliable information about food consumption by infants than by older children. The physical examination is mainly useful in providing evidence of medical problems that increase energy expenditures or interfere with food intake or nutrient utilization.

Size (weight for age or length for age) is a crude index of nutritional status. Much more useful is gain in weight and gain in length. The latter are sensitive indexes during the period of rapid growth in early infancy but somewhat less sensitive indexes in later infancy and childhood. Laboratory studies are most valuable in providing confirmation of disorders suspected on the basis of the medical history. However, iron deficiency anemia is sufficiently prevalent in infancy to warrant routine determination of hemoglobin or hematocrit.

NOTES

1. S.J. Fomon and R.G. Strauss, "Nutrient Deficiencies in Breast-Fed Infants," *New England Journal of Medicine* 299 (1978): 355–357.

2. P.A. Lane and W.E. Hathaway, "Vitamin K in Infancy," *Journal of Pediatrics* 106 (1985): 351–359.

3. S.A. Bock, "Prospective Appraisal of Complaints of Adverse Reactions to Foods in Children During the First 3 Years of Life." *Pediatrics* 79 (1987): 683–688.

4. S.J. Fomon, *Infant Nutrition*, 2nd ed. (Philadelphia: W.B. Saunders Co., 1974), 465–466.

5. P.V.V. Hamill et al., *NCHS Growth Charts, 1976*, Vital and Health Statistics, Series II (Rockville, MD: Health Resources Administration, DHEW, 1976).

6. Fomon, *Infant Nutrition*, 35–37.

7. P. Karlberg et al., "The Development of Children in a Swedish Urban Community: A Prospective Longitudinal Study. III. Physical Growth During the First Three Years of Life," *Acta Paediatrica Scandinavia*, (Supplement 187) 48 (1968): 1–148.

8. R.M. Malina et al., "Head and Chest Circumferences in Rural Guatemalan Ladino Children, Birth to Seven Years of Age," *American Journal of Clinical Nutrition* 28 (1975): 1061–1070.

9. J.D. Cook, C.A. Finch, and N.J. Smith, "Evaluation of the Iron Status of a Population," *Blood* 48 (1976): 449–455.

Chapter 7

Environmental Management of the Infant
(Birth Through Two Years)

Veronica D. Feeg

OVERVIEW

The birth of an infant marks the physical separation of mother and child, but the growth and nurturance of that newborn remains dependent on interaction with its caregivers. During this sensitive period, the environment influences the child's nutritional adequacy more than it does during any other developmental period of life. In addition to infants' physiological health status and developmental competencies, they are totally dependent on their caregivers for providing food and on their environments for supporting the feeding process.

While the act of infant feeding might appear to be a simple exchange of the caregiver providing food and the baby ingesting it, the process of feeding an infant is more complex. A complete assessment of the parent as a feeding agent and the environment as a supportive milieu is necessary to identify potential feeding problems and children at risk for inadequate nutrition.

ASSESSMENT: ENVIRONMENTAL DOMAINS

To assess the environment for factors that foster or inhibit good nutrition, the practitioner needs to observe feeding patterns of infant and caregiver in five assessment domains:

1. parent cognition/knowledge of nutrition
2. parent-infant interaction
3. social support
4. physical space and resources
5. economic and cultural influences and constraints

These five domains represent categories of evaluation that provide a framework for systematic data collection. The goals of promoting adequate nutrition in infancy for each domain and the age-specific criteria for evaluating effectiveness of teaching or counseling interventions are listed in Table 7-1.

Parent's Cognition/Knowledge of Nutrition

Throughout infancy and most of childhood, parents are the primary suppliers of food. But they can provide adequate nutrition only if (1) they have been given relevant information, (2) they comprehend that information, and (3) they are motivated and able to follow that information to feed their infant accordingly.

The parents' ability to read and understand informational content presented in their contacts with service providers is essential and needs to be determined. The health care practitioner should assess the infant caregiver's level of knowledge in general, as related to principles of nutrition, including the following:

- Is the caregiver capable of understanding the fundamentals of good nutrition?
- Can the caregiver state nutritional requirements for the infant?
- Can the caregiver identify foods that provide required nutrients?
- Does the caregiver expect appropriate developmental behaviors from the infant, particularly related to eating and feeding (see chapter 8)?

In general, the parent's knowledge and ability to learn are the foundations upon which the practitioner structures interventions. If the caregiver is not competent to understand specific diet instructions, especially if the infant requires a major therapeutic diet regimen, additional intervention must be sought, including substitute or alternative caregivers for feeding and eating activities. If the parent is incapable of providing nourishment for the infant, referral is necessary.

Parent-Infant Interaction

One of the major tasks of the mother and child during the first year of life is the development of attachment. Attachment, a unique emotional relationship between two individuals, has been deemed critical for later social, cognitive, and (indirectly) physical growth and development.

The newborn elicits certain behaviors—such as grasping, clinging, cuddling, following with the eyes, smiling, and crying—that promote or maintain contact with the mother. The mother's responsiveness to the infant's cues contributes to a pattern of interaction. The reciprocal relationship locks together mother and child

Table 7-1 Environmental Domains of Influence on Infant Nutrition

Assessment Domains	General Goals	Age-Specific Criteria
Parent/caregiver knowledge	Caregiver, as feeding agent, is cognitively competent, adequately informed, and understands the infant's need for nutrition to grow and develop normally.	Birth–6 months: Parent recognizes importance of breast milk (preferable) and/or infant formula as total source of nutrition for the first 6 months.[1] 6–12 months: Parent understands the principles of introducing new foods to milk diet of infant. 12–24 months: Parent understands the need to effect a transition for the child to table food and family mealtime.
Parent-infant interaction	Caregiver and infant are eventually satisfied in the feeding process.	Birth–6 months: Mother or caregiver and infant interact positively in the breastfeeding or bottlefeeding situation. 6–12 months: Parent and infant respond positively to each other's cues in the feeding situation. 12–24 months: Child achieves greater independence with parental support during feedings.
Social support	Infant feeding is supported and enhanced by family and significant others.	Birth–6 months: Breastfeeding (and/or bottlefeeding) activity is encouraged, accepted, and supported by significant others, siblings, and family. 6–12 months: Family shares in infant-feeding activities and new foods initiated. 12–24 months: Child is included as member of family during mealtime.

continued

Table 7-1 continued

Assessment Domains	General Goals	Age-Specific Criteria
Physical space and resources	Home or alternate feeding facilities are adequate in space and appropriate and conducive for feeding infant.	Birth–6 months: Physical space is clean and comfortable for breastfeeding and/or bottle feeding and promotes mother-infant interaction. 6–12 months: Facilities and resources are clean and adequate for infant-feeding activity. 12–24 months: Child eating area and utensils are age-appropriate and adequate for independent eating with family.
Economic or cultural constraints	Family can adjust infant's foods with economic or cultural limitations to maintain nutritionally adequate feedings.	Birth–6 months: Necessary breastfeeding or bottlefeeding supplies are available for use and cleaned adequately. 6–12 months: Baby foods, commercial or home-prepared, are low-cost, safe, and developmentally appropriate. 12–24 months: Child meals are adequately prepared and balanced for good nutrition with economic and cultural considerations.

and mediates all types of communication, including nurturing activities. The health care practitioner needs to assess the interaction between mother and child as the environmental basis for infant nutrition. This assessment should answer the following questions:

- Does the caregiver make eye contact with the infant during feeding?
- Does the caregiver talk to the child?
- How is the child handled?
- Does the child vocalize during feeding?

An evaluation of the mother-infant interaction can be based on observations of the interaction during the feeding situation. The learning resource manual *Nursing Child Assessment Satellite*, developed by Barnard, provides a detailed approach to assessing feeding behaviors.[2] This approach requires extensive training but can yield diagnostically useful data for the practitioner.

The *Nursing Child Assessment Feeding Scale (NCAFS)*, consisting of 76 behavioral items to observe during feeding, is applicable to infants of all ages during the first year of life. It can be obtained from the University of Washington, NCAST (Nursing Child Assessment Training), M-S WJ-10, Seattle, Washington, 98195.

Social Support

The family exerts a powerful influence on the infant's growth and development. Beyond the mother-infant relationship in breastfeeding, early socialization activities of the child with others often center around playing and eating activities. The infant's behavior and developmental competencies influence how early and to what extent the infant is integrated into the family's daily life.

Factors in the social environment can promote good patterns of eating as well as present barriers to attaining optimum nutrition for the infant. The practitioner needs to identify the social support and social interferences concerning siblings and significant others that are related to infant nutrition. The practitioner should seek answers to the following questions:

- Does the family and/or significant others support the mother-infant relationship in breastfeeding?
- How does the family interact with the infant regarding eating patterns?
- How many siblings are there (age and number), and how does the family view mealtime and eating together?
- How ready is the family to integrate the new member into the family's eating activities? How do young siblings respond? Does mealtime precipitate behavior difficulties that interfere with eating?

The social environment, important to the mother in the early infancy period, becomes more and more important to children as they get older, particularly as it relates to food selections and eating behaviors. The mother is influenced by the support or lack of support in the social environment in her efforts to breastfeed successfully. The infant's socialization needs are developmental: the newborn receives nourishment and social reinforcement with breastfeeding, beginning with a simple dyadic relationship; and the child then progresses toward greater independence and multiple relationships in self-feeding and social behaviors at family mealtime. The health care practitioner needs to identify potential problems in the social environment accordingly.

Physical Space and Resources

The physical space and resources available for infant feeding will help to determine the adequacy of infant nutrition. Facilities in the home or in alternative feeding settings need to be clean, functional, and comfortable to enable the caregiver and infant to interact. The practitioner needs to identify factors in the physical environment that may inhibit breastfeeding, bottlefeeding, and child self-feeding activities. Food, supplies and utensils need to be available, clean, and age-appropriate for the infant.

The assessment of the physical environment should answer questions regarding:

- where the mother usually breastfeeds and if she is comfortable in her physical setting
- where food is prepared and what supplies are used or needed
- how safe the area is that the child will eat in, for example, is it provided with high chair, table, and portable (sassy) seat and does it allow appropriate positioning for oral-motor activities of chewing and swallowing?

Economic and Cultural Influences and Constraints

The practitioner needs to identify economic limitations and cultural practices of the infant's family in order to adequately consider recommendations for good nutrition. The availability of foods and supplies or resources will depend on the economic situation of the family, but it will also be influenced by the family's cultural attitudes and practices related to eating. When economic or cultural factors interfere with the provision of adequate nutrition, adjustments in the practitioner's nutritional guidance should be made, aimed at alleviating the constraints.

In difficult situations, the practitioner should prioritize necessities over the goals of optimal nutrition. If equipment and supplies are limited because of inadequate financial resources, the practitioner should determine whether the limitations are health-threatening and, if so, should seek additional support services. Suggestions on cost-effective meal planning and infant feeding can be offered, using principles of a balanced diet, hygiene, and safety.

ENVIRONMENTAL ANALYSIS OF AGE GROUPS

Birth to Six Months

For the first few months of life, breastfeeding gives all newborns a good start in development (see chapter 8). According to the American Academy of Pediatrics, breastfeeding should supply the newborn with total nutritional needs for at least the first six months of life.[3-5] However, in spite of increases in the incidence and duration of breastfeeding, the majority of all infants are still not breastfed for the four- to six-month recommended time period.

Assessment

Although breastfeeding provides nutritional and immunological benefits to most infants, many women either fail to initiate breastfeeding in the critical first few hours of the infant's life or they terminate breastfeeding earlier than they would desire.[6] Lack of "success" in breastfeeding is viewed by some experts to be related to factors that could have been overcome with adequate assessment and early intervention. The practitioner needs to identify these factors in the environmental assessment, including:

- the mother's knowledge of breastfeeding and the specific mechanics of positioning the infant to breast, information related to care of nipples and expressed breast milk, and the mother's knowledge of her own need for nutrition and hydration to ensure an adequate milk supply
- the mother-infant interaction, including positioning, cueing, and responsiveness to infant stress
- the mother's support by significant others and family members in her decision to breastfeed, and her personal attitudes and feelings regarding the act of breastfeeding
- physical space that is clean and comfortable for the mother to breastfeed the infant in privacy, if that is the mother's personal preference, and the resources available for care of the mother while breastfeeding
- adequate financial resources and cultural practices that support good nutrition for the breastfeeding mother

In the event that breastfeeding is not possible or is contraindicated, appropriate infant formula should be safely prepared for bottlefeeding, and the instructions must be accurately followed. The health care practitioner needs to determine that the mother is able to read labels and understand directions for diluting mixtures. The bottlefeeding activity can also provide the infant with warmth of mothering; the practitioner should look for similar indicators of maternal-infant interaction that promote good bottlefeeding activities. Infants meet their nutritional, security,

Table 7-2 Potential Environmental Feeding Problems, Birth to Six Months

Potential Problems	Recommendations for Intervention
Inability to breastfeed successfully due to: • lack of information • lack of social support • maternal physical problems • interfering activities/poor physical environment	• Provide information and reinforce teaching efforts with other means. • Discuss communicating with family and other health professionals regarding feelings about breastfeeding. • Identify source of physical problems while continuing to support breastfeeding if possible (pump, supplements, etc.). • Teach breast-pump interventions for supplemental feedings or if separated from infant. • Assist in identifying environment that is comfortable and minimizes distractions.
Poor mother-infant interaction related to: • mother's inability to read cues • infant's physical characteristics and temperament • mother's lack of knowledge or confidence in mothering	• Assist mother to recognize infant signals and cues that promote satisfying relationship. • Discuss uniqueness of infant. • Discuss comfortable feeding positions. • Assess for serious attachment difficulties and refer to other professionals if necessary.
Lack of maternal cognition/knowledge relating to: • positioning for feedings • developmental expectations for infant • preparation of formulas and foods (see chapter 8) • care of feeding equipment and work area (see Table 7-4)	• Assist with audio/visual materials, as well as written materials at mother's reading level. • Use demonstrations and return demonstrations; "model" behavior expected from mother. • Review storing and cleaning information for bottles and supplies. • Find substitute caregiver or support person for feeding activities. • Correct errors with discussion, demonstration, and return demonstration.
Limited resources	• Refer to social services for adequate maternal nutrition. • Discuss low-cost alternatives for feeding.

and physiological needs for comfort simultaneously with frequent, positive breast-feeding or bottlefeeding interactions with mother.

Potential Problems

With a systematic and comprehensive assessment of the infant's environment with regard to nutrition, potential growth and feeding problems can often be avoided. Early detection of the barriers to breastfeeding and good nutrition and identification of factors that promote good health can aid in preventing more serious nutritional problems that would otherwise not be manifested until the infant's growth pattern changes (see Table 7-2).

Six to Twelve Months

Having complied with the recommendations not to introduce solid foods for 4 to 6 months, and not to introduce cow's milk until at least 6 months,[7] the parent of the 6- to 12-month-old infant faces the challenge of adding new and strange nonmilk nourishments to the inexperienced infant (see chapter 8). This period requires the parent to take care in exposing the child to more difficult chewing consistencies, while observing the infant's responses to foods and visceral reactions to potential allergens.

Assessment

Feeding the 6- to 12-month-old infant becomes an adventure. With time, the caregiver should soon become skillful in mastering the mechanics of presenting food to an open or less willing mouth. The practitioner should discuss the principles of sequencing solid foods introduced to the infant (see Exhibit 8-1) and provide support and reassurance to the parent for independent decision making in the feeding activity. The assessment should cover the following five environmental factors:

1. caregiver's knowledge of preparation and care of foods to be given to infant
2. caregiver's ability to effectively introduce new foods to the infant with appropriate pacing and developmental expectations, and the infant's satisfaction or pleasurable response to feeding attempts
3. family participation in the delight of feeding the infant and acceptance of the infant's sometimes messy attempts to be an ''eating'' member of the family
4. a physical set-up (high chair, sassy seat, and so forth) that promotes good eating posture and positioning, adequate resources and supplies, and knowledge related to preparation of commercial or home-prepared foods (see Exhibit 7-1)
5. adequate financial resources and cultural practices to allow for provision of a variety of foods with good nutritional quality

Parents can be encouraged to use feeding activities as a means of exploring new events in the world with the infant. The infant's delight at experiencing new tastes, smells, and consistencies can stimulate the parents to share in this pleasure. The health care practitioner can assist the parent to identify these pleasurable moments as compensation for some of the more frustrating ones that accompany the feeding situation.

Exhibit 7-1 Form for Assessing Use of Commercial and Home-Prepared Infant Foods

	Yes	No
Commercial food criteria:		
• Uses a variety of commercial baby foods available, including meats, vegetables, and fruits		
• Introduces new foods sequentially, with enough time to identify potential allergies		
• Stores opened jars adequately		
• Prepares baby foods safely, with particular attention to temperature and cleanliness		
• Can read labels and follow instructions for food preparation and storage		
Home-prepared food criteria:		
• Uses clean equipment for preparing food and prepares food adequately for long-term storage		
• Stores home-prepared food appropriately		
• Grinds or chops food to developmentally appropriate consistencies		
• Knows foods to avoid and those that infant will not digest or tolerate; limits seasoning, sugar, and salt		
• Progresses foods sequentially, taking care to observe for allergic reactions or sensitivity		

Potential Problems

In this period, as throughout most of early childhood, feeding problems and nutritional inadequacies are manifested by poor growth and/or failure to thrive along an expected range. A careful assessment of the environmental factors in feeding the 6- to 12-month-old infant can reveal some of the subtle problems that can become overt feeding difficulties in the future (see Table 7-3).

Twelve to Twenty-Four Months

The period of rapid growth of the child continues well into the beginning of the second year, with monumental developmental gains. Language, fine and gross motor abilities, and the eagerness to explore the environment reflect unfolding skills that strongly influence the child's intake of foods. This is the period when sitting down for food may not be what the child has in mind. Thus, the caregiver needs to master a variety of new skills, patiently allowing the child to become more and more independent in eating.

Table 7-3 Potential Environmental Feeding Problems, 6 to 12 Months

Potential Problems	*Recommendations for Intervention*
Lack of knowledge related to introduction of new foods Infant exhibits multiple allergies of unknown causes	• Discuss developmental readiness of infant (see chapter 8). • Suggest sequence of new foods introduced (e.g., single vegetables, fruits, meats over several weeks). • Provide assistance in structuring introduction of new foods to diet.
Maternal feeding activities inappropriate related to: • poor pacing and tempo • distractions and interferences • infant behavior expectations • preparing, handling, or storing foods	• Discuss motor mechanics of infant feeding, chewing, and swallowing. • Demonstrate or "model" good feeding situation with infant, pointing out tempo, technique, and sequence.
Poor maternal feeding behaviors, including: • poor positioning—infant lying, standing, or seated on inappropriate chair • feeding activities complicated by games, competing toys, or unstructured behaviors • isolating infant from other family members	• Discuss infant's need to be prepared for foods coming. • Discuss creating the eating situation with infant as similar to mealtime situations and preparing infant for future mealtime environment.

Assessment

The early emergence of eating problems and the development of subsequent nutritional deficits are identifiable in this period. These are usually related to the child's characteristics, behavior, and the environment in which the eating occurs. The child should be gradually introduced to table foods and table behaviors, and the family should continue to integrate the child into the family's social activities of mealtime. In this period, the health care practitioner needs to assess the behavioral, social, and nutritional needs of the child, including the following:

• the caregiver's knowledge about progressing to table foods and understanding of those foods that should be avoided for safety or intolerance reasons
• caregiver-child interactions, including patience with and understanding of the child's behaviors, assistance to the child in gaining continuing independ-

Table 7-4 Assessing the Physical and Family Environment of the 12- to 24-Month-Old Child

Environmental Factors	Helpful Hints
Physical Space	
Feeding area and equipment support the child's need for:	• Allow the child to sit at the table, to permit the feet to be flat on floor or foot rest.
• growing independence with self-feeding	• Limit space and restrict the child to focus on eating activities.
• exploring and manipulating things	• Offer finger foods that are easy to "chew" and manipulate independently, gradually introducing other foods and allowing the child to master self-feeding.
• Participating socially with family	
• good eating posture and positioning	
• ability to anticipate presentation of foods	• Take a casual, relaxed approach to the child's meals, limit snacks before meals, and discourage continuous snacking.
• a structured and controlled eating experience	
Social Environment	
Family table and mealtime atmosphere provides the child with:	• Gradually move the child closer to the family table.
• opportunities for family interaction	• Engage the child in family discussion and activities that accompany eating.
• opportunities for expressing self	• Set a good example.
• positive modeling for trying new tastes and textures	
• pleasurable experiences associated with eating and mealtime	

ence with self-feeding, and gradual integration of the child into the family mealtime

• family support and encouragement of child participation at family mealtime (see Table 7-4)

• a physical set-up that supports self-feeding and minimizes behavioral complications (for example, spilling, acting out)

• financial resources and cultural patterns that allow the child to have balanced diets and increasing autonomy

Table 7-5 Potential Environmental Feeding Problems, 12 to 24 Months

Potential Problems	Specific Recommendations for Intervention
Child eating problems, including:	
• has finicky appetite	• Do not coerce or make games of eating.
• refuses milk	• Serve milk with colored straw, offer milk substitutes.
• drinks too much milk	• Offer milk after meals only, offer water or juices between meals.
• refuses meat	• Provide bite-size pieces, child-size portions, easy to chew meats, or meat substitutes (eggs, peanut butter).
• refuses fruits or vegetables	• Add fruits to cereals, gelatin dessert, puddings, ice cream; introduce bite-size pieces of vegetables.
• refuses breads or cereals	• Add raisins or fresh fruit to cereal.
• eats too many sweets	• Offer "natural" sweets (fruits); do not use sweets as a reward for good behavior.
Poor family interaction at mealtime including:	
• acting out behavior	• Set limits and use time-out.
• chaotic interactions or poor "modeling"	
Lack of independence or excessive independence	• Provide activities in which the child will be successful, including assistance with self-feeding behaviors.

Source: Reproduced with permission from P.M. Queen and R.R. Henry, "Growth and Nutrient Requirements of Children" in R.J. Grand, J.L. Sutphen, and W.H. Dietz, eds., *Pediatric Nutrition: Theory and Practice* (Stoneham, MA: Butterworth Publishers, 1987).

Potential Problems

The second year of the child's life is a time for gaining mastery over formerly dependent activities, such as feeding. Parents often view the labile eating behaviors of the child with concern, but long-term eating disturbances need to be differentiated from normal finicky eating patterns. The practitioner needs to assess environmental contributions to the feeding behaviors of the child in order to facilitate early detection of serious nutritional deficits. The practitioner can also suggest to the caregiver ways of managing these sometimes trying experiences (see Table 7-5).

NOTES

1. American Academy of Pediatrics, Committee on Nutrition, "The Use of Whole Cow's Milk in Infancy," *Pediatrics* 72 (1983): 253–255.

2. K. Barnard, *Learning Resource Manual: Nursing Child Assessment Satellite Training*. (University of Washington, School of Nursing: Nursing Child Assessment Project, 1978), 17–62.

3. American Academy of Pediatrics, Nutrition Committee of the Canadian Pediatrics Society, and Committee on Nutrition of the American Academy of Pediatrics, "Breastfeeding," *Pediatrics* 62 (1978): 591–601.

4. American Academy of Pediatrics, Committee on Nutrition, "Encouraging Breastfeeding," *Pediatrics* 65 (1980): 657–658.

5. American Academy of Pediatrics, "Policy Statement Based on Task Force Report: The Promotion of Breastfeeding," *Pediatrics* 69 (1982): 654–661.

6. C. Rogers, S. Morris, and L.J. Taper, "Weaning from the Breast: Influences on Maternal Decisions," *Pediatric Nursing* 13 (1987): 341–345.

7. American Academy of Pediatrics, Committee on Nutrition, "The Use of Whole Cow's Milk," 253–255.

Chapter 8

Dietary Assessment and Management of the Infant
(Birth Through Two Years)

Claudette Austin

- What are the types of infant formula, and what are the advantages of each?
- What action is recommended for infant feeding difficulties?
- When should one introduce solid foods to infants?
- What feeding practices can lead to tooth decay in infants?

DIETARY ASSESSMENT

Overview

Assessment of the nutritional adequacy of infants' diets plays a major role in determining their growth, development, and overall health. The first year of life is characterized as a period of very rapid growth. The infant's nutrient requirements per unit of body weight are greater at this time than at any other age. This is a period when problems of undernutrition and overnutrition are likely to develop, and it is critical that the diet provide the necessary nutrients to support optimum growth.

Methods of Assessing the Diet

Dietary assessment measures both the quality and quantity of food intake. It can also identify other factors that affect present and past food intake, such as activity level, food intolerances and/or allergies, current feeding patterns, and age-appropriate feeding skills. Information about food intake can be collected in several ways. Currently in use are the 24-hour recall (see appendix A-2) and 3-to-7-day feeding histories, which illustrate usual feeding patterns (see appendix A-4 on the Food Diary, which may be adapted for this purpose). Whichever methodology is used, it has been found that, generally, caretakers of underweight infants overestimate and caretakers of overweight infants underestimate the amounts of food consumed.

Breastfeeding

Human milk is generally regarded as the best source of nourishment for the young infant. Its unique biological composition and antiinfective properties offer unsurpassed advantages to the growing infant. The quality of human milk is known to be affected by many variables: the mother's health and nutritional status, the stage of lactation, the time of day, and individual differences.

The following advantages of breastfeeding may be cited:

- Colostrum and breast milk provide immunological properties against certain bacteriological infections.
- Its chemical composition makes it easily digestible and absorbable by infants.
- Breastfeeding may promote desirable maternal-infant bonding.
- Breastfeeding may promote better mouth and jaw development because the infant has to suck harder.
- Breast milk is sterile, readily available, and low in cost.

Here are some helpful tips about breastfeeding:

- The newborn infant should be allowed to suck for five minutes on each breast on the first day in order to achieve a let-down reflex. At the end of ten days, the infant should be nursing for ten minutes on each side.
- Milk supply is equal to demand; the more frequently an infant is put to the breast, the greater the milk supply.
- The greatest flow of breast milk is in the first five to ten minutes, but infants need to continue nursing to satisfy their need to suck.
- Initially, infants will need to be fed every two to three hours but later will settle into their own sleep-feeding schedule.
- There is no need for introduction of solids until the infant is four to six months of age; until then, the infant will thrive on breast milk alone.

Formulas

When breastfeeding is not possible or desirable, a commercial infant formula is the best alternative for meeting the infant's nutritional needs. Unmodified milks (cow, goat) do not meet the nutritional needs of the infant and are not considered appropriate infant nourishment. The nutrient composition of all marketed formulas is regulated by standards established by the Infant Formula Act of 1980. Formulas are sold in powder, liquid concentrate, and ready-to-use formulas. The correct dilution of powder and liquid concentrate formulas is extremely important, so time should be spent in explaining to the client the need to follow directions carefully. This is especially important when working with non-English-speaking clients. In any event, it is useful to review the instructions on the selected formula can with the parent or caregiver and then to have the parent or caregiver repeat the relevant information.

Four major types of formulas are used in infant feeding:

1. Humanized, cow's milk formulas are designed to resemble breast milk in composition and to provide comparable nutritional benefits. They are made from nonfat cow's milk with the following modifications:
   - The protein is heat-treated to produce a more digestible curd; and demineralized whey is added to achieve a whey/casein ratio of 60:40, which approaches the 80:20 whey/casein ratio of human milk.
   - Vegetable oils are added to provide essential fatty acids and calories.
   - Vitamins and minerals are added to approach comparable levels in human milk.
   - These formulas are available in two forms: low-iron or unfortified, and iron-fortified (12 mg Fe/liter).
2. Soy-protein-based, lactose-free formulas are designed for the infants who are sensitive to cow's milk, have galactose intolerance, or have a congenital or acquired lactase deficiency. These formulas contain soy protein isolate, supplemented with L-methionine, vegetable oils, and carbohydrates, such as sucrose and corn syrup solids. Soy formulas contain iron and vitamin/mineral supplements. When consumed in adequate quantities, no additional supplementation is needed, except for fluoride in areas where indicated.
3. Protein-modified formulas are for infants with allergies or sensitivity to cow's milk or soy protein and for infants with chronic diarrhea or malabsorption.
4. Specialized, medically indicated formulas are used with infants who have inborn errors of metabolism and other specific problems; the emphasis in this publication is on formulas for normal-term infants.

Table 8-1 compares nutrients in commercial formulas. Table 8-2 provides a guide for formula feeding.

Table 8-1 Selected Infant Feedings

	Vol/100 Cal	Na/100 Cal	Protein Source	CHO Source	Fat Source	Indications for Use	Comment
Mature human milk	135 ml	25 mg	Whey/casein ratio: 80:20	Lactose	Fatty acids	Best source of nutrition for full-term infants during first months of life	Need vitamin C and D supplement (see Table 8-4)
Cow's milk (whole)*	150 ml	76 mg	Whey/casein ratio: 18:82	Lactose	Butter fat	Undiluted cow's milk not recommended for at least the first six months, preferably for one year	Supplement with iron and vitamin C, A, and D if not fortified
				Commercial Infant Formulas			
SMA 12 (Wyeth)	148 ml	22 mg	Nonfat cow's milk, demineralized whey; whey/casein ratio: 60:40	Lactose	Oleo, coconut, oleic, and soy oils	For full-term infants with no special nutritional requirements	Available fortified with iron
Enfamil (Mead-Johnson)	148 ml	22 mg	Nonfat cow's milk, demineralized whey; whey/casein ratio 60:40	Lactose	Soy, coconut oils	For full-term and premature infants with no special nutritional requirements	Available fortified with iron, 12 mg/L
Similac (Ross)	148 ml	32 mg	Nonfat cow's milk; whey/casein ratio: 18:82	Lactose	Soy and coconut oils, mono- and diglycerides	For full-term and premature infants with no special nutritional requirements	Available fortified with iron, 12 mg/L
			Products for Milk-Protein-Sensitive Infants ("Milk Allergy")				
Prosobee (Mead Johnson)	148 ml	36 mg	Soy protein isolate	Corn syrup solids	Soy and coconut oils	With milk protein allergy, lactose intolerance, lactase deficiency, galactosemia	Hypoallergenic, zero-band antigen, lactose- and sucrose-free

Product	Volume	Protein source	Carbohydrate source	Fat source	Indications	Comments
Isomil (Ross)	148 ml	Soy protein isolate	Corn syrup sucrose	Soy and coconut oils	With milk protein allergy, lactose intolerance, lactase deficiency, galactosemia	Soy protein isolate, lactose-free
Isomil SF (Ross)	148 ml	Soy protein isolate	Corn syrup solids	Soy and coconut oils	With milk protein allergy or sucrose intolerance	Sucrose- and lactose-free
Nursoy (Wyeth)	148 ml	Soy protein isolate	Sucrose	Oleo, coconut, oleic, and soy oils	Lactose free	Allergy lactose intolerance, galactosemia

Products for Infants with Malabsorption Syndromes

Product	Volume	Protein source	Carbohydrate source	Fat source	Indications	Comments
Portagen (Mead Johnson)		Sodium caseinate	Corn syrup solids, sucrose	MCT (coconut source) and corn oil	For impaired fat absorption secondary to pancreatic insufficiency, bile acid deficiency, intestinal resection, lymphatic anomalies	Fat: 87% MCT, 12% corn oil; nutritionally complete
Nutramigen (Mead Johnson)		Casein hydrolysate Amino acid premix	Sucrose, modified tapioca starch, corn syrup solids, cornstarch	Corn oil	For infants and children intolerant to food proteins, for use in galactosemic patients	Enzymatic hydrolysate of casein, hyperallergenic formula, nutritionally complete

*The American Academy of Pediatrics Committee on Nutrition recommends that reduced fat milk not be used for infants.[1]

Source: Adapted from D. Wong and L. Whaley, *Clinical Handbook of Pediatric Nutrition*, 2nd ed. (St. Louis, MO: The C.V. Mosby Co, 1986), 125–126; American Academy of Pediatrics, Committee on Nutrition, "Commentary on Breast Feeding and Infant Formulas Including Proposed Standards for Formulas," *Pediatrics* 57 (1976): 278; and American Academy of Pediatrics, Committee on Nutrition, "Nutritional Needs of Low-Birth-Weight Infants," *Pediatrics* 60 (1977): 519, modified from C.H. Kempe, H.K. Silver, and D. O'Brien, eds. *Current Pediatric Diagnosis and Treatment* (Los Altos, Calif.: Lange Medical Publications, 1984).

Table 8-2 Guide for Formula Feeding

Age	Average Number of Feedings/24 Hours	Average Volume Per Feeding
Birth to 2 weeks	6–8	2–3 ozs.
2 weeks–2 months	6-7	3-4 ozs.
2 months–4 months	5-6	5-6 ozs.
4 months–6 months	4-5	6-7 ozs.
6 months–9 months	3-4	6-8 ozs.
10 months–12 months	3	8 ozs.

Introduction of Solid Food

Guidelines

Exhibit 8-1 illustrates the steps to infant feeding and serves as a guide for adding solids to the infant's diet. This guide can also be used as an instructional tool with clients.

Practical Hints

The following practical hints will be useful when introducing new foods:

- Introduce one new food every five to seven days. This allows the infant to become familiar with the food; and, if allergies are present, the cause can be identified. If such symptoms as irritability, rash, diarrhea, or vomiting occur, eliminate the new food.
- Offer very small amounts of the new food (a teaspoonful) at the beginning.
- Use a very thin soup-like consistency when starting solids.
- Give solids by spoon, not diluted in the infant's bottle. Foods offered in the bottle do not contribute to the development of balanced eating patterns (for example, they may lead to later refusal of solid foods).
- On initiation of spoonfeeding, offer the infant a few ounces of breast milk or formula to take the edge off hunger. This will permit acceptance of the new food. After the infant is accustomed to spoonfeeding, new foods can be offered at the beginning of the feeding.
- Infants are entitled to likes and dislikes. Offer rejected foods a week or two later.
- Use foods of smooth consistency at first, for example, strained or pureed fruits, vegetables, and meats.

- Infants' appetites vary. Never force infants to eat more of a food than they are willing to take.
- Prepare homemade baby foods by mashing, blending, or grinding to a smooth consistency. Do not add salt, sugar, or spices. Recipes may be helpful.[2]
- When buying commercial infant foods, purchase jars of single foods. Mixed dinners, meats and vegetables, and desserts have less nutritional quality by weight.

Table 8-3 lists foods to avoid during infancy.

Vitamin-Mineral Supplements

Normal, healthy infants consuming a varied diet do not require nutrient supplements. Infants fed iron-fortified commercial infant formulas require only fluoride supplements in areas where indicated. If a low-iron-containing formula is being used, alternative sources of iron must be offered. Enriched infant cereals provide a convenient and reliable source of bioavailable iron. Guidelines for vitamin/mineral supplementation are given in Table 8-4.

Epidemiological studies have shown an inverse relationship between fluoride ingestion and dental caries. It is recommended that, if possible, concentrated formulas be prepared with fluoridated water. Supplemental fluoride is recommended

---

Table 8-3 Foods to Avoid in Infancy

Home-prepared Baby Foods	Foods That May Cause Choking	Allergy-related Foods	Foods That Are Difficult to Digest
Do not use canned vegetables or preseasoned family food because of the high sodium content	Candies Celery Cookies Corn	Cocoa Chocolate Corn Peanuts	Bacon Sausage Fatty foods Fried foods
	Fruits with seeds	Citrus	Highly spiced foods
Avoid use of home-prepared, high-nitrate-containing vegetables such as beets, spinach, turnips, mustard, and collard greens	Hot dogs Nuts Popcorn Potato chips Raisins	Tomatoes Wheat Milk Egg whites	Whole-kernel corn

NEVER INTRODUCE COW'S MILK EARLIER THAN SIX MONTHS OF AGE, AS IT MAY CAUSE GASTROINTESTINAL BLOOD LOSS AND/OR IRON DEFICIENCY ANEMIA.[3]

Exhibit 8-1 Infant Feeding Guide

	BIRTH 1 2 3	4 5 6	7	8 9	10 11 12	13 14
FEEDING GUIDE	BREAST MILK or FORMULA and BOILED WATER	ADD IRON FORTIFIED CEREAL 2-3 T*	ADD STRAINED OR PUREED FRUIT & VEGETABLES 4-6 T	ADD STRAINED MEAT, POULTRY, COTTAGE CHEESE, PLAIN YOGURT 2-4 T	ADD CHOPPED FOODS— VEGETABLES, FRUITS, 4 T MEAT, POULTRY 2-4 T, EGG YOLK ½ (Hard cooked) TABLE FOODS (Chopped)	
AGE (— MONTH —)	BIRTH 1 2 3	4 5 6	7	8 9	10 11 12	13 14
FEEDING RECOMMENDATIONS	NO SOLID FOODS	START WITH RICE CEREAL, THEN ADD OTHERS USE WITH BREAST MILK OR FORMULA	PLAIN FRUIT & VEGETABLES START FRUIT JUICE (non-acid) FROM A CUP WHOLE MILK CAN BE STARTED	ADD STRAINED MEAT & EGG YOLK TOWARD END OF 9 MONTHS	BEGINNING OF SELF FEEDING TRANSITION FROM STRAINED & PUREED FOOD TO COARSER TEXTURED FOOD LIKE CHOPPED FOOD	TRANSITION TO 3 MEALS SNACKS CHOPPED TABLE FOODS DRINK ALL LIQUIDS FROM A CUP BECOME ACCLIMATED TO FAMILY DIET
DEVELOPMENTAL PATTERNS	ROOTING REFLEX SUCKS ONLY	BEGIN SWALLOWING PATTERN TRANSFER FOOD FROM FRONT OF TONGUE TO BACK		BEGIN CHEWING PATTERN	FINGER FEEDING DRINKING FROM A CUP	MATURATION OF BITING, CHEWING, AND SWALLOWING

*T = Tablespoon

Table 8-4 Supplementation of Diets of Infants and Toddlers

	Desirable Daily Supplements		
Milk or Formula	Vitamin D 400 IU	Vitamin C 35 mg	Iron 7 mg
Human milk	+	−	+
Cow milk			
Whole, homogenized, D-fortified	−	+	+
Evaporated	−	+	+
Commercially prepared formula-Fe-fortified	−	−	−

Source: Reprinted from *Vitamin and Mineral Supplement Needs in Normal Children in the United States,* American Academy of Pediatrics, Committee on Nutrition, © 1979.

Table 8-5 Supplemental Fluoride Dosage Schedule (mg/day)

	Concentration of Fluoride in Drinking Water (ppm)		
Age	<0.3	0.3-0.7	>0.7
2 weeks–2 years	0.25	0.00	0.00
2–3 years	0.50	0.25	0.00
3–16 years	1.00	0.50	0.00

Note: 2.2 mg sodium fluoride contains 1 mg fluoride.

Source: Reproduced by permission of *Pediatrics*, Vol. 63, page 150, Copyright 1979.

for infants receiving breast milk and formulas prepared with nonfluoridated water. Table 8-5 provides guidelines for fluoride supplementation.

COMMON NUTRITIONAL PROBLEMS OF THE INFANT

Table 8-6 contains information about common nutritional problems during infancy. It also provides further assessment questions, recommended action, and steps in evaluation.

Table 8-6 Common Nutritional Problems in Infancy

I. FEEDING DIFFICULTIES

Feeding difficulties are identified by (1) frequent crying, (2) a need to be fed frequently (every two hours or less), and (3) constant sucking and mouthing movements without satisfaction.

These can occur if the infant has a weak suck, poor feeding techniques are used, the infant has a reaction to parental anxieties, or improper feeding equipment is used.

Assessment	Action
How is the infant fed? Breast, formula, partial breast/formula?	Review kinds of milk with mother.
How often is feeding, and what is the volume?	Review frequency of feeding and amount taken with mother. Calculate how much milk baby is taking.
Are the bottle nipples too firm or the holes too small?	Check nipples for firmness and speed of flow.
What is the feeding position?	Set up a calm, relaxed feeding situation with the mother. Talk the mother through a feeding session, showing her how to relax and position the infant and bottle.
	After feeding, demonstrate reflexive rooting and sucking actions—even though the baby has been fed.
How do mother and child interact?	See chapter 7.
Are there parental anxieties?	See chapter 7.
What are the number and ages of other children in the home?	Make suggestions for activities for others, such as giving them a favorite toy while the infant is being fed.

Evaluation

Review progress with mother at follow-up visits. Look for improved intake and reduced frequency of feeding and a more nurturing relationship between mother and infant.

Evaluate weight gain of infant and compare with growth charts (chapter 6). Determine if infant is gaining as expected.

If problem persists, redemonstrate methods of feeding for several feedings until symptoms have diminished.

II. OVERWEIGHT/OBESITY

Defined as a gross discrepancy between length and weight.[4]

Some feeding practices that contribute to the problem are (1) overconcentration of formula, (2) overuse of bottlefeedings, and (3) general overfeeding.

Causes are usually multifactorial.

A study by Garza and Stuff reported that breastfed infants consumed an average of 30,000 fewer calories than bottlefed infants by age eight months. Current standards for calorie requirements for infants may be inaccurate.[5]

Table 8-6 continued

Assessment	Action
How is the formula diluted?	Review and demonstrate correct dilution of formula. Advise regarding use of ready-to-feed formulas.
How frequent is the feeding, and what is the volume?	Provide list of suggested amounts to be fed for age of child (see Table 8-2 and Exhibit 8-1).
How much nonformula liquids are used (i.e., solids, such as cereal, put in bottle)?	Instruct the parent to offer foods other than milk in cup or by spoon.
How many caretakers are responsible for feeding?	Assist the parent in developing a written feeding schedule.
	Instruct parents/caregivers to expect fluctuations of appetite. Infants should not be forced to finish all of their bottles and solids that are offered.
What is the family attitude toward the child's weight?	Discuss problems of obesity in children. The fat baby is not necessarily healthy. Offer nonoral ways to comfort and reward the infant.
What is the activity level? Is the child confined to playpen or crib?	Encourage the parents to allow the infant free movement of the entire body and extremities (also see chapter 7).

Evaluation

Anthropometric measurements should demonstrate:

a. a decrease in percentile value for weight for age, but no change in length for age

b. a decrease in percentile value for weight for length

If problem persists, refer to a registered dietitian (R.D.) for individualized care plan for infant and family education.

III. NURSING BOTTLE CARIES

Caries are identified by rampant decay of the upper incisors.

This occurs when infants are put to bed with a bottle of milk, formula, fruit juice, or any sugary liquid or they are breastfed when they sleep with their mothers.

The liquid pools around the upper front teeth while the child sleeps. Sugar in the liquid combines with the natural bacteria in the mouth and produces acid, which causes demineralization of the enamel.

Assessment	Action
What is the current method of feeding— Breast or bottle?	Routinely explain to the mother the effect of sugary materials on the teeth. Point out that sugar is found in breast milk, formula and other foods.

Table 8-6 continued

What are the solids in the diet? Types? Quantity?	Educate the parent on sugar content of foods. Suggest less sweet foods (e.g., crackers instead of cookies, low-sugar cereals, and fruits instead of sweet desserts).
What are the other nonmilk liquids in the diet?	Educate the parents on the sugar content of liquids and show them how to read labels to determine the sugar content of liquids. Suggest that fruit juices be drunk from a cup.
Is the infant put to nap or to bed with a nursing bottle?	Discuss how this practice leads to tooth decay. Encourage the mother/caregiver to offer plain water before nap or bedtime. The infant will adapt to this change if the caregiver is consistent.
Is there bedtime snacking?	Instruct on effective daily cleaning of teeth, especially at bedtime.
Are sweetened pacifiers used?	Discourage use.
Are fluoride supplements used?	Recommend use of fluoride supplementation in areas where warranted (see Table 8-5).

Evaluation

At the next visit, complete a 24-hour recall with the mother (see appendix A-2). Look for reduction in intake of sugary beverages and foods. Look for positive change in feeding practices.

Review home care of teeth and mouth.

If problem persists, refer to a pedodontist.

IV. REFUSAL TO EAT

Refusal to eat is characterized by refusal to bite, chew, or drink large quantities of milk or other liquids.

This can occur when (1) solids are offered in the bottle or (2) spoonfeeding is delayed.

Assessment	Action
Does the child have a hypersensitive gag reflex? Is there hand-to-mouth action? Is the child able to hold the spoon? Is the motor development at expected level?	Have a speech and physical therapist evaluate oral-motor skill.
Is food preparation compatible with developmental stage?	If the child demonstrates appropriate skills, have the parent choose a food the child enjoys and place it between the back molars.

Table 8-6 continued

Encourage serving some finger foods at each meal.

Suggest that parents provide a small amount at mealtime with only one food that requires chewing.

Offer liquids in a cup at the end of the meal.

Also see chapter 7.

Evaluation

At the next visit, complete a 24-hour recall of the infant's intake with the mother (see appendix A-2). Evaluate intake and look for food behavior change.

Evaluate weight gain of infant and compare with growth grid.

If problem persists, refer to a registered dietitian (R.D.) for further evaluation and in-depth counseling.

V. FAILURE TO GAIN WEIGHT

Failure to gain weight is characterized by a drop in percentile values of weight for age.

Assessment	Action
What is the average 24-hour intake of food and formula?	Compare 24-hour intake with amounts expected to be consumed in that period.
What is the frequency, quantity, and adequacy of feeding?	Advise the parent regarding appropriate feeding recommendations with regard to amounts, frequency, and types of food (see Exhibit 8-1).
What is the formula dilution?	Discuss formula preparation with the parent; focus on correct measurement, since this is a common error.
Has there been a recent bout of prolonged vomiting, diarrhea, or other illness that could have contributed to weight loss?	Recommend methods of fluid replacement. If condition has been persistent, refer to physician.
What is the number of caretakers and their meal responsibilities?	Help the parent prepare a feeding chart, listing amounts and kinds of food required for the infant. This can be provided to all caretakers to ensure a consistent feeding schedule.
Are there feeding difficulties?	Suggest smaller, more frequent feedings. This technique may increase amounts consumed.

Table 8-6 continued

Evaluation

During follow-up visits, evaluate actual weight gain against expected weight gain for age and sex (see Figures 6-1 through 6-6).

If there is a reason to question home conditions, refer to social worker for assessment of housing and income needs.

If the problem persists, refer to a registered dietitian (R.D.) for a personalized nutrition care plan and exploration of need for supplemental food program.

NOTES

1. American Academy of Pediatrics, Committee on Nutrition, *Pediatric Nutrition Handbook*, 2nd ed. (Elk Grove Village, Ill.: American Academy of Pediatrics, 1985), 25.

2. A. Natow and J. Heslin, *No Nonsense Nutrition For Your Baby's First Year*, 2nd ed. (New York: Prentice Hall Press, 1988), 122–156.

3. American Academy of Pediatrics, Committee on Nutrition, *Pediatric Nutrition Handbook*, 2nd ed. (Elk Grove Village, Ill.: American Academy of Pediatrics, 1985), 23, 25.

4. S.J. Fomon, *Infant Nutrition*, 2nd ed. (Philadelphia: W.B. Saunders Co., 1974), 22.

5. "Infants RDAs and Growth Rates May Be Inaccurate." *CNI Weekly Report* (Washington, D.C.: Community Nutrition Institute: April 14, 1988), 7.

Part IV

The Young Child

Chapter 9

Nutrition Assessment of the Young Child
(Two Through Six Years)

Susan R. Rosenthal and Celia Z. Padron

OVERVIEW

A thorough nutrition assessment of the young child is important in order to identify the child at risk for growth problems. The nutrients in food provide energy for growing tissues. Growth is synonymous with a diet that provides those necessary nutrients.

In the United States, both primary protein-calorie malnutrition (PCM) and Kwashiorkor or protein depletion in the young child are unusual. However, drastic elimination diets for food allergy, the lack of education, and altered maternal-child interaction may all be causes of primary protein-calorie malnutrition.[1,2] More often, malnutrition is secondary to malabsorption or decreased intake caused by an underlying chronic disease.

HEALTH HISTORY

Review of the child's past medical history should focus on past illnesses caused by or related to nutritional deficiencies. Frequent infections (more than six per year) are often associated with chronic malnutrition. The cell mediated immune response is depressed in malnourished children.

Both acute and chronic diarrhea may be intimately associated with underlying malnutrition.[3] Acute diarrhea may be secondary to viral, bacterial, or parasitic causes. Chronic diarrhea is multifactorial in its etiology. Most probably, a combination of small-bowel mucosal damage, pancreatic insufficiency, small-bowel bacterial overgrowth with resultant bile acid malabsorption, and depressed cellular immunity all play a role.[4,5]

Frank vitamin deficiency, secondary to inadequate intake, is uncommon in the United States. However, the development of rickets, vitamin B_{12} deficiency, and riboflavin deficiency have been associated with strict vegetarian diets.[6] Patients with malabsorption of fat solute vitamins (A, E, D, K) will have symptoms referable to these vitamin deficiencies.

Poor school performance, lethargy, anorexia, and irritability may be symptoms of iron deficiency. Iron deficiency has also been associated with pica, a craving for nonfood substances, such as clay, dirt or lead paint.[7] However, there is no definitive evidence that pica is caused by iron deficiency.

Allergies

Food allergies are often felt by parents to be the cause of diarrhea and failure to gain weight in the young child. A family history combined with observation of other systemic symptoms of an IgE-mediated response—such as eye, skin, or lung manifestations after ingestion of specific foods—is useful in making the diagnosis of food allergy. Manifestations of allergy by dietary protein ingestion include eczema, atopic dermatitis, and bronchospasm. However, ''food sensitivity'' with manifestations related only to the GI tract has been described.[8] Foods commonly causing local and systemic allergies include cows milk, egg, peanuts, wheat, and corn[9] (see Table 14-1, Section V, Allergy).

Clinical features of dietary protein intolerance include diarrhea, vomiting, edema secondary to intestinal protein loss, anorexia, anemia, and poor growth. Children between the ages of six months to three years are most commonly affected.[10] The clinical symptoms improve with withdrawal of the offending antigen.

Family History

Family history should include information on family growth patterns, obesity, and eating habits. Familial disease associated with malnutrition, cardiovascular problems, hypertension (see Table 12-1), hypercholesterolemia, and diabetes mellitus needs to be identified. In addition, a history of family food allergies must be established and ruled out.

PHYSICAL ASSESSMENT

Examination

In physical assessment of young children, attention should be focused on symptoms referable to nutrient deficiencies or excesses (see appendix C-1). In addition, the following areas may be of particular concern for this age group.

Diarrhea, when accompanied by poor weight gain, is an important indicator of nutrient malabsorption. A history of abdominal distension and increased flatus may be present with carbohydrate malabsorption. Parents of the child may also report floating stools or foul-smelling, bulky stools. In these cases, steatorrhea should be suspected.

Some of the conditions that need to be excluded with such a history are cystic fibrosis, celiac disease, postenteritis syndrome, milk protein intolerance, and giardiasis. Cystic fibrosis of the pancreas results in decreased pancreatic exocrine secretion, with secondary malabsorption of fat and protein. In such cases, symptoms of steatorrhea may be present. Diarrhea may be the presenting symptom. Celiac sprue, or gluten-sensitive enteropathy, is a permanent intestinal intolerance to all forms of gluten. Gluten is present in wheat, rye, oats, and barley. The small intestinal mucosa in such children is flattened, leading to numerous nutritional deficiencies. However, some children may exhibit only a failure to grow properly. Primary lactose intolerance is rare in the young child. However, a secondary inability to absorb lactose or sucrose following a viral enteritis may occur (see Table 11-2, Section II, Lactose Intolerance). Occasionally, an intolerance to monosaccharides is seen as well. Giardia may invade the small intestinal mucosa, causing secondary lactose intolerance as well as steatorrhea.

Medications

Many drugs affect the absorption, metabolism, and excretion of nutrients. Drugs used in the preschool age group include anticonvulsants, which decrease absorption of vitamin D, folic acid, and riboflavin. Osteomalacia due to vitamin D deficiency has been recognized as a complication of anticonvulsant therapy.[11] Antimicrobials may cause decreased synthesis of vitamin K, reduced intestinal lactose levels and folate, and B_{12} deficiency. Mineral oil laxatives may interfere with vitamins A, D, E, and K absorption (see Table 9-1).

ANTHROPOMETRIC ASSESSMENT

The purpose of anthropometric assessment is to compare a child's body size and rate of growth with reference standards. Consistency in a child's growth pattern is important, since it may diverge significantly from the norm for the child's age due to genetic factors (see appendix D).

Changes in weight for age may reflect growth, or they may reflect only increased or decreased fat stores. Because weight can be lost and regained several times, variation in weight is an indicator of acute changes in nutrient intake.

Weight for height most accurately assesses body build and distinguishes wasting from constitutional short stature. Decreased weight for height indicates acute

Table 9-1 Drug and Nutrient Interactions

Drug	Nutrient Considerations	Possible Gastrointestinal Side Effects
Antacids (general)	Increased excretion of phosphate, calcium, and fluoride by the formation of insoluble aluminum salts; high sodium content may cause fluid retention; alkaline destruction of thiamine increased; absorption of iron, vitamin A, and magnesium decreased	Constipation, diarrhea, and steatorrhea
Anticholinergic (general)	Possible decreased absorption of electrolytes and iron; increased absorption of monosaccharides	Can cause nausea, vomiting, constipation, and decreased taste acuity
Anticonvulsants	Decreased vitamin D levels; decreased absorption and competitive inhibition of folic acid and vitamin B_{12} (with megaloblastic anemia); osteomalacia or rickets due to accelerated vitamin D and bone metabolism; vitamins K, B_6, and C and calcium and magnesium levels are decreased	Hyperplasia of gums; gastric irritation with nausea, anorexia, and vomiting
Phenytoin	Altered vitamin D metabolism with reduction in vitamin D and calcium; decreased levels of folic acid and vitamins B_{12} and B_6	
Primidone	Decreased levels of vitamins D and K due to altered vitamin D metabolism	
Ritalin		Appetite suppression; depression of height and weight
Antiinflammatory agents		
Aspirin	Decreased uptake of vitamin C in thrombocytes and leukocytes; decreased protein binding of folacin; loss of iron with blood loss	GI irritation

Table 9-1 continued

Drug	Nutrient Considerations	Possible Gastrointestinal Side Effects
Corticosteroids	Increased protein catabolism; decreased glucose tolerance; increased sodium retention; decreased absorption or increased excretion of zinc, potassium, vitamin C, calcium, and iron; accelerated vitamin D metabolism; increased vitamin B_6 requirement	Increased appetite; height suppression
Antimicrobials (general)	Decreased synthesis of vitamin K by gut microflora; nonabsorbed antibiotics reduce lactase levels; some are folate and vitamin B_{12} antagonists with increased incidence of megaloblastic anemia	Diarrhea, nausea, vomiting, decreased taste acuity, and lactose deficiency; damage to intestinal cell wall; steatorrhea
Clindamycin	Decreased potassium	
Cycloserine	Vitamin B_6 antagonist; decreased intestinal absorption of niacin, calcium, and magnesium	
Gentamicin	Increased urinary excretion of potassium and magnesium	
Isoniazid	Increased excretion of vitamin B_6, lowered levels of niacin	
Neomycin	Precipitation of bile salts with decreased absorption of fat and vitamins A, D, K, B_{12}; decreased absorption of potassium, sodium, calcium, lactose, sucrose, d-xylose, and magnesium	
p-Amino salicylic acid	Inhibition of absorptive enzymes and of vitamin B_{12}, folic acid, iron, and cholesterol absorption	
Penicillin	Aftertaste with food; suppression of appetite; inhibition of glutathione; increased urinary and potassium excretion	
Sulfonamides	Decreased synthesis of folic acid, B vitamins, and vitamin K; decreased iron absorption	
Tetracyclines	Binding to bone calcium; decreased zinc and iron	

continued

Table 9-1 continued

Drug	Nutrient Considerations	Possible Gastrointestinal Side Effects
Chloramphenicol	Altered protein and hemoglobulin synthesis; increased excretion of B_6; lowered niacin levels	
Antineoplastics Methotrexate	Folic acid antagonists block normal metabolism, causing megaloblastic anemia in some cases; damage to intestinal wall with nonspecific decrease in absorption	Anorexia, stomatitis, nausea, vomiting, diarrhea, oral ulcerations, constipation, and decreased taste acuity
Cathartic Laxatives	Fluid and electrolyte losses may occur; lubricants decrease absorption of fat-soluble vitamins and calcium; bulk agents may bind certain trace elements	Mucosal irritation with abdominal cramps and diarrhea
Calomil	Decreased phosphorus absorption	
Bisacodyl	Decreased intestinal uptake of glucose	
Mannitol	Damage to intestinal wall; absorption of glucose, water, and sodium	
Mineral oil	Interference with micelle formation and decreased vitamins A, D, E, K; carotene and calcium absorption	
Phenolphthalein	Increased transit time with decreased absorption of vitamin D, calcium, riboflavin, and potassium	
Chelating agent (general)	Increased excretion of heavy metals	Decreased taste acuity and aftertaste with suppression of appetite, nausea, and vomiting
Penicillamine	Chelating of metals; decreased iron, zinc, and copper levels; increased renal excretion of B_6	
Diuretics (general)	Increased renal excretion or retention of potassium; calcium, magnesium; decreased B_6, thiamine, and carbohydrate tolerance	Gastric irritation, nausea, vomiting, and abdominal pain

Table 9-1 continued

Drug	Nutrient Considerations	Possible Gastrointestinal Side Effects
Furosemide	Increased renal losses of zinc	
Electrolyte repletion Potassium chloride	Decreased absorption of B_{12}; secondary to decreased ileal pH	

Source: Adapted from *Nutrition in Pediatrics* by W.A. Walker and J.B. Watkins (Eds.), pp. 882–884, with permission of Little, Brown & Company, © 1985.

---

malnutrition. A normal weight for height when both are below the 5th percentile may indicate chronic undernutrition or "nutritional dwarfism." Measurements that fall within the 50th percentile indicate appropriate weight for height. Deviation from this indicates over- or undernutrition.[12]

Any loss of weight in a young child may be significant. Malabsorption, anorexia secondary to chronic disease, and behavioral disturbances may be implicated.

Height is the best indicator of the child's long-term nutritional status. Height for age below the 5th percentile may indicate a chronic severe nutritional deficit. However, it may also be indicative of constitutional short stature. Knowledge of the heights of the parents and siblings is essential in making a judgment about the meaning of the data. Measurements between the fifth to tenth percentile should be evaluated further (see Table 12-2). Steady linear growth is a reassuring indicator of the adequacy of the child's diet.

The measurement of growth velocity evaluates the change in rate of growth over a specified time period. Standard charts used are those developed by Tanner[13] (see Figures 15-1 through 15-4). These charts are very useful for early identification of children with undernutrition and secondary growth failure. Slight changes in growth percentiles on standard height charts are more easily seen in these charts.

LABORATORY ASSESSMENT

Laboratory tests can provide confirmation of nutritional deficiencies previously suspected by the history and physical examination. In addition, deficiencies that are not apparent clinically may be detected (see appendix C-1). Nutrient levels and biochemical changes may be evaluated by examination of tissue, blood, and urine.

Liver secretory proteins are useful markers of visceral protein status. Synthesis of albumin is reduced after protein depletion. Since the half life of albumin is

20 days, it reflects chronic protein depletion. Proteins with shorter half lives have been proposed as markers of acute protein calorie malnutrition. These are pre-albumin, transferrin, ferritin, retinol-binding protein, and complement.[14]

Protein status can also be assessed by urinary excretion of protein breakdown substances. The creatinine height index has been widely used to measure protein depletion. Urinary excretion of creatinine correlates with lean body mass, because creatinine is a degradation product of muscle creatinine.

Since height remains unaltered with acute malnutrition, it is useful to compare a 24-hour urinary creatinine excretion with body height to determine the creatinine-height index (see appendix C-2).

Other tests that appear to be clinically useful in the malnourished child are total lymphocyte count and intradermal skin testing. Nutritional deprivation causes decreased cellular immune response. Lymphopenia indicates impaired immune function. Total lymphocyte count (TLC) less than $1,500/mm^3$ falls more than two standard deviations below the mean at any age; values less than $1,000/mm^3$ indicate severe lymphopenia.[15] TLC is calculated with the following equation:

$$TLC = \frac{\% \text{ lymphocytes} \times \text{ white blood cells}}{100}$$

Children with compromised cellular immune response secondary to malnutrition will show a loss of delayed-type skin hypersensitivity. Therefore, there is no cutaneous induration (anergy) when a number of antigens, such as monilia and mumps, are introduced intradermally. Skin tests are normally positive (5 mm induration after 72 hours) in children with an intact immune system. As nutritional status improves, this anergic response will be reversed. Infections, steroid therapy, and malignancies may also cause anergy.

Analysis of trace minerals in hair and nails is not an accepted method of determining nutritional status because they reflect deposition of stores over a long period of time, rather than recent dietary intake. These tissues are also constantly contaminated by external agents such as cosmetics and shampoos.[16]

SUMMARY

Nutritional considerations should always be kept in mind when evaluating the health of the young child. Many factors influence nutritional status. They include the environment, cultural factors, family history, and intercurrent or chronic disease states. Clinical examination and laboratory assessment, when used in conjunction with a detailed history, will uncover most nutritional deficiencies.

NOTES

1. R.M. Suskind, ed., *Textbook of Pediatric Nutrition*, 4th ed. (New York: Raven Press, 1981), 297–299.

2. A. Walker and J.B. Watkins, eds., *Nutrition in Pediatrics: Basic Science and Clinical Application* (Boston: Little Brown & Co., 1985), 551–554.

3. J.A. Walker-Smith and A.S. McNeish, *Diarrhea and Malnutrition in Childhood* (London: Butterworth & Co., Ltd., 1986), 1–5.

4. Ibid., 4.

5. R. Edelman, "Cell Mediated Immune Response in Protein-Calorie Malnutrition: A Review," in *Malnutrition and Immune Response*, ed. R.M. Suskind (New York: Raven Press, 1981), 47.

6. Suskind, *Textbook*, 295.

7. W.H. Crosby, "Pica: A Full Report," *JAMA* 235 (1976): 2765.

8. Walker and Watkins, *Nutrition in Pediatrics*, 152.

9. Ibid., 152.

10. Ibid., 153.

11. W.C. McLean and G. Graham, *Pediatric Nutrition in Clinical Practice* (Addison-Wesley Publishing Co., 1982), 8.

12. S.J. Fomon, *Nutritional Disorders of Children: Prevention, Screening, and Followup* (Rockville, Md.: U.S. Department of Health, Education and Welfare, Public Health Service, Health Services Administration, 1978), 32.

13. J.M. Tanner and R.H. Whitehouse, "Clinical Longitudinal Standards for Height, Weight, Height Velocity, Weight Velocity and Stages of Puberty," *Archives of Diseases in Childhood* 51 (1976): 170.

14. Suskind, *Textbook*, 294.

15. Ibid., 297.

16. Walker and Watkins, *Nutrition in Pediatrics*, 552.

Chapter 10

Environmental Management
of the Young Child
(Two Through Six Years)

Rosemary Liguori and Donna Wong

OVERVIEW

Young children continue to grow and exercise newly developed skills in their increasingly expanded environment. Motor skills become refined, and social skills are discovered. The young child is eager to learn and grow. Optimal nutrition is a key ingredient to the child's success.

Generally, young children spend the majority of their time in the home and perhaps day care and/or nursery school. Some young children of working mothers are cared for in the homes of others, or a caregiver comes into their home. Therefore, to evaluate the impact of the environment for nutritional purposes, the home, family, and child care arrangements are the primary aspects. Intervention to improve nutrition must be structured to include all of these environmental factors.

ENVIRONMENTAL ASSESSMENT

Home and Family

The family is the catalyst in the child's development. Food and mealtime have many meanings to us. Culture, socialization, health, and love all come into play when we speak of the family and food. The family is where we learn the meaning of food and the importance of nutrition and develop food patterns and habits that will affect us for a lifetime. Cultural factors can influence the nutrition of children. In some subcultures, for example, it is thought that, if some family members are obese, it is acceptable for other family members to be obese;[1] what the father prefers to eat dictates what is purchased and prepared for the entire family.

In general, the greater the cohesiveness of the family, the better the diet; whereas the more disorganized the family, the poorer the diet.[2] The family members stimulate and influence one another. The extroverted family allows the child to explore new foods within the family and among friends. In contrast, the isolated family tends to depend on experts to direct them to community programs.

School and Day Care

Because of the increase in the number of working mothers and single-parent families, the need for alternative modes of child care has increased dramatically. Head Start and day care facilities have partially met this challenge, servicing many socioeconomic levels. Thus, just as the family plays an important role in setting the stage for a healthy nutritional life, the alternative care setting is having an increased impact on the preschool child.

In any event, whether the child care is provided in the home or at a center-based day care facility, it is important that nutrition and eating habits be carefully discussed. The child's adjustment or maladjustment to the situation may be reflected by eating behaviors.

Community and Socioeconomic Factors

In lower socioeconomic families, there is a tendency toward consumption of foods that contain higher calories and higher concentrations of salt and are nonnutritious. In lower-income families, there are less restrictions on such foods, and the result is often a poor diet. Such a diet contributes to obesity and dental caries, which, in turn, cause increased morbidity and mortality.[3]

In short, there is an increased risk for the young child in lower-income families. Brown et al. found that in lower-income children there is a higher incidence of anemia, underweight, short stature, and elevated erythro protoporphy (EP) levels.[4] Lower-income families purchase more dairy products, spend more on nonnutritious foods, and shop at many different stores. These families are concerned more with food preferences than with cost and nutrition. They tend to have poorer shopping habits, are more disorganized, frequently shop (many times a week), spend more money, and do not compare prices.

In contrast, higher-socioeconomic family members have a greater body size and higher hemoglobin, hematocrit, and iron levels. Also, they have higher vitamin-A and ascorbic acid levels. Vitamin supplements are often given to children in such families, even if they do not need them. Also, children whose parents are better educated tend to be leaner and healthier.[5]

Food shopping behaviors and food use by well-educated parents reflect more concern for cost than preference. They select more protein food, plan their shopping, read labels, and are aware of the importance of nutrition. For example, they consume a higher amount of animal and vegetable protein, fruit, and vegetables and a lower amount of cereal and bread.[6]

Thus, health care practitioners should be aware of the socioeconomic levels of their clients so that, when necessary, they can assist them with better nutritional choices, encourage them to read labels, demonstrate cost-effective shopping, and prevent possible nutrition deficiencies.

INTERVENTIONS FOR A HEALTHY ENVIRONMENT

Mealtime for the Hurried Family

Mornings are often hectic for working parents. To help this situation, Hirsch suggests that, for the family's breakfast, leftovers from the previous night's supper should be creamed, warmed on the stove or microwave, and placed in pita bread or on top of a baked potato. Leftover mashed potatoes could be mixed with a beaten egg, then fried like a potato pancake and served with applesauce. Or one could fry an egg, place it over some warmed spinach and put it on a toasted English muffin. Alternatively, one could put warm beef over waffles.[7] Some other quick, but nutritious, breakfast ideas are listed in Table 10-1. Similarly, it is often difficult to be creative when planning lunch, especially in packing lunches. Some ideas to spark the lunch menu are also listed in Table 10-1.

Table 10-1 Suggestions for the Hurried Family

Quick and nutritious breakfast foods:
Yogurt with fresh fruit	Yogurt over cereal
Toasted cheese bread	Rice cakes with peanut butter
Granola	English muffin minipizza
Tuna melt	Salad
Frozen yogurt sprinkled with raisins	

For an efficient start in the morning:
Set the table the night before.
Line up breakfast cereal or other nonperishable foods ahead of time.
Use paper plates.
Allow the preschooler to help as much as possible.

Lunch fun and fancy:
Fruit on a stick
Pita bread or bagel in lieu of bread
Tuna, peanut butter, or cottage cheese on celery
Sandwiches made with a cookie cutter
Rolled-up, thin slices of lean meat or cheese
Foods served in a muffin tin or egg carton
Banana on a hot dog bun and spread with peanut butter

Dealing with Picky Eaters

Many times parents are dissatisfied with their child's lack of interest in foods, especially if the child picks at foods or refuses to eat vegetables or drink milk. Yet food inconsistencies, food jags, and lack of variety in a child's diet are actually very typical. These do not necessarily reflect willful disobedience. Young children are becoming social beings and are interested in their environment. They may experience mealtime as hurried, boring, filled with tension, or interrupting their play. The most important rule is to relax and not to pressure, nag, bribe, force, or cajole. Unfortunately, food and mealtime often provide ammunition for a battle, with the child victorious in the end. In such situations, the parents need reassurance that both they and the child will survive this stage (see Table 11-2, Section VI, Refusal to Eat.). In many ways, young children are like adults, with the major difference being the child's proportionately smaller perspective. Thus, it is helpful to remember that the young child

- eats when hungry
- can be responsible in food consumption
- stops when filled
- loves rituals
- can be made more comfortable with proportionally sized equipment (utensils, table, chairs)
- may not be ready to sit through an entire meal
- enjoys participating in food selection and preparation

Some children who are poor eaters need extra encouragement. One approach that provides additional motivation at mealtime is the use of a daily food chart, based on the principles of reinforcement (see Exhibit 10-1). The child is given points for each serving in each of the four food groups. If the child accumulates the correct number of points for each food group (four for fruit and vegetables, four for grains, three for dairy, and two for meat), the child is given a star or sticker. Parents might add a special reward for any day in which every food group has a star. To help the child understand the concept of food groups, the family might make a poster by cutting out pictures of appropriate foods from magazines (food coupons work well) and pasting them in a section marked with the number of required servings for each group. Posters and brochures on various food groups are also available; for example, the poster *Every Day Eat the 3-2-4-4 Way* is available from the National Dairy Council, 6300 North River Road, Rosemont, IL 60018-4233. Finally, to ensure the correct serving size, parents can use measuring cups; children often find such cups interesting new utensils.

Exhibit 10-1 My Own Daily Food Chart

	Fruit & Vegetable				Bread & Cereal				Milk				Meat				★
	B	L	D	S	B	L	D	S	B	L	D	S	B	L	D	S	
MON																	
TUES																	
WED																	
THURS																	
FRI																	
SAT																	
SUN																	

Child Care and Day Care

There are five issues to consider in the nutrition of the young child under alternative child care arrangement:

1. nutritional needs of the child
2. the parent and child care provider communicating those needs
3. nutrition education
4. exercise
5. sleep needs

Nutritional Needs

If the day care facility is licensed by the state, there are regulations for nutrition and food preparation that must be followed. Head Start, which is federally sponsored, has nutrition performance standards that are more stringent than those for day care facilities. The regulations for day care facilities may be obtained by contacting the appropriate state agency. For Head Start, the United States Department of Health and Human Services should be contacted.

Children who are in a child care setting for less than four hours should receive one-third of the total nutritional requirements for the day. Children who are in a child care setting for more than four hours a day should receive one-half to two-thirds of their daily nutritional needs.

Communication Between Parents and Child Care Provider

When parents are considering an alternative child care setting, they should be encouraged to interview the child care provider about such nutritional practices as meal planning, preparing, and service. Table 10-2 presents suggestions to assist the parent in such interviews. The parents should be encouraged to write down their questions before the interview to facilitate collecting relevant information.

Child care providers supplement and augment the family away from home. It is thus imperative that there be communication with such providers via letters, educational meetings, or conferences. A comprehensive history should be given to the provider. This should include information on nutrition, family health, food likes, food dislikes, and allergies. A physician's note regarding any milk or milk-product allergies should be placed on file, since many state and federal regulations enforce milk consumption.

Nutrition Education

In the environment of a day care center, numerous opportunities for nutrition education exist. For example, the serving of ethnic foods can provide the child of a different culture with a feeling of confidence and familiarity.[8] By respecting cultural differences in food preferences, the child can be given a sense of worth. Thus, early learning about various ethnic and cultural environments could be included in the day care curriculum. For example, food sources—such as pita bread, bagels, spaghetti, and rice—could be used to represent different ethnic groups.

In a study by Gillis, Gould, and Henderson concerning the use of food in learning activities for young children, it was found that educators felt that nutrition education is too expensive and too messy, and that the staff is lacking to carry out such programs. Ironically, in the same study, the educators considered proper nutrition for the child as essential.[9]

Table 10-2 Suggestions for Parents' Questions to the Child Care Provider

What types of food are served?
Where do the children eat, and how is the food served (family style, one course at a time, or all at the same time)?
How are food dislikes handled?
What emphasis is placed on manners?
Are snacks provided?
Are there nutritional guidelines that the center has to meet?
Are there set times for eating, or can the children eat or have a snack at any time?
Is there a breakfast program?

Keane reported changes that can occur in the preschool child after such educational programs. He found a decrease in the wasting of food, an increase in nutrition knowledge, and more nutritious food choices by the children.[10] Concepts that can be addressed in such nutrition programs include food preparation, processing, and shopping. Food preparation may incorporate fine motor manipulation, appreciation of color and consistency (soft/hard), and sensory exploration.

To emphasize low salt, low cholesterol, low sugar, and increased consumption of complete carbohydrates, Stark et al. used a method for labeling foods.[11] A red label identified "don't-eat" foods, such as cookies, candies, chips, and so on; and a green label identified "do-eat" foods, such as fruits and vegetables. The children were rewarded with stickers for the right food choices. This approach appeared to be very effective, especially when parents were involved. Stark et al. found that, without parental participation, the children easily returned to their previous eating behaviors.

Exercise

Children who play hard burn more calories, but they then replenish them without much encouragement. During the hot weather, children will not play as hard and therefore will require fewer calories. Fortunately, nature is able to facilitate this fine-tuning of calories and energy requirements.

The lack of physical activity and the watching of television, often with nonnutritious snacks, contribute to an obesity problem for many young children.[12] Children are exposed to as many as 20,000 commercials per year.[13] Many of these promote foods, especially highly sugared, nonnutritious choices, and are designed to attract children's attention. Older children are more resistant to such advertisements; in many cases, they are just interested in the "box." In any case, parents who are themselves physically active can serve as role models for their children. They can encourage their children to participate in sports and to be concerned about physical fitness.

If exercise is not a daily habit, the environment of the home might be altered to allow its development. Changes might include less TV-viewing, especially while eating; no TV-viewing at all at certain times; and exercise with the children, for example, roller skating, sleigh riding or just going for a brisk walk. Remember to suggest extra fluids in warm weather.

Sleep Needs

Children have different sleep-awake cycles, reflecting different sleep needs. These circadian rhythms constitute a biological cycle, recurring every 24 hours, that governs our sleep and awakening, activity and rest, hunger and eating, body temperature, and hormone activity. The hormone cortisol secreted by the adrenal gland regulates this cycle, dropping off in the evening and rising in the morning.[14]

If children awake when their cortisol levels are low, they will have difficulty sleeping at night or be cranky during the day. When sleep-wake cycles are irregular, mealtime schedules can become quite variable.[15]

Nibbling on protein snacks from 3 P.M. on to bedtime can help some children sleep better. Tryptophan, an amino acid found in red meats and other protein-rich foods, causes drowsiness and encourages sleep.[16] Protein-rich foods include peanut butter, nuts, cheese, and yogurt. Calcium-rich foods have a calming effect on sleep. Foods high in calcium include dairy products—such as hard and cottage cheese, milk, and yogurt—broccoli, and green leafy vegetables.[17] Sugary desserts and foods that are high in carbohydrates should be avoided at bedtime because they raise the blood sugar level and then make it fall rapidly during the night, disturbing the sleep pattern.

ROLE OF THE HEALTH CARE PRACTITIONER

The health care practitioner can provide essential services to assist the family in meeting the nutritional needs of the preschool child. First, it is important that the professional obtain a complete nutrition history. Many times the chief concerns in such a history are "just tickets in the door;" for example, the child who constantly refuses foods may be doing so as part of a power struggle with parents who are divorcing; the divorce is thus the real issue, not the refusal of food.

Anticipatory guidance should be a part of the counseling, addressing such issues as food jags, food preferences, and food dislikes. To make the counseling effective, it is necessary that the professional know how the family perceives food and nutrition. The approach should be family-centered, permitting the entire family to benefit, not just the child.

The health care practitioner screens, assesses, identifies, and formulates a plan of care with input from the family; helps the family set goals and develop a healthy lifestyle (this is a slow process); counsels and makes suggestions and recommendations; evaluates the results; and then, if necessary, refers to other professionals. For example, if there is a weight problem, the health care practitioner may refer to a psychologist to identify the underlying strategy or to an exercise or diet program.

Nutrition education may be done on an individual, family, or community basis. Often the professional is asked to speak on nutritional issues to groups, both professional or lay people. Indeed, the practitioner should be a resource person for the family and the community.[18] Identifying additional nutrition support—for example, from such local, state, or federally funded programs as Women, Infant, and Children (WIC), the Food Stamp Program, the Food Distribution Program, the School Breakfast and Lunch Program, and the Special Milk Program—is an important aspect of the health care practitioner's role.[19]

NOTES

1. M. Venters and R. Mullis, "Family-Oriented Nutrition Education and Preschool Obesity," *Journal of Nutrition Education* 16 (1984): 159–161.

2. Ibid., 160.

3. J. Brown et al., "Ethnic Group Difference in Nutritional Status of Young Children from Low-Income Areas of an Urban Country," *American Journal of Clinical Nutrition* 44 (1986): 938–944.

4. Ibid., 942.

5. E. Bassler and K. Newell, "Food Shopping Behaviors and Food Use by Well Educated Young People," *Journal of Nutrition Education* 14 (1982): 146–149.

6. Ibid., 149.

7. R. Hirsch, *Super Working Mom's Handbook* (New York: Warner Books, 1986), 84–85.

8. J. Slattery, C. Pearson, and C. Torre, *Maternal and Child Nutrition, Assessment and Counseling* (New York: Appleton-Century-Crofts, 1979), 21.

9. D. Gillis, E. Gould, and J. Henderson, "Day Care Teachers: Nutrition, Knowledge, Opinion and Use of Food," *Journal of Nutrition Education* 12 (1980): 200–204.

10. M. Keane, "A Comparison of Two Modes of Nutrition Education on Preschoolers' Nutrition Knowledge and Consumption of Foods at the Noon Meals." *Dissertation Abstracts International* 45 (1985): 3470.

11. L. Stark et al., "Food Choices in Preschoolers," *Journal of Applied Behavior Analysis* 19 (1986): 367–379.

12. W.H. Dietz, "Childhood Obesity," in *Annals of the New York Academy of Science* (New York: New York Academy of Science, 1987), 47–53.

13. P. Pipes, *Nutrition in Infancy and Children* (St. Louis, Mo.: C.V. Mosby Co., 1985), 199.

14. L. Smith, *Improving Your Child's Behavior and Chemistry* (New York: Prentice-Hall, 1977), 123.

15. R. Ferber, *Solve Your Child's Sleep Problem* (New York: Simon & Schuster, 1985), 34.

16. Smith, *Improving Your Child's Behavior*, 125.

17. Ibid., 126.

18. L. Whaley and D. Wong, *Care of Children and Infants* (St. Louis, Mo.: C.V. Mosby Co., 1987), 15.

19. M. Egan, "Federal Nutrition Support Programs for Children," in *Pediatric Nutrition Handbook* (Evanston, Ill.: AAP Publishers, 1979), 161–173.

Chapter 11

Dietary Assessment and Management of the Young Child
(Two Through Six Years)

Jeannette B. Endres

- Should young children be served artificial sweeteners or sugar?
- Is there a relationship between diet and hyperactivity in young children?
- Is brown sugar more nutritious than granulated sugar?
- What foods can be recommended if the young child is lactose-intolerant?

DIETARY ASSESSMENT

Overview

Young children, ages two to six, include the group known as "toddlers" and "preschoolers." Recommended dietary allowances (RDA) for these children include two categories, for ages one to three, and for ages four to six (see appendix B-2). For these children, health care practitioners must address such issues as anemia, obesity, lactose intolerance, snack-food consumption, cardiovascular disease, sweetener use, and hyperactivity. No one assessment procedure will suffice when evaluating the nutritional well being of the child in this age group; all relevant measurements must be considered.

Assessing the Diet of the Young Child

Using the Nutrition Questionnaire and the 24-Hour Recall Form (see appendixes A-1 and A-2), the health care practitioner should determine what the child is currently eating in relation to height and weight (see appendix D). Assessing the nutritional status of the young child is usually the first step in reassuring the caregiver that the child is progressing according to accepted standards or in helping the caregiver modify certain dietary practices. The practitioner should listen to the caregiver's concerns related to the family and the child, specifically watching for concerns related to height and weight measurements while the assessments are being made.

The health care practitioner should assess and evaluate height and weight, other anthropometric data, developmental readiness, dietary intake, the setting in which the child eats, and exercise patterns and plan goals for change with the caregiver. The child should be viewed as a member in an ever-changing family. If a specific diet has been prescribed, the problems of dietary change should be reviewed.

The health care practitioner should allow and encourage the caregiver to choose and take responsibility for specific activities to modify the child's behavior, for example, dietary intake, exercise, mealtime environment, and skill development. Specific changes should be planned with the caregiver/family regarding the food behavior of the family or child to be measured and completed by the next visit. In this process, the following questions may be asked by the health professional to help the mother (caregiver) succeed with any changes:[1]

- What do you see that could be changed or improved?
- What is a realistic goal for you?
- What problems are likely to interfere with your plans?
- How can you modify (change) your time schedule, home setting, or physical environment to help you and your child achieve any changes?
- Who can help; what can they do?
- What can you do to help during the next few weeks?
- What encouraging things can you say to yourself when confronted with doubts?
- How are you going to keep track of behaviors to see changes?

Developmental Skills

All 20 primary (baby) teeth have usually erupted when the child is 2 1/2 to 3 years of age. When children have mastered the eating process and foods can be given directly from the family table, they may experience a less than enthusiastic desire for food. Yet, developmentally, the child is ready for a wide range of foods from the family table. There are new food tastes for the child; commercially prepared, ground, or chopped foods have a taste- and mouth-feel that is different from that of the same food served at the family table.

Many children are developmentally ready to use small flatware in eating food at the table. Spoons and forks can be offered for the 23-month-old, and a knife can be added for the four-to-six-year-old. Using equipment may encourage food intake.

Glasses or cups with heavy bottoms can help prevent spills. Filling a glass only partially full not only gives the child the opportunity to ask for more but also limits the amount the caregiver needs to clean up if accidents occur. Clear plastic glasses allow the caregiver and the child to judge the quantity to serve.

Developmental scales are quick and easy to use with the family, ensuring that the child is feeding and eating according to developmental readiness. (See chapter 8, Exhibit 8-1, for skills or abilities that can be expected at various age levels.)

Diet and Hyperactivity

Caregivers/parents sometimes raise questions about the relationship of diet to hyperactivity. The scientific community, the National Institutes of Health, the Food and Drug Administration, and the National Education Association have all made recommendations relevant to the caregiver and parents regarding diet and hyperactivity.[2] Two conclusions may be drawn from these recommendations:

1. There is no evidence to justify recommending a ban on foods containing artificial food colorings in federally supported food programs used by caregivers.
2. Because the diet usually suggested for hyperactivity has no apparent harmful effects and because the nonspecific effects of the dietary treatment are frequently beneficial to families, there is no reason to discourage families that wish to use the diet as long as other therapy is continued and the child's nutritional status is monitored.

Sweeteners

Health care practitioners are often asked, "Should I serve artificial sweeteners or sugar to young children?" Nutritionists are often tempted to answer with another question, "Is either really necessary?" In fact, it is difficult to find evidence in the scientific literature indicating that consumption of table sugar per se is detrimental to the preschooler's health. However, reduction of simple sugars is advisable for the treatment of diabetes, the treatment and prevention of obesity, and the prevention of dental caries.

Fructose, sorbitol, and xylitol are sweeteners that have the same caloric value as table sugar, but they are used differently by the body, often requiring less insulin for the initial stages of metabolism. Many "sugar-free" candies and gums that are sweetened with sorbitol and xylitol can cause diarrhea, especially in young children. Therefore, although candy or gum may be labeled sugar-free, it may still contain calories and in some cases cause the preschooler gastric distress and diarrhea. One must read the labels! Sweeteners that are commonly used in food preparation and contain nutrients and energy are listed in Table 11-1.

Table 11-1 Calorie and Iron Content of Selected Natural Sweeteners

Sweetener (1 tbsp)	Kilocalories	Iron (mg)
Molasses, blackstrap		
Dark	43	3.20
Light	50	0.90
Syrup		
Corn (light and dark)	59	0.80
Maple	50	0.20
Brown sugar, dark (packed)	51	0.47
Honey	64	0.10
Granulated sugar	46	Trace
Crystalline fructose	42	Trace

Source: Reprinted from *Food, Nutrition and the Young Child*, 2nd ed., by J.B. Endres and R.E. Rockwell, p. 154, Copyright © 1985 Charles E. Merrill Publishing Company, Columbus, Ohio. Used with permission.

Health care professionals can evaluate the nutrient contribution of various options. The energy and iron content of natural sweeteners indicates that the primary nutrient is carbohydrate, with a small amount of iron. Blackstrap molasses (first extraction) is the exception; in addition to iron, it contains calcium (one tablespoon is equal to one-half cup of milk). However, very few children enjoy the flavor of this molasses; most children prefer a syrup made from molasses and high-fructose corn syrup.

Consuming sweeteners for the purpose of obtaining iron is hard to justify in light of their high energy value. The amount of iron found in one tablespoon of packed brown sugar is equal that in about one-half slice of whole wheat bread (0.4 mg). However, one-half slice of bread, in addition to supplying other nutrients, has approximately 30 to 35 kcal, while one tablespoon of brown sugar supplies 51 kcal.

Although safe for use by the whole family, sweeteners should be used along with a balanced diet, not in place of foods that provide a wide variety of nutrients. Thus, a sugar replacement or table sugar can be limited or omitted from the child's diet. If included, it should be used only in order to enhance an already balanced diet.

Data Analysis

Diet information obtained from the 24-hour recall and/or the nutrition questionnaire should be evaluated in terms of the nutritional needs of each child. The child's diet can be quickly compared with the suggested foods and amounts shown in the food groups (see appendix B-1). Time generally does not permit a more detailed calculation of nutrients in milligram amounts that can be checked against the RDA (see appendix B-2).

A diet should not be evaluated for the young child without consideration of activity patterns. A useful tool is a Food and Activity Record (see appendix A-5) that can be adapted for the young child. Calories consumed can be estimated from this record. The record can also help in evaluating the amount of time the child watches television or participates in other activities and the times when snacks and other foods are eaten.

If the child's eating pattern appears to be typical of children in that age group and the weight in relation to height is within an acceptable range, there is little need to recommend a change in energy allowance. However, the nutrient density or the composition of the foods eaten may still need to be modified.

There are two methods by which energy needs may be assessed. In the first method, the amount eaten is compared with a standard. The simplest, but not always the most accurate, procedure may be to roughly estimate energy, using a base of 1,000 calories and adding 100 calories for each year of age. However this method does not relate easily to the RDA. Based upon the mean and range given in RDA tables for energy, the need per kilogram or pound of body weight decreases as age increases:

Birth–6 months	115 kcal/kg (47.7)
6 months–1 year	105 kcal/kg (52.3)
1–3 years	100 kcal/kg (44.8/lb)
4–6 years	85 kcal/kg (38.6/lb)

Thus, in calculating the needs of an actual child using the RDA, kcal per height is often the most meaningful:

1–3 years	37.1 kcal/in (14.4/cm)
4–6 years	38.6 kcal/in (15.2/cm)

The energy in the diet of the two-to-six-year-old should be from 37 to 39 kcal per inch.

COMMON NUTRITIONAL PROBLEMS OF THE YOUNG CHILD

Information about common nutritional problems of the young child is provided in Table 11-2. This table also provides additional assessment questions, recommended actions, and ways to evaluate outcomes. Actions recommended by health care practitioners for specific weight problems are shown in Exhibit 11-1. Food combinations that supply complete protein are listed in Table 11-3. Nutrient-dense snacks that provide educational opportunities for children are listed in Table 11-4.

Table 11-2 Common Nutritional Problems of the Young Child

I. OBESITY

In one study of nursery school children, as many as 12 percent of the children were considered obese and could have been identified by earlier measurements of height and weight in order to initiate preventive measures.[3]

Using the height-for-weight grids, measurements greater than the 95th percentile indicate obesity[4] (see appendix D).

The health care provider should be cautious when recommending dietary restrictions for the young child based only upon height-weight grids and should take into consideration the family history of obesity as well as the environment.

According to the committee on Nutrition of the American Academy of Pediatrics, most obese children, unlike adults, have an increase in lean body mass for height, accounting for as much as 50 percent of the obese child's excess weight.[5]

Genetic factors can be influenced by environmental factors. The genetic tendency toward fatness can be expressed or repressed depending on the food supply and emphasis on exercise.[6]

"No one has enough information to predict which children will spontaneously lose their excess fat, which will do so with some treatment, and which will always be fat."[7]

Assessment	Action

Exhibit 11-1, Recommended Actions of Health Care Practitioners for Weight Problems by Degree of Severity and Age, provides assessments and actions for all children. Also, see chapters 8 and 14 for further suggestions regarding childhood obesity.

II. LACTOSE INTOLERANCE

Lactose, the carbohydrate found in milk and milk products, is consumed in its natural form and in a variety of manufactured and processed products.

Lactose intolerance is a lack of sufficient quantities of the digestive enzyme lactase.

Tolerance of lactose and large quantities of milk is peculiar to northern European and white American ethnic groups, but many adults in the world cannot tolerate large quantities of milk because of lactose intolerance.

Evidence of lactose malabsorption is seen in almost 33 percent of black children ages 5 to 6 years.

Lactose activity can be influenced by transit time (how fast the food moves through the intestinal tract), the food (cheese, milk, yogurt) through which the lactose is consumed, and/or intake of additional foods along with lactose.

A child may not be able to tolerate a glass of milk taken alone, but, after the consumption of other foods, milk may be well-tolerated.

Cheese may be tolerated when cow's milk gives gastric distress.

Because milk is an important food source for many vitamins, minerals, and protein, lactase can be purchased under the trade name of Lact-Aid and added to dairy products to predigest the milk sugar (lactose). Enzyme-treated milk is also available in some supermarkets.

The caregiver can try cheese and yogurt, since much of the lactose is broken down in the fermentation process.

Table 11-2 continued

Supplementation with calcium may be necessary in some cases; 800 mg of calcium a day is recommended for children two to five years old (see appendixes B-2 and F).

Assessment	Action
Is lactose intolerance suspected, or has it been diagnosed?	Determine foods child has been eating by 24-hour recall with the caregiver (see appendix A-2).
What foods has the child been consuming that contain lactose?	Evaluate the intake for sources of lactose.
What foods should be eliminated from the child's diet?	Plan a diet with the caregiver that eliminates sources of lactose. Instruct the caregiver on how to find calcium substitutes, hidden sources of lactose, where foods can be purchased, and methods of food preparation. Instruct in label reading.

Evaluation

Have caregiver keep a three-day food diary (see appendix A-4) and bring to next visit. Evaluate for sources of lactose.

Monitor diet for calcium, vitamin D, and riboflavin.

If child is not symptom-free, review diet plan again and emphasize hidden sources of lactose to be avoided.

If the symptoms persist, refer caretaker and child to a registered dietitian (R.D.) for in-depth counseling.

III. ANEMIA

Anemia is a condition in which the concentration of hemoglobin (measurement of the color of the red blood cells) and hematocrit (measurement of the quantity of red blood cells) is below a certain standard.

One of the most common causes of anemia is an iron-deficient diet.

The transition from infant feeding regimens, often including fortified formulas and infant cereals, to family foods can affect the iron content of the diet and subsequently the iron status of the child.

As the child reaches two to three years, iron can be supplied in the form of "red" meats, legumes, breads, iron-fortified cereals, and certain vegetables and fruits.

Iron from red meats is more readily available to the body than iron supplied from plant products.

Fifteen mg per day is recommended for children one to three years old; 10 mg per day for four to six year olds.

Assessment	Action
Are the hemoglobin and/or hematocrit levels below the normal range?	Determine foods child has been eating by completing a 24-hour recall with the caregiver (see appendix A-2).

Table 11-2 continued

Is the child still using a bottle? What is put in the bottle? How much milk is the child consuming?	Discourage use of bottle for any drink or food at this age. (See chapters 7, 8, and 10 for feeding suggestions.)
Is the child consuming meat? Are cereals and breads fortified with iron?	Plan a diet with the caregiver that will provide an increase in iron-containing foods. (See appendix F for sources of iron. See appendix B-1 for suggested foods and amounts for this age group.)
	Have caregiver keep a three-day food record to bring to next visit.

Evaluation

Evaluate three-day food record for iron-containing foods and total adequacy. Check amounts of milk consumed.

Note hemoglobin and hematocrit levels. If not improved, review diet plan carefully with caregiver and emphasize offering iron-containing foods.

If hemoglobin/hematocrit levels do not improve at subsequent visits, refer to registered dietitian (R.D.) for in-depth counseling and/or to physician to consider supplemental iron.

IV. VEGETARIAN DIET

The use of vegetarian diets must be taken into consideration when evaluating the child's diet, especially the iron status.

A pure or strict vegetarian diet excludes all food of animal origin (e.g., meat, poultry, fish, eggs, and dairy products). The group known as vegans often avoids one or more other food groups, such as processed foods, cooked foods, legumes, cereals, grains, or fruits. Fruitarians limit their food intake to raw and cooked fruits, nuts, honey, and oil.

For lacto and lacto-ovo-vegetarian diets, see chapter 17 and appendix H.

Children's diets that are restricted in animal products should contain fortified soy milk.

Tofu is another good protein alternative. Tofu is the curd produced from clotting soy milk (soybean product).

Combination dishes that have complementary proteins or include milk products and eggs and complement the plant food are good choices (see Table 11-3, Food Combinations that Supply Complete Protein).

Use of a vegetarian diet that allows ample energy or kilocalories and adequate supplies of iron-fortified cereals, dairy products, and eggs is safe for children.

If diets are more restricted in animal foods, the child's growth can be affected.[8]

Parents who wish to have their children follow a vegetarian diet should be made aware of the implications for the young child.

For assessment, action, and evaluation, see chapters 14 and 17.

V. CARDIOVASCULAR DISEASE AND DIET MODIFICATION (also see chapters 14 and 17)

The American Academy of Pediatrics provides recommendations for a prudent approach to diets of children: "Current dietary trends in the United States toward a decreased consumption of saturated fats, cholesterol, and salt and an increased intake of polyunsaturated fats should be followed with moderation. AVOID DIETS THAT ARE EXTREME FOR CHILDREN."[9]

Table 11-2 continued

The increase in cereal grains with high fiber at the expense of animal protein leads to a decrease in essential nutrients, such as iron, which come with animal proteins.

Menus that meet the dietary guidelines for children over five years of age have been published.[10]

No attempt should be made to restrict the child's intake of a variety of nutrient-dense foods on the basis of fat, sodium, or cholesterol content.

Assessment	Action
If there is a family history of elevated blood lipids, assess the child's diet for high amounts of fat and sodium.	Determine the child's food intake by completing a 24-hour recall with the caregiver (see appendix A-2).
Is the child consuming large quantities of foods that contain excess amounts of sodium and fat?	Plan a diet for the child with the caregiver that will meet the nutritional needs of the child. Suggest nutrient-dense foods. See appendixes F and G-1, and Table 16-1. Discourage use of high-fat and salty foods, such as potato chips, pickles, and salted meats.
	Have the caregiver keep a three-day food record to bring to next visit (see appendix A-4).

Evaluation

Evaluate the three-day record for nutritional adequacy and intake of "empty calories" that are high in fat, sugar, and sodium.

If necessary, review instruction in a high-nutrient-dense, adequate diet for a young child with emphasis on avoidance of large quantities of fat, sugar, and sodium.

Encourage the caregiver to continue to offer the child a prudent, well-balanced diet.

VI. REFUSAL TO EAT (See also chapters 7, 8, and 10)

Refusal to eat in the young child is generally characterized by refusal to eat foods offered at the family mealtime. Only small amounts may be eaten or all foods may be left unconsumed.

If refusal to eat is reported, the reasons should be explored.

Assessment	Action
Is the child developmentally ready for the foods and equipment?	See Exhibit 8-1, Infant Feeding Guide
Is the child hungry?	Complete a 24-hour recall with the caregiver to determine quantity and quality of foods eaten. Portions may be too large; feedings may be too frequent; low nutrient density foods—such as candy, soda pop, and snack foods—may be given too frequently and dull the child's appetite.

Table 11-2 continued

Is the child exerting independence?	Suggest to the caregiver that it may be wise to ignore the refusal to eat for a time but offer three nutritious meals and two snacks that contribute to nutrient intake. Remove uneaten food quietly after several minutes with no comment; do not give additional food until the next eating period. See Table 11-4, Nutrient Dense Snacks that Provide Educational Opportunities for Children.[11]
Is the child too busy and "on the go," exploring the environment?	Suggest that the caregiver schedule a "quiet time" before meal period to prepare the child for eating the meal.
Is the child tired, needing sleep more than food?	Suggest setting up routines for eating and sleeping so that the child is not overtired at mealtime.
Is the child expected to eat foods not eaten by other family members?	Suggest that, whenever possible, the child be offered the same foods as the other family members.
Are the utensils, chair, and table the right size?	Suggest ways to elevate the child at the family table. Support for feet is also important. While certain utensils and equipment may make the child comfortable, they may also make the child feel isolated.
Are portions appropriate size?	Use food models to determine the amounts of food. Suggest smaller portions for the young child. (See appendix B-1 for recommended amounts of food for the young child.)
Is the child getting sick or recovering from an illness?	Explain to the caregiver that the child may not be able to eat because of illness. Suggest such nutrient-dense liquids as soups; juices and plain carbohydrate foods may also be suggested for a short period.

Evaluation

Have the caregiver keep a three-day food record and bring it to next visit. Evaluate quantity and quality of foods eaten.

If the caretaker reports that the child still refuses to eat, try to determine the cause and reinforce recommended action.

If the child continues to refuse to eat and is not gaining weight as expected, refer to a registered dietitian (R.D.) for in-depth counseling with the caregiver.

Source: Adapted from *Food, Nutrition and the Young Child,* 2nd ed., by J.B. Endres and R.E. Rockwell, pp. 88–162, copyright © 1985 Charles E. Merrill Publishing Company, Columbus, Ohio. Used with permission.

Exhibit 11-1 Recommended Actions of Health Care Practitioners for Weight Problems, by Degree of Severity and Age

		Degree of Overweight*		
		Mild**	**Moderate****	**Severe**
Weight for Height Percentile		75–89	90–94	95 and above
Developmental Stage	**Age Range**	**Levels of Activities**		
Infant	0–12 mo	Action 1	Action 1	Action 1
Toddler	1–2 yrs	Action 1	Action 1	Action 2
Preschool	3–5 yrs	Action 1	Action 2	Action 2
Schoolage	6–9 yrs	Action 1	Action 2	Action 3
		Mild	**Moderate**	**Severe**
Percent overweight for height, age, sex		120–139	140–159	160 and above
Preadolescent	varies	Action 1	Action 2	Action 3
Adolescent	15–18	Action 1	Action 2	Action 3

Levels of Activity Related to Prevention and Treatment

Action 1

A. Ascertain history of the child's physical growth by use of National Center for Health Statistics growth charts if possible. If there is a marked change from the child's usual pattern of growth, move to Action 2.

B. Ascertain family history of obesity: Neither parent obese—low risk of child becoming more obese; may need to explore other causes of obesity; one parent obese—moderate risk of child becoming more obese; Two parents obese—high risk of child becoming more obese. If moderate or high risk automatically move to Action 2.

C. Ascertain caretakers' or individual's knowledge, attitudes, and practices related to the following items and provide education where needed. Normal growth patterns; Body size and shape; Nutrient and food needs; Normal psychosocial development, especially in relation to food intake, discipline and control; Physical activity.

Action 2

A. A thorough assessment of the problem by a health practitioner who has an understanding of the many aspects of the problem and is capable of recognizing when referral is required, i.e., dietitian-nutritionist, pediatrician or other M.D. or nurse with special expertise in this practice.

B. Intervention program based on individual need for a period of time (6–12 months) to bring about change in behavior of caretaker and/or child. If unsuccessful move to Action 3.

Exhibit 11-1 continued

Action 3

A health assessment and the development of an intervention program by a multidisciplinary team at a specialized clinic. This program could then be carried out by a team of local professionals if the clinic is a distance from the home community.

*Based on NCHS growth charts.
**Mild and Moderate may be actually heaviness due to factors other than fat, i.e., muscularity and/or heavy body frame. Skinfold measurements can substantiate fatness.

Source: Reprinted from *Children and Weight: A Changing Perspective* by E.B. Peck and H.D. Ullrich with permission of Nutrition Communications Associates, © 1985.

Table 11-3 Food Combinations That Supply Complete Protein

Baked beans and brown bread	Cheese sandwich
Lentil soup with rice	Peanut butter sandwich
Hopping John (beans and rice) and peas and rice	Tamale pie with beans and cheese
Split pea soup with bread	Toast and eggs
Cereal,* hot or cold, with milk	Granola with cereal, nuts, and seeds
Cereal* cooked with milk	Cheese vegetable casserole
Pizza, cheese, with whole wheat crust	Cheese souffles

*Use iron-fortified

Table 11-4 Nutrient-Dense Snacks That Provide Educational Opportunities for Children

Activity	Snack
To pour and drink	Natural fruit juices, milk, protein shake (½ C milk, ½ C orange juice, ¼ C powdered milk), water
For fingers	Fruit*
	Orange, grapefruit, tangerine, banana slices, apple, pear, peach slices, pineapple wedges, dried apricots, dates, raisins, grapes, plums, cherries, berries, papaya, mango
	Popsicle made from fruit juice or pureed fruit, fruit leather (fruit pureed and dried)
	Vegetables
	Cherry tomatoes and other vegetables, raw or cooked crunchy—cucumber, zucchini, potato, turnip, green beans, cauliflower, green pepper strips or wedges, asparagus, broccoli, brussel sprouts, peas (for older children), lima beans
To spread on	Peanut butter, yogurt dips, flavored margarine (make your own)
To use fork, spoon	Yogurt,** cottage cheese, cold meat cubes, whole-grain crackers and cookies (limit sugar and fat), whole-grain bread, whole-grain or fortified cereals

*Most fresh or canned fruit (e.g., bananas cut in disks or pieces, oranges, grapefruit, pineapple, etc.) can be frozen on a tray, brought out ten minutes before snack time, and enjoyed as a crunch snack.

**Plain yogurt may be sweetened by adding fresh fruit.

NOTES

1. B.B. Holli and R.V. Calabrese, *Communication and Education Skills: The Dietitian's Guide* (Philadelphia: Lea & Febiger, 1986), 202.

2. M.A. Lipton and J.P. Mayo, "Diet and Hyperkinesis—An Update," *Journal of the American Dietetic Association* 83 (1983): 132–134.

3. F. Ginsberg-Fellner et al., "Overweight Obesity in Preschool Children in New York City," *American Journal of Clinical Nutrition* 34 (1981): 2236–2241.

4. W.H. Dietz, "Obesity in Infants, Children and Adolescents in the United States. Identification, National History and After Effects." *Nutrition Research* 1 (1981): 117.

5. American Academy of Pediatrics, Committee on Nutrition, "Nutritional Aspects of Obesity in Infancy and Childhood," *Pediatrics* 68 (1981): 880–883.

6. A.J. Stunkard et al., "An Adoption Study of Human Obesity," *New England Journal of Medicine* 314 (23 January 1986): 193–198.

7. E.B. Peck and H.D. Ullrich, *Children and Weight: A Changing Perspective.* (Berkeley, Calif.: Nutrition Communications Associates, 1985): 13.

8. J.T. Dwyer et al., "Growth in 'New' Vegetarian Preschool Children Using the Jenss-Bayley Curve Fitting Technique," *American Journal of Clinical Nutrition* 37 (1983): 815.

9. American Academy of Pediatrics, Committee on Nutrition, "Toward a Prudent Diet for Children," *Pediatrics* 71 (1983): 78–80.

10. J. Dwyer, "Diets for Children and Adolescents That Meet the Dietary Goals," *American Journal of the Disabled Child* 134 (1980): 1073–1080.

11. J. Endres and R. Rockwell, *Food Nutrition and the Young Child* (Columbus, Ohio: Merrill Publishing Company, 1985), 149.

Part V

The School Age Child

Chapter 12

Nutrition Assessment of the School Age Child

Kathleen A. Mammel

OVERVIEW

Undernutrition is the most important cause of growth retardation in school-aged children, and it is preventable. Obesity is the most common nutritional disorder of children in America.[1] Five to 25 percent of children are obese,[2] and 80 percent of obese children become obese adults.[3] The use of the nutrition assessment at the time of routine health exams in children may detect nutritional deficits, including malnutrition, as well as obesity. Only when nutritional disorders are detected can interventions be instituted.

HEALTH HISTORY

Pediatric

The pediatric health history includes history of present illness (or current health concerns), past medical history, review of systems, family medical history, and social history. The majority of the nutrition history will be included in the past medical history and review of systems.

Inquiry should be made regarding the history of severe or chronic illnesses, particularly gastrointestinal or renal, and their duration; the use of medications (for example, antibiotics, anticonvulsants, steroids, diet pills, laxatives, or diuretics— see also Table 9-1);[4,5] and immunization status. Concerns by the child or parent about weight or rate of growth should be addressed, including losses, gains, or poor gains. Older children should be asked about their satisfaction with their height and weight, since body image becomes more important to them around pubescence. It may be best to obtain this information while talking with the child alone.

The parents can be asked whether they notice any unusual eating habits, such as food refusal, hoarding or hiding foods, pica, bingeing, or vomiting. A history of gastrointestinal symptoms—such as nausea, vomiting, diarrhea, constipation, or changes in appetite—can be obtained in the review of systems. In addition, it is important to know the amount and frequency of physical exercise, particularly in an obese child or in an active underweight child. For females a menstruation history is also essential.

The nutritional history can detect deficits, and it may also help focus the work-up of a child with growth problems (see chapter 14).

Family

The family history should include questions about the parents' stature, tendency toward obesity, and race or ethnic group. In addition, information regarding family history of hyperlipidemia, hypertension, cardiovascular disease (coronary heart disease, coronary artery or peripheral bypass surgery, or stroke at less than 60 years of age), diabetes mellitus, or gout should be obtained.[5,6]

Familial, genetic, and environmental factors all contribute to obesity. A small percentage of obese children may have an endocrine disorder, such as hypothyroidism or Cushing's disease, but this can generally be ruled out by physical exam. Obesity is associated with hypertension, hypertriglyceridemia, diabetes mellitus, gallbladder disease, musculoskeletal defects, endometrial cancer,[7] pregnancy complications, and cerebrovascular accidents. But the greatest hazards of obesity in the child may be psychosocial.

Children with obesity, diabetes mellitus, hypertension, or a family history of these diseases are at risk for hypercholesterolemia and should be screened by two serum cholesterol levels.[8,9]

PHYSICAL ASSESSMENT

Much of the physical assessment of nutritional status can begin with a general inspection. One can note the fat distribution (truncal obesity or a buffalo hump) or the presence of emaciation with diminished subcutaneous fat, muscle wasting, and redundant skin folds. The hydration status can be assessed by checking the skin turgor, perfusion, and the moistness of the mucous membranes. Inspection of the skin may reveal pallor, edema, unusual rashes (petechiae, ecchymoses, hyperketatosis, folliculosis), skin breakdown, or poor wound healing. Vitamin deficiencies need to be considered with rashes. There may be abnormal hair distribution, lanugo hair, or loss of the shine or curl.

Head, eyes, ears, nose, and throat (HEENT) examination may reveal glossitis, stomatitis, bleeding gingiva, corneal xerosis (drying), or angular palpebritis—all of which can be associated with vitamin deficiencies. A careful inspection of the mouth and teeth is essential. Nutrition plays a key role in the development and acquisition of newly errupting teeth, as well as in their susceptibility and maintenance. Teeth should be inspected for caries, mottling, and enamel defects. Malocclusion may be contributory to digestive and gastrointestinal problems. Chronic allergic rhinitis or enlarged tonsils may be interfering with taste and swallowing. Thyroid should be palpated for enlargement.

Examination of the chest may reveal a pigeon chest, rachitic rosary, or Harrison's groove of the rib cage. Breast development should be evaluated in staging the level of development in females (see Table 15-1). It should be noted that breast development follows prepubescent fat accumulation; therefore, weight gain in school age females will precede the onset of secondary sex characteristics.

Cardiovascular assessment should include auscultation and vital signs. Bradycardia, hypotension, or hypothermia may be anorexic indicators.[10] Tachycardia, arrhythmias, and hypertension may be predictors of future cardiovascular problems or vitamin imbalance. Serial blood pressure measurements can aid in the early detection of hypertension. Systolic pressure and both the fourth (muffling of sound) and fifth (disappearance of sound) Korotkoff phases should be recorded, since the true diastolic pressure in children usually falls between the two.[11,12] See Table 12-1 for suspicious (greater than 95th percentile) blood pressure levels in children.

It should be noted if the abdomen is scaphoid or obese, if the rectus muscles are well-defined, and if there is any hepatosplenomegaly or mass. The genital examination is important in Tanner staging (see Table 15-1) the level of pubertal development in the older child.

The musculoskeletal examination evaluates for muscle wasting or weakness. The spine should be inspected for any deviations or displacement (kyphosis, lordosis, scoliosis). Extremities should be symmetric; nutritional deficits may be reflected in knock-knees, bowed legs, or flared epiphyses.

Table 12-1 Suspected Hypertensive Levels in Children and Adolescents

Age (Yr)	Pressure (mm Hg)
3–6	$\geq$110/70
6–9	$\geq$120/75
10–13	$\geq$130/80
14–19	$\geq$140/85

Source: (Adapted from Londe, S., Goldring, D.: Am. J. Cardiol. 37:650, 1976), and reproduced with permission from Watkins, L.O., and Strong, W.B.: The Child: When to Begin Preventive Cardiology, in Lockhart, J.D., et al. (eds.): *Current Problems in Pediatrics*, Vol. XIV, No. 6, p. 27. Copyright © 1984 by Year Book Medical Publishers, Inc., Chicago.

Neurological examination may detect confusion or irritability, abnormalities of the cranial nerves (swallowing), loss of motor strength, tenderness of the calves, diminished vibratory sensation, or deep tendon reflexes. Short attention span and learning difficulties may be indicative of long-standing nutritional inadequacies.[13]

Assessment for indicators of nutritional deficiencies should be incorporated into the physical examination. Appendix C-1 lists signs associated with nutritional deficiencies.

ANTHROPOMETRIC ASSESSMENT

Children will grow an average of two inches per year; they will grow one to two feet between the ages of 6 to 12. They increase weight about 4½ to 6½ pounds per year, almost doubling in weight between those ages.[14]

Height and weight may be plotted against age on National Center for Health Statistics (NCHS) charts for 2-to-18-year-olds by sex (see appendix D) and compared with the standardized percentile curves (5th, 10th, 25th, 50th, 75th, 90th, and 95th percentiles) as well as with the previous measurements for the patient.

Weight for stature (see appendix D) can also be plotted until the advent of pubescence, when it becomes unreliable because of the variation in patterns of growth. A diminished weight for height is indicative of acute undernutrition, and a decreased height for age suggests chronic undernutrition. The normal growth curve should parallel one of the percentile lines, except during pubescence when the timing of the growth spurt varies, resulting in crossing of percentile lines.

When a child is growing at an unusual rate, one needs to identify the cause and treat it if possible. Children at the extremes of the growth curves (less than the 5th percentile or greater than the 95th percentile) are more likely to have a growth disorder than those near the 50th percentile. Measurements and recordings need to be verified whenever a deviation is noted.

Growth failure may be primary—from inadequate intake as in malnutrition, psychosocial deprivation, or eating disorders—or it may be secondary to an underlying chronic disease, infection, or excessive losses. Merritt and Suskind found one-third of hospitalized patients at a pediatric referral center to show evidence of acute malnutrition and nearly one-half to manifest chronic malnutrition.[15]

Table 12-2 lists factors responsible for growth parameters less than the 5th percentile and greater than the 95th percentile. Growth failure is usually more common and more serious. Nutritional inadequacy may be caused by dietary inadequacy, failure to absorb, failure to utilize, hastened excretion, or increased requirement.

Table 12-2 Some Reasons for a Child Being Below the 5th Percentile or Above the 95th Percentile

Measurement	Below the 5th Percentile	Above the 95th Percentile
Weight	shortness malnutrition chronic renal disease psychosocial deprivation infectious disease iron-deficiency anemia	tallness obesity edema
Length or stature	short parents malnutrition psychosocial deprivation delayed malnutrition chronic renal disease hypothyroidism hypopituitarism Turner syndrome	tall parents accelerated maturation Marfan syndrome pituitary gigantism
Weight-for-length	recent febrile illness recent malnutrition Marfan syndrome	obesity edema achondroplasia
Head circumference	microcephaly, e.g., fetal alcohol syndrome craniostenosis	hydrocephaly
Triceps skinfold thickness	malnutrition chronic illness, e.g., cystic fibrosis	obesity

Source: Reprinted with permission of Ross Laboratories, Columbus, Ohio 43216, from *Pediatric Anthropometry* by W.M. Moore and A.F. Roche, pp. 20–21, © 1983.

The weight index is the ratio of the actual weight to the ideal weight for age. A weight index of 0.9–1.1 is normal, greater than 1.1 indicates overweight, and greater than 1.2 indicates obesity. Less than 0.9 reflects leanness. Muscular children will be classified as overweight, but triceps skinfold measures can rule this out[16] (see chapter 2).

Obesity is characterized by the presence of excessive body fat, a weight index greater than 1.2, and/or a triceps skinfold more than one standard deviation above the mean. Although some clinicians consider those with skinfold thickness greater than the 90th percentile to be obese, it is reasonable to begin intervention at the 75th percentile. Body weight is the most commonly used measure of fatness; but, because it is a function of age, sex, height, frame, and Tanner stage, it tends to underestimate fatness in children under six or seven years old and overestimate fatness in adolescents (see chapter 15). Triceps skinfold is the best way to measure obesity in children and teenagers.

A bone age determined from a radiograph of the left hand may be helpful in interpreting whether an unusual rate of maturation is responsible for a deviation from the growth curve. If the bone age equals the chronologic age, this possibility can be ruled out.

LABORATORY ASSESSMENT

Laboratory data may be useful in detecting a biochemical abnormality—such as protein, vitamin, or mineral deficiencies—before they would otherwise be apparent on clinical examination. They may be confirmed by anthropometric values or dietary or clinical data. See appendix C-2 for suggested laboratory assessments and diagnostic implications.

Twenty-four-hour creatinine excretion reflects the amount of muscle mass. The creatinine-height index may be calculated from the milligrams of creatinine excreted in 24 hours, divided by the milligrams of creatinine excreted by a normal person of the same height, times 100.[17] Total protein and albumin may be measured in the serum. Visceral protein status may be assessed by measuring albumin, prealbumin, transferrin, retinol-binding protein, complement, and ribonuclease—all of which are proteins of short half-life synthesized by the liver.[18]

Vitamins and minerals are important for normal cellular composition and function. Levels may be measured directly or by an enzyme assay.

Hemoglobin or hematocrit should be used to screen for anemia; if present, further evaluation may be done to determine the cause. Common nutritional causes of anemia include iron deficiency, folate or vitamin B_{12} deficiency, and lead intoxication.

Table 12-3 Median and 95th Percentiles for Serum Lipid and Lipoprotein Values in Children, by Age

| Age, yr | Cholesterol, mg/dL (Percentile) | | | | | | | | Triglycerides, mg/dL (Percentile) | |
| | Total | | HDL* | | LDL* | | VLDL* | | | |
	50th	95th	50th	95th	50th	95th	50th	95th	50th	95th
2–3	157	203	61	87	92	131	5	18	58	115
4–5	159	204	60	90	91	135	4	17	53	104
6–7	160	208	61	93	92	138	4	19	52	109
8–9	161	207	64	94	91	136	5	23	55	130
10–11	162	212	61	93	93	142	6	24	57	132
12–13	154	203	61	93	88	133	7	23	58	124
14–15	149	206	59	90	83	131	7	23	60	124
16–17	148	200	58	90	81	129	7	23	60	126
18–19	152	190	59	85	83	122	8	25	64	162

Note: Lipid values are from fasting children.

*HDL = high-density lipoprotein (α-lipoprotein), LDL = low-density lipoprotein (β-lipoprotein), VLDL = very-low-density lipoprotein (pre-β-lipoprotein).

Source: Reprinted from *American Journal of Diseases of Children,* Vol. 136, p. 855, with permission of American Medical Association. Copyright 1982, American Medical Association.

Total peripheral lymphocyte count and intradermal skin testing may be used to screen for immune dysfunction that can occur secondary to severe malnutrition. An absolute lymphocyte count less than 1,500 indicates a child at risk for malnutrition, and a count of less than 1,000 is probably indicative of malnutrition.[19,20] There may be diminished cell-mediated immunity and diminished complement protein and hemolytic complement activity, placing the malnourished child at risk of recurrent and/or significant infection.[21]

Cholesterol should be measured in obese patients as well as those with a family history of elevated lipids or premature cardiovascular disease, essential hypertension, diabetes mellitus, or gout.[22,23] Table 12-3 gives median and 95th percentile lipid data on a biracial population of children.

SUMMARY

All children should have nutritional screening at the time of routine health maintenance examinations. The screening should include the historical questions stated in the Health History section as well as height and weight plotted for age and sex. Blood pressure should be followed to allow early detection of hypertension. Hemoglobin or hematocrit should be checked, and lipids should be evaluated in obese children or those with a family history of cardiovascular disease. Counseling regarding regular exercise, maintenance of ideal body weight, and the dangers of smoking should be included in all health maintenance visits.[24] Advice on an appropriate diet, including cholesterol and salt intake, should also be given.

If malnutrition is suspected or obesity is present, a comprehensive nutrition assessment should be performed, including clinical and dietary evaluation, anthropometric measurements, and laboratory data.

Frequent follow-up of malnourished children is necessary for the monitoring of growth until the etiology can be determined and treatment is underway. Obese children also require regular follow-up for motivational purposes, as well as to be certain that weight loss does not occur too rapidly.

Much work remains to be done in the areas of fitness, the prevention and successful treatment of obesity and eating disorders, and the identification of childhood risk factors for coronary heart disease and the proper dietary recommendations for its prevention.

NOTES

1. W.H. Dietz, "Childhood Obesity: Susceptibility, Cause, and Management." *Journal of Pediatrics* 103 (1983): 676–686.

2. G.B. Forbes, "Prevalence of Obesity in Childhood," in *Obesity in Perspective,* vol. 2, DHEW Publication no. (NIH) 75–708, ed. G.A. Bray (Washington, D.C.: U.S. Government Printing Office, 1975), 205–207.

3. S. Abraham and M. Nordsieck, "Relationship of Excess Weight in Children and Adults," *Public Health Report* 75 (1960): 263–273.

4. G.M. Owen, "Physical Examination as an Assessment Tool," in *Nutrition Assessment: A Comprehensive Guide for Planning Intervention*, ed. M. Simko, C. Cowell, and J. Gilbride (Rockville, Md.: Aspen Publishers, Inc., 1984), 58.

5. J.H. Forster, "Elevated Lipids: Whom to Screen and How to Treat," *Contemporary Pediatrics*, April 1985: 22–32.

6. American Academy of Pediatrics, Committee on Nutrition, "Prudent Life-Style for Children: Dietary Fat and Cholesterol," *Pediatrics* 78 (1983): 521–525.

7. P.W. Blitzer, E.C. Blitzer, and A.A. Rimm, "Association Between Teenage Obesity and Cancer," *Preventive Medicine* 5 (1976): 20.

8. American Academy of Pediatrics, Committee on Nutrition, "Prudent Life-Style for Children," 523.

9. "NIH Consensus Conference: Lowering Blood Cholesterol to Prevent Heart Disease," *Journal of the American Medical Association* 253 (1985): 2080–2086.

10. Task Force on Nomenclature and Statistics, *Diagnostic and Statistical Manual of Mental Disorders*, 3rd ed. (Washington, D.C.: American Psychiatric Association, 1980), 67–69.

11. L.O. Watkins and W.B. Strong, "The Child: When to Begin Preventive Cardiology," *Current Problems in Pediatrics* 14 (1984): 1–71.

12. A.J. Moss and F.H. Adams, "Index of Indirect Estimation of Diastolic Blood Pressure: Muffling Versus Complete Cessation of Vascular Sounds," *American Journal of Diseases of Children* 106 (1963): 364.

13. J.R. Galler, "Examining for Long-Term Consequences of Undernutrition," *Pediatric Basics* 47 (1987): 2–4.

14. L.F. Whaley and D.L. Wong, *Nursing Care of Infants and Children*, 3rd ed. (St. Louis, Mo.: C.V. Mosby Co., 1987), 704.

15. R.J. Merritt and R.M. Suskind, "Nutritional Survey of Hospitalized Pediatric Patients," *American Journal of Clinical Nutrition* 32 (1979): 1320–1325.

16. R.H. Durant and C.W. Linder, "An Evaluation of Five Indexes of Relative Body Weight for Use with Children," *Journal of the American Dietetic Association* 78 (1981): 35.

17. F.E. Viteri and J. Alvarado, "The Creatinine Height Index: Its Use in the Estimation of the Degree of Protein Depletion and Repletion in Protein Calorie Malnourished Children," *Pediatrics* 46 (1970): 696–706.

18. G.L. Blackburn et al., "Nutritional and Metabolic Assessment of the Hospitalized Patient," *Journal of Parenteral Enteral Nutrition* 1 (1977): 11–22.

19. Merritt and Suskind, "Nutritional Survey," 1324.

20. C.G. Neumann et al., "Immunologic Responses in Malnourished Children," *American Journal of Clinical Nutrition* 28 (1975): 89–104.

21. Ibid., 97.

22. Forster, "Elevated Lipids," 28.

23. American Academy of Pediatrics, Committee on Nutrition, "Prudent Life-Style for Children," 524.

24. Ibid., 524.

Chapter 13

Environmental Management of the School Age Child

Judith B. Igoe and Georgia L. Heiberger

OVERVIEW

School age children spend the majority of their time in three distinct environments: home, school and community. A typical grade-school day is 7 to 8 hours. If this is coupled with an average of 9 hours sleep per night, the child has less than 8 hours to play, eat, do homework and chores, and participate in recreational activities. The child's 24-hour day can be divided into three equal parts, with one-third of it spent in school, one-third spent sleeping, and the last third spent on personal and family requirements. It can be seen that any efforts to evaluate the school age child's environment for nutritional purposes must include the home, school, and the community. Additionally, interventions aimed at improving nutrition must be structured so that they can be applicable to one or all of these environments. Public Laws 94-142 and 99-457 require a free, appropriate, public school education for all handicapped children. Although some of these children will have unusual nutritional requirements, many of them will be well served by the nutritional guidelines offered in this chapter.

ENVIRONMENTAL ASSESSMENT

To obtain a complete picture of the school age child's environment, information should be gathered about the home, school, and community (see Figure 13-1). According to a comprehensive study of childhood health and illness conducted by the U.S. Department of Health and Human Services, there are physical, social, and emotional barriers to adequate nutrition for the school age child.[1] These barriers must be addressed as a part of the total assessment of the child.

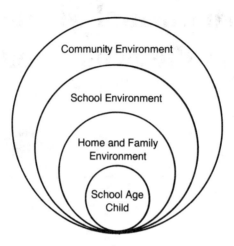

Home and Family	School	Community
physical and social development of child	educational structure	education, health, and welfare systems
	integrated health/ nutrition curriculum	availability and access to resources
family health, nutrition beliefs, habits, and practices	(kindergarten through grade 12)	by all families
	school feeding programs	parent education and involvement
daily living and home management skills		

Figure 13-1 Assessment of the School Age Child's Environments. *Source:* Adapted from "A Theoretical Framework for Studying School Nutrition Education Programs" by A.H. Gillespie in *Journal of Nutrition Education*, Vol. 13, No. 4, pp. 150–156, with permission of Society for Nutrition Education. © 1981 Society for Nutrition Education.

Home and Family Environment

The home is where the child first interacts with siblings and adults in the family environment; it is also where a number of factors can limit access to adequate nutrition. Inadequate financial resources can restrict a family's ability to purchase sufficient amounts of food and provide a livable and safe shelter for a child. Limited food choices and poor dietary habits may result in temporary deviations from normal growth and developmental milestones. In family settings where adults are illiterate, there is usually poor understanding of health and nutrition information. Such families may have poor health habits, especially regarding such preventive health care as well-child examinations, immunizations, and dental checkups.

Among the social barriers to a child having adequate nutrition is the changing lifestyles of families. There are now more single-parent homes and more women who are heading households. Society is experiencing what is described as the "feminization of poverty," with the majority of children in these households living at the poverty level. Additionally, there are more homeless families and an increasing number of children in out-of-home child-care programs.[2] These shifts contribute to a social climate in the home in which child rearing and home-management skills are not a priority. Routine health care may be considered a luxury that can be ill afforded in the family budget. Limited cooking utensils and lack of menu planning compound the problem of providing the food available to a child.

Children who are without adult supervision or who are exposed to inappropriate guidance may spend excessive hours sitting and watching television and TV commercials that promote consumption of "fast foods" and "empty-calorie" snacks. Eating such snack foods and being inactive may lead to childhood obesity and sometimes hypertension, which, without detection and early intervention, can lead to costly health problems in adulthood.

Lack of family support systems may pose a problem of emotional instability for a child. A child who has a poor self-image or lacks self-esteem may show learning disabilities or behavioral problems. Over a period of time, these limitations may become significant mental, as well as physical, health problems. Table 13-1 lists questions that should be considered in planning an assessment of the child's home situation.

School Environment

A primary barrier to adequate nutrition can exist in the school environment. Tight school schedules and noisy, crowded school lunchrooms may limit a child's

---

Table 13-1 Assessment of the Child's Home Situation

- What is the family's financial situation?
- Can the family afford nutritious foods?
- Do primary caretakers know how to select and buy low-cost, nutritious foods?
- Who supervises the children at mealtimes?
- Is mealtime a family time, or is everyone rushed?
- Is a responsible adult available before and after school to encourage the consumption of nourishing snacks?
- Do the children know how to choose appropriate snacks?
- Do the children have any understanding of the food groups and their importance to health?

time for meals during the day.[3] The school breakfast and lunch programs are the major source of food for some children. Currently, under the Federal School Lunch Program lunches are served in approximately 75 percent and school breakfasts in about 25 percent of all public schools. Participation by children eligible for these meals is about 50 percent and 25 percent, respectively.[4] School food menus that contain unfamiliar foods or foods that are not traditionally part of the ethnic diet of a child are often rejected by the children. This results in a large amount of food waste. Table 13-2 lists questions that can be useful in assessing the nutritional potential of school environment.

Community Environment

An improved quality of life for the child and family can be achieved where there is community support for a school board composed of concerned parents who have an agenda for the education, health, and welfare of school age children. Parents who are knowledgeable will fully utilize all resources to achieve these goals. Where there is a lack of broad-based support for quality education, especially for sound school and community feeding programs, the child suffers. Concurrently, a lack of local health services available to the child and family places them at high risk for a range of health- and nutrition-related problems.

INTERVENTION STRATEGIES

Schools are a primary agency for nutrition intervention for the following reasons:

- School-age children have special nutritional needs.
- Life-long food habits and preferences are formed at an early age.

Table 13-2 Assessing the Nutritional Potential of School Environment

- Are vending machines present in the school? If so, do they contain nutritious foods?
- Are school personnel good role models for children?
- Are school employees interested in nutrition programs?
- Are health-promotion events part of school activities?
- Do the school children participate in sports, and are these sports "safe" for them?
- Is any type of nutrition education provided in the school?

Source: Reprinted from *Achieving the 1990 Health Objectives for the Nation: Agenda for the Nation's Schools* by D.D. Allensworth and C.A. Wolford, Office of Disease Prevention and Health Promotion, U.S. Department of Health and Human Services and the American School Health Association.

- Poor nutrition slows intellectual development.
- Many needed changes in dietary practice can be accomplished only through the socializing process of education.[5]

Evidence is accumulating about the effects of nutrition and social environments on attention, memory, cognitive performance, emotional affect, and social function—all of which directly influence the academic achievement of students. The need to modify nutrition and social environmental hazards in order to improve the health status, and potentially the learning ability, of children has been recognized. Health education task forces have singled out the nation's schools as a primary, if not *the* primary, vehicle through which school age children and youth should be informed about factors that will influence their health.[6]

Health promotion authorities estimate that approximately 30 percent of the nation's health promotion objectives for school age children could be directly or indirectly realized in the school:

The nation's schools provide an appropriate and efficient vehicle by which our population can be educated about increasingly complex risks to their health and well-being and about individual and societal means available to control such risks. Since 1909, schools have been called upon by numerous agencies of society to provide timely and effective health education for our young people. . . . Furthermore, the need to educate children and youth is underscored by the fact that the cause of much premature disease and disability is due to the adoption of health debilitating behaviors. These behaviors or habits such as dietary choice, smoking, alcohol abuse, or a sedentary lifestyle have their roots in the behavioral choices—the habits—established during youth.[7]

The agenda for achieving nutritional goals by using the school setting is extensive, involving three major aspects of the school health program: health service, health instruction, and promotion of a healthful school environment.[8,9]

Health Services

Nutrition interventions involving health services in the school include the following:[9]

- periodic screening to ascertain lean body mass and nutritional status, as part of a permanent record
- dissemination of basic information on sound nutritional practices in conjunction with screening clinics

- provision of counseling services for students on appropriate nutritional practices, fad diets, and the relationship between diet and specific diseases
- safe weight-reduction and weight-control classes, including self-help support groups for safe weight reduction, weight control, and exercising
- provision of other health/nutrition services emphasizing self-care activities for primary problems (including obesity) presented by students
- coordination of school-site activities on health promotion and nutrition for faculty and staff.[10]

Health Instruction

A brief review of the literature suggests areas in which nutrition education is needed. One study has indicated a high correlation between childhood obesity and adult obesity.[11] Another study showed that suboptimal nutrition was closely tied to poverty groups; as income rose, so did height, weight, and general nutritional status.[12]

Eating disorders, such as anorexia nervosa and bulimia, and poor eating habits often start before the school age child leaves elementary school. Elementary-school athletes often adopt controversial dietary plans, such as carbohydrate loading, in the hope of increasing their stamina and performance.[13] Teachers have noted that many of their students consume high-calorie snack foods rather than nutritious ones for both lunch and breakfast.[14] Such evidence affirms the need for integrated nutrition education programs for school age children, from kindergarten through 12th grade.

Nutrition education must be formalized and specifically planned into the curriculum, recognizing its importance to a child's comprehensive education plan. Therefore, in order for nutrition education to be effective it is vital to obtain administrative support for the curriculum design.

Some interesting suggestions for providing health instruction in the schools, focused on nutrition, are listed in Table 13-3.

Promotion of a Healthy School Environment

Ways to make the school environment a more nutrition conscious and healthy place might include the following:

- Identify one week in the school year in which all content areas and pupil service areas integrate and coordinate the central theme of nutrition in course work and programs.

Table 13-3 Classroom Learning Activities in Nutrition Instruction

1. Hold a mock election and elect the "Nutrient of the Year." Divide students into teams to prepare campaign speeches for each nutrient.
2. Using a nutrition questionnaire (see appendix A-1), have children assess their own nutritional adequacy.
3. Using a food diary (see Appendix A-2), have children evaluate their diet for promoting or retarding the following: heart disease, high blood pressure, dental caries, cancer, and obesity (see chapter 20).
4. Evaluate the risks associated with popular fad diets (see chapter 20).
5. Plan a simple monthly nutritious menu for the family, and involve the family in a home assignment, using the menu.
6. Organize a taste-testing contest involving wholesome, nutritious, low-calorie, low-cholesterol, low-sodium, and high-fiber foods.
7. Monitor and evaluate eating practices in the school cafeteria; project long-term health outcomes if current practices continue.
8. Analyze a list of nutritional myths; have children share their own.
9. Have the class prepare a newsletter "News-Trition" on health and eating. Have the students write and document articles on the dangers of fad diets, bulimia, anorexia, etc.
10. Contract for a specific period of time to eliminate from the diet specific foods that are of low or poor nutritional value.

Source: Reprinted from *Achieving the 1990 Health Objectives for the Nation: Agenda for the Nation's Schools* by D.D. Allensworth and C.A. Wolford, Office of Disease Prevention and Health Promotion, U.S. Department of Health and Human Services and the American School Health Association.

- Promote low-calorie, low-cholesterol, low-salt, and high-fiber food selections in vending machines and in fund raising.
- Promote the labeling of low-calorie, low-cholesterol, low-salt food selections in cafeteria food lines and vending machines.

THE ROLE OF THE SCHOOL HEALTH CARE PROFESSIONAL

In order to have a meaningful influence on the nutritional well-being of the school age child, the health care professional must know and be known by the local school system, the board of education, and local parent-teacher groups. The health care professional should be recognized and solicited for input regarding curriculum development, policy making, and budget discussions that affect nutrition and health promotion in the schools. Also, a reciprocal or collaborative relationship with the school nurse and other school personnel is necessary to implement suggested strategies.

Studies conducted by the University of Colorado School Health Programs, a training and research center for health professionals, reveal that school nurses are actively engaged in formal and informal health promotion activities. Their school health clinics, as well as actual classrooms, are seen as actual opportunities for nutrition education. They provide various health services, such as counseling for eating disorders, that can enhance the nutritional status of students. The school nurse study committee of the American School Health Association has been working diligently to improve nutritional conditions in the schools. The association's position is that the "school nurse should provide guidance in the maintenance of nutritious school lunch programs and food sales in school stores and during extracurricular activities."[15]

School age children have many nutritional needs that must be addressed. Nutrition education and health promotion through nutrition are entitlements for all school age children. Indeed, the strategies for promoting health through nutrition are both cost-effective and appropriate to an educational setting. The role of the health care professional working with school aged children is to take an active, indeed a leading, role to champion such strategies.

NOTES

1. *Better Health For Our Children: A National Strategy*, vol. 1, Report of the Select Panel for the Promotion of Child Health (Washington, D.C.: US Government Printing Office, 1980), 112–113.

2. J. Gephart, M.C. Egan, and V.L. Hutchins, "Perspectives on Health of School-Age Children: Expectations for the Future," *Journal of School Health* 54 (1984): 11–16.

3. M.K. Koster, "Self-Care: Health Behavior for the School-Age Child," *Topics in Clinical Nursing* 4 (1983): 29–40.

4. *Better Health for Our Children*, p. 113.

5. C.N. D'Onofrio and R. Singer, "Unplanned Nutrition Education in the Schools: Sugar in Elementary Reading Texts," *Journal of School Health* 53 (1983): 521–526.

6. D.C. Iverson and L.J. Kolbe, "Evolution of the National Disease Prevention and Health Promotion Strategy: Establishing a Role for the Schools," *Journal of School Health* 53 (1983): 294–302.

7. D.D. Allensworth and C.A. Wolford, *Achieving the 1990 Health Objectives for the Nation: Agenda for the Nation's Schools* (Kent, Ohio: Office of Disease Prevention and Health Promotion, U.S. Department of Health and Human Services, and American School Health Association, 1988), 190–199.

8. Ibid.

9. *Healthy People: The Surgeon General's Report on Health Promotion and Disease Prevention* (Washington, DC: Department of Health and Human Services, 1979), 38–39.

10. Allensworth and Wolford, *Achieving the 1990 Health Objectives*, 190–199.

11. A. D'Augelli and H. Smicklas-Wright, "The Case for Primary Prevention of Overweight Through the Family," *Journal of Nutrition Education* 10 (April/June 1978): 76–78.

12. S. Garn and D. Clark, "Nutrition, Growth, Development and Maturation: Findings from the Ten-State Nutrition Survey of 1968–1970," *Pediatrics* 56 (1975): 306–319.

13. S. Cheung, "Controversies in School Health," *Journal of School Health* 55 (1985): 35–37.

14. M.A. Poolton, "What Can We Do About Food Habits?" *Journal of School Health* 1 (1978): 646–648.

15. "Disease Prevention, Health Promotion, and Health Protection Programs: The Role of the School Nurse" (Paper prepared by the School Nurse Study Committee of the American School Health Association, 1988), 7.

Chapter 14

Dietary Assessment and Management of the School Age Child

Deborah Thomas-Dobersen

- Can a school-age child get a balanced diet from a vegetarian diet?
- What effect does television have on eating habits?
- What are the indicators for limiting fats?
- Is a weight reduction diet ever safe for children?

DIETARY ASSESSMENT

Overview

The school age years are an important period in the formation of attitudes toward food. Children will select sweet foods over more nutritious foods if given the choice.[1] Children need guidance in selecting a nutritious diet and parents need to limit sweets and other empty-calorie foods to amounts that will not interfere with the healthy food choices needed for a balanced meal plan.

By the school age years, food likes and dislikes have been established, but they can be changed. Repetitious food choices are common, but they seldom seriously compromise nutrient adequacy.

Assessing the Diet of the School Age Child

To determine the eating style of the child, it is necessary to find out what is eaten, how frequently it is eaten, where it is eaten, and with whom. This information should be obtained during the first visit. If the child is interviewed with the parent, the diet quality may increase; thus it is recommended that information gained separately from the parent and child be combined. Some children cannot report reliable amounts, but they can tell you what they eat. Each situation should be judged individually.

Recommendations to enhance the nutritional quality of the diet may be necessary. To be effective in getting the child to actually eat the recommended foods, it is important to make suggestions that will fit in with the eating style of the child.[2]

Special attention should be given to meal patterns. Does the child eat breakfast? Breakfast is an important meal, yet often the child eats alone or in a hurried, chaotic environment; or breakfast may be skipped if the child is trying to diet or is staying up late at night and getting up too late in the morning. Children who eat breakfast have a better attitude, school record, and problem-solving ability than do nonbreakfast eaters.[3]

Lunch is also an important meal. If the lunch is bought at school, what is actually eaten? One should find out what is bought (just milk and ice cream?), and what is traded or wasted. If lunch is carried from home, the potential still exists for trading and selling the original items. In any event, home-prepared lunches, when compared with school lunches, have been shown to provide significantly fewer nutrients and to offer little variety.[4]

Snacks are important in contributing to the child's nutrient intake and eating style. The quality of the snacks may determine whether nutrient requirements are met. Is the mother in the home to supervise snacking? Is money used to buy treats at a store on the way home from school? Is snacking done in front of television? How many hours a day is the child watching television? What is the frequency of snacking? The frequency of snacks is a factor that may contribute to dental caries.[5] One researcher has found a positive correlation between the hours of television watched and body fatness.[6]

A variety of tools can be used to assess the child's diet. The child or the child and parent can fill out a nutrition questionnaire (see appendix A-1) or complete a food diary (see appendix A-4) to describe the child's current intake. The nutrition questionnaire and food diary will provide a food-intake pattern of the child and be useful when making any diet modifications.

In assessing the diet, a combination of tools may be used. But the most important factor in eliciting honest reporting are concerned not so much with the method that is used, but rather with the need to (1) establish rapport with the child and parent and (2) ask questions in such a manner that the expected answer is not automatically conveyed or approval or disapproval with the answers is displayed.

Data Analysis

Diet information obtained from the initial records should be evaluated in terms of nutritional needs of the child. Time may not permit calculations of nutrients in milligram amounts. However, the diet can be quickly assessed against the food groups (see appendix B-1). In this way, excessively high-calorie or low-nutrient foods, bizarre diets, and the omission of certain categories of food can be noted.

Nutrients reported most often to be in less than appropriate amounts in the diet of school age children are vitamins A, C, and B_6 and the minerals calcium and iron.[7,8] Children from low-income families are frequently shorter, indicating that limited caloric intake may be causing their growth to be stunted. The lower the economic status of the family, the more likely a nutritional deficiency will be found.[9] Intake of iron in the school age child is not as much of a problem as it is for other age groups. The Ten State Nutrition Survey, however, shows that for low-income children iron deficiency anemia is much more prevalent[10] (see appendix F, Selected Nutrients and Major Food Sources).

COMMON NUTRITIONAL PROBLEMS OF THE SCHOOL AGE CHILD

Information about common nutritional problems of the school age child is provided in Table 14-1. The table also suggests further assessment questions, recommended actions, and ways to evaluate outcomes. In Table 14-2, tips for helping parents with food shopping, food storage and preparation, and mealtime arrangements are listed.

Table 14-1 Common Nutritional Problems of the School Age Child

---

I. OBESITY/OVERWEIGHT (see also chapters 12 and 17)

Obesity onset may be in infancy or preadolescence.[11]

Fat children have a tendency to remain fat.[12]

American children consume too many sugar-containing foods.[13]

Intervention should be early and in earnest.[14]

Assessment	Action
What is the present degree of overweight? (See chapter 12.)	Calorie levels should be individually determined, depending on age and sex.
	Diet should not be below 1,200 kilocalories per day nor less than 30 percent from fat (see appendixes E-1 and D-1).
What is the current eating behavior pattern of parents and family? (see appendixes A-4 and A-5.)	Diet modification should be tailored to the child's and family's eating habits to provide sufficient nutrients for growth and development.
What kinds of food are consumed? Quantity? Nutritional quality?	Recommendations for changing eating patterns:
	Change types of food purchased (fewer potato chips, more bread sticks, fruits, and vegetables).

Table 14-1 continued

	Change nutritional quality of snacks (snacks prepared and left by working parents) (see Table 16-1).
	Change beverage of parents and child from soda pop to milk (see also Table 14-2).
Are the child and parents motivated to join a weight-loss program?	Include parents in the treatment program (they may be seen separately from the child).
	Encourage parents to motivate the child with recognition and awards of coloring books or similar nonfoods instead of sweets.
What is the current level of energy expenditure? Family exercise pattern? Number of hours of TV viewing?	Encourage parents to model exercise by brisk walking, jogging, aerobic dancing, or any other activity that the child will enjoy and that will increase the child's kilocaloric expenditure.
	Suggest home contracts or weekly records incorporating goals and number of exercise points and the use of a graph to color.

Evaluation

When evaluating weight loss, an appropriate goal is weight maintenance during growth in height.

Examine the child's records of food intake and exercise for behavior change.

The long-term maintenance of lowered body fat is the final evaluation of success.

If excess weight continues to be a problem, consider referring to a clinic that runs weight-control groups for children. If there are financial resources and sufficient interest, employ a registered dietitian (R.D.).

One suggestion for teaching about calories and good nutrition is use of the traffic light diet.[15]

Special programs may also be available in local hospitals. One such program is the Body Shop for children of both sexes, aged 8 to 12 years. The program can be purchased from Linda Munro-Cailliez, Methodist Hospital, 6500 Excelsior Blvd., St. Louis Park, MN 55426.

II. ALTERNATIVE FOOD PRACTICES (see also chapter 17)

Vegetarian diets should be scrutinized closely for nutritional deficiencies; extreme types of vegetarian diets can significantly retard growth.[16] (see appendix H).

Vitamin and mineral deficiencies are most common in the vegan diet category.[17]

Assessing for possible toxic doses of vitamins and minerals is imperative in children's health assessment.

Any consumption of vitamins and minerals above the RDA should be discouraged unless medically indicated.

Table 14-1 continued

Assessment	Action
Is the growth rate inadequate?	Monitor the child's growth rate carefully (see chapter 12).
What kind of alternative diet is being followed? What foods are avoided?	Encourage a more healthful diet by increasing child's and parent's knowledge about the food the child is eating and what is needed.
Which nutrients are likely to be inadequate in this child's diet?	If the child is on a vegan diet (eating only plant foods), supplements of vitamin D, B_{12}, and iron are recommended.
What foods containing these nutrients might be acceptable to the child?	Recommend fortified soy milk or calcium supplements for a child on a vegan diet.
Is the child taking supplemental vitamins and minerals? What kind? What is the dosage? Are megadoses used?	Caution should be observed in recommending nutrient supplements to rectify poor quality diet. The American Academy of Pediatrics indicates specific high-risk children for whom supplements may be indicated.[18]

Evaluation

A repeat dietary assessment at the next clinic visit can be used to evaluate changes in nutrient quality.

If nutrient quality is not improved and if growth still appears to be a problem, refer to a registered dietitian (R.D.) for evaluation and intervention.

III. EARLY DETECTION OF EATING DISORDERS

Eating in general is a sensitive indicator of emotional state and the parent-child interaction.[19]

Preoccupation with weight and figure can be seen among girls as young as nine to ten years.[20]

Characteristics for identifying children at risk for developing disorders include decreased self-esteem; perfectionistic attitude; preoccupation with body weight and food; rigid ideas about "bad" foods and the need to follow a hard and depriving diet perfectly; marked parental dependence; oversensitivity to criticism and rejection; aspirations to be a jockey, wrestler, gymnast, model, actor or actress, or ballet dancer or to be like a parent in such an occupation.

Family characteristics for identifying children at risk for developing eating disorders include a family member with an eating disorder; a family excessively critical of a child's weight and eating patterns; parental attitudes and behavior around the child's eating that seem bizarre; and exaggerated parental concern and vehemence regarding the child's eating behavior.

Educational programs and early intervention are needed to prevent morbidity in this age group.[21]

Assessment	Action
Initial questions may help identify some children who are already trying rigid diets or who are preoccupied with their figures.	

Table 14-1 continued

Are you trying to lose weight?	Help the child understand energy needs for growth and the importance of vitamins and minerals.
Do you eat very little breakfast and lunch to lose weight?	Distribute calories more evenly throughout the day by setting realistic eating patterns.
What is your weight goal?	Set appropriate weight goal and help shape realistic and healthy attitudes toward body weight.
	Help the child examine problems with fad diets.
Do you feel some foods are "bad?"	Try to add some of the foods the child perceives as "bad" or "fattening."
What is the family's view of the child's attempt to lose weight?	Get the family involved.
Does the family eat together?	If not, encourage this practice.

Evaluation

Monitor the child for appropriate weight and nutritional status.

Reanalyze eating patterns. Are they less bizarre? Is talk about weight gain more realistic?

If problem is not corrected, refer for assessment for eating disorders.

IV. ATHLETIC DIETARY REGIMENS (see also chapter 17)

It is important to determine the athletic dietary regimen being followed by the child.

Basal metabolic rate and activity take priority over growth. The child may suffer suboptimal growth if the calories are not sufficient.

The American Academy of Pediatrics stresses that there are few, if any, indications to manipulate body fatness for sports participation in the school age child.[22]

Children require more attention in preventing dehydration and heat disorders because they have a lower sweat capacity and a greater heat production.[23]

Assessment	Action
Is the athlete consuming an adequate diet?	Have the athlete bring in a three-day food record (see appendix A-4).
Assess the diet for energy intake; monitor growth (see chapter 12).	Instruct in principles of an adequate diet with additional calories to allow for athletic performance.
Why is energy intake low? No time to eat? Inadequate food at home? Attempt to lose weight rapidly?	Discuss dangers of inappropriate weight loss.
Assess protein intake. Is athlete taking protein supplements?	Explain that protein supplements are unnecessary and will not lead to an increase in muscle mass.[24] Only training will lead to an increase in muscle mass.

Table 14-1 continued

With regard to vitamins and minerals, determine if the athlete is using supplements, salt tablets, or electrolyte drinks.	Explain that the need for vitamins and minerals will be met if the diet contains a variety of nutritious foods.
Determine fluid intake.	Instruct that fluids should never be restricted as a means of weight control.
Determine the kind and amounts. Is fluid restricted? Are adequate fluids present at activity? If activity is intense and prolonged, is scheduled drinking enforced? Is electrolyte drink provided? Is athlete at risk for heat-related illness?	Explain that cool, plain water is the best fluid for athletes. Electrolyte drinks are not recommended. Even if sweating is profuse, the basic mixed diet will satisfy mineral losses of sodium and potassium. Salt tablets may be dangerous.
Are carbohydrates being taken? Candy or sugar-drinks before activity? High-carbohydrate meals or premeals? Carbohydrate loading?	High sugar intake prior to exercise may lead to low blood sugar, thus impairing performance.[25] Sugar, preferably in the form of fruit juices, taken during exercise tends to maintain blood glucose. Both high-carbohydrate diets and carbohydrates provided during the activity enhance athletic performance.[26] Carbohydrate loading is probably not indicated for this age group.
	Relevant information may need to be provided to the coach, parents, and/or trainer as well as the child.

Evaluation

If growth is restored and progressing, intervention has been successful.

A repeat of a three-day food diary or appropriate questions can be used to assess if the desired behaviors have changed. If not, assess why.

If further intervention is needed, a registered dietitian (R.D.) specializing in sports nutrition can help with setting up an individualized program for weight loss/gain, optimal distribution of calories, fluid schedules, and other diet-related problems.

V. ALLERGY

The most common allergens are cow's milk protein, eggs, fish, nuts, wheat, citrus fruits, pork, and food additives.

There is no strong evidence to link food allergy or sugar with hyperactivity.[27,28]

Malnutrition could result from long-term use of elimination diets.

Assessment	Action
Identification of the specific food allergens by blinded oral challenge may more accurately predict food allergy than patient history and skin tests.[29]	

Table 14-1 continued

Diagnosis should be firmly established before starting the child on any restrictive diet.

Eliminate food(s) identified by the oral challenge.

Instruct parents on the following: (1) how to identify hidden sources of allergens in foods, (2) how to find acceptable substitute foods, (3) where these foods can be purchased.

Instruct parents on methods of food preparation, menu planning, and appropriate cookbooks/recipes.

If the allergy eliminates multiple foods or involves foods basic to the diet, such as milk, wheat, eggs, and corn, enlist the services of a registered dietitian (R.D.).

Evaluation

Monitor the child for energy and nutrient intake. Multiple allergies should be monitored especially carefully.

If milk is restricted, monitor for adequate calcium, riboflavin, and vitamin D.

If citrus is restricted, monitor for adequate vitamin C.

VI. DENTAL HEALTH

Dental caries represents the destruction of tooth enamel and dentin by acid demineralization.

The process of tooth decay involves plaque, a sticky, colorless layer of bacteria that turns fermentable carbohydrate from food into acids.

The acid then attacks and dissolves tooth enamel.

Assessment	Action
If the nutrition assessment indicates that the child has incidence of dental caries, further dietary assessment should be made.	Review meal and snacking pattern with child and parent. Suggest alternative foods to replace sugars and sugar-containing food.
Question child and parent in depth regarding intake of sucrose, sugary foods, and complex carbohydrates.	Suggest taking any sugar- and starch-containing foods with meals, since they are less likely to cause caries if eaten as part of the meal.[30]
Elicit information regarding the frequency of food intake.	Have the child and parent consider no more than three snacks a day.
	Discourage eating of foods that tend to stick to the teeth, like toffee or dried fruit, or foods that are sucked for a long time, like lollipops and hard candy.
Question the child and parent about brushing habits and techniques, including frequency of brushing.	Discuss appropriate tooth brushing and flossing and the importance of regular dental checkups.

Table 14-1 continued

Evaluation

Assess to determine if the child has reduced the risk factors for caries production.

Behavior changes in eating habits: kind of food, frequency of snacks.

Changes in care of teeth: frequency of brushing, use of fluoride.

Because dental caries is a disease of slow progress, the reduction rate is not immediate.

If caries persists, refer to a registered dietitian (R.D.) for in-depth nutrition education.

VII. PREVENTION OF CARDIAC DISEASE (see also chapter 17)

Coronary heart disease is a pediatric disease, and it is likely that intervention early in life would be most effective.[31]

Diet has been shown to be related to elevations in serum lipids in infancy and childhood.[32]

Obesity and lack of physical fitness are risk factors in coronary heart disease.[33]

Assessment	Action
If there is a family history of elevated blood lipids, assess child for lipid levels (see Table 12-3)	
Assess current nutritional patterns with regard to cholesterol, total fat, saturated fat, and sodium and calorie content. Review eating away from home, type(s) of restaurant visited, frequency of visits, and kinds of food most often selected.	Have child and/or parent complete a three-day food diary (see appendix A-4). Plan an individualized diet with the child and/or parents with calorie levels appropriate for growth and maintenance of ideal body weight. The American Heart Association Nutrition Committee recommends a decrease in total fat to 30 percent of calories, a decrease in saturated fat to 10 percent of calories, a level of polyunsaturated fat that is 10 percent of calories,[34] a decrease in cholesterol to 100 mg/1,000 calories, a level of protein that is approximately 15 percent of calories, an increase in carbohydrates to 55 percent of calories, and an increase in dietary fiber.
Review snack patterns and type of food consumed; look for sources of fat and sodium.	Teach practical skills, e.g., how to prepare low-fat foods and snacks. Target specific behaviors for change, e.g., reducing fatty and salty foods. Encourage exercise and the achievement and maintenance of ideal body weight. Encourage family involvement as essential for successful nutritional changes.

Table 14-1 continued

Refer to the local Heart Association for books, pamphlets, and possible food-preparation classes.

If possible, refer to a registered dietitian (R.D.) for in-depth diet counseling.

Evaluation

At follow-up, review what the child is eating; assess for behavior changes.

Reinforce changes made, reevaluate goals, and suggest further changes that need to be made.

If the child is at risk with a family history of elevated serum cholesterol or hypertension, refer to a physician and a registered dietitian (R.D.) for further evaluation.

Table 14-2 Tips for Helping Parents

Food shopping

- Use a list; avoid "impulse buying."
- Include child in short food shopping trips; avoid lengthy trips.
- Plan food shopping trips after meals instead of when hungry.
- Buy more low-calorie foods and fewer high-calorie foods.

Food storage and preparation

- Keep low-calorie foods where child has easy access to them.
- Store high-calorie foods out of sight.

Mealtime

- Use small portions and allow for seconds.
- Praise child to reinforce desired eating/health behaviors.
- Avoid using food as reward or punishment.
- Do not encourage child to always clean the plate.

Source: Adapted from "Behavior Therapy Techniques Applied to Eating, Exercise, and Diet Modification in Childhood Obesity" by J.W. Varni and H.T. Banis in *Developmental and Behavioral Pediatrics*, Vol. 6, No. 6, pp. 367–372, © by American Society of Parenteral and Enteral Nutrition, 1985.

NOTES

1. M. Story and J. Brown, "Do Young Children Instinctively Know What to Eat?" *New England Journal of Medicine* 316 (1987): 103–106.

2. J.J. Wurtman, "What Do Children Eat? Eating Styles of the Preschool, Elementary School, and Adolescent Child," in *Textbook of Pediatric Nutrition*, 3rd ed., ed. R.M. Suskind (New York: Raven Press, 1981), 597–607.

3. E. Pollitt, R.L. Leibel, and D. Greenfield, "Brief Fasting, Stress and Cognition in Children," *American Journal of Clinical Nutrition* 34 (1981): 1526.

4. Centers for Disease Control, *Ten-State Nutrition Survey, 1968-1970*, DHEW Publication no. (HSM) 72–8133 (Washington, D.C.: U.S. Department of Health, Education, and Welfare, Human Services and Mental Health Administration, 1972), 310.

5. U.S. Department of Health and Human Services, *Dental Health in Children with Phenylketonuria*, Publication no. HRS-D-MC 84-1 (Rockville, Md.: U.S. Department of Health and Human Services, 1984), 13.

6. W.H. Dietz and S.L. Gortmaker. "Do We Fatten Our Children at the Television Set? Obesity and Television Viewing in Children and Adolescents," *Pediatrics* 75 (1985): 807–812.

7. Centers for Disease Control, *Ten-State Nutrition Survey*, 81–85.

8. F.W. Lowenstein, "Preliminary Clinical and Anthropometric Findings From the First Health and Nutrition Examination Survey, USA, 1971-1972." *American Journal of Clinical Nutrition*, Vol. 29 (1976): 918.

9. G.M. Owen et al., "A Study of Nutritional Status of Preschool Children in the United States, 1968-1970," *Pediatrics* 53 (1974): 597.

10. Centers for Disease Control, *Ten-State Nutrition Survey*, 3–8.

11. J. Knittle, et al., "Childhood Obesity," in *Textbook of Pediatric Nutrition*, ed. R. Suskind (New York: Raven Press, 1981), 415–431.

12. K.D. Brownell, T.A. Wadden, and G.D. Foster, "A Comprehensive Treatment Plan for Obese Children and Adolescents: Principles and Practice," *Pediatrician* 12 (1983-1985): 89–96.

13. K.J. Morgan and M.E. Zabik, "Amount and Food Sources of Total Sugar Intake by Children Ages 5 to 12 years," *American Journal of Clinical Nutrition* 34 (1981): 404.

14. G. Kolata, "Obese Children, a Growing Problem," *Science* 232 (1986): 20–21.

15. L.H. Epstein, R.R. Wing, and A. Valoski. "Childhood Obesity." *Pediatric Clinics of North America* 32 (1985): 363–379.

16. W.H. Dietz and J.T. Dwyer, "Nutritional Implications of Vegetarianism in Children," in *Textbook of Pediatric Nutrition*, 3rd ed., ed. R.M. Suskind (New York: Raven Press, 1981), 179–188.

17. R. Harring and S. Zlotkin, "Unconventional Eating Practices and Their Health Implications," *Pediatric Clinics of North America* 32 (1985): 429–445.

18. G.B. Forbes and C.W. Woodruff, eds., *Pediatric Nutrition Handbook*, 2nd ed. (Elk Grove Village, Ill.: Committee on Nutrition, American Academy of Pediatrics, 1985), 45.

19. E.M. Satter, "Childhood Eating Disorders," *Journal of American Dietetic Association* 86 (1986): 357–361.

20. J. Yager, "Bulimia," *Resident and Staff Physician* 30 (1984): 43–55.

21. American College of Physicians, Health and Public Policy Committee, "Eating Disorders: Anorexia Nervose and Bulimia," *Annals of Internal Medicine* 105 (1986): 790–794.

22. American Academy of Pediatrics, Committee on Sports Medicine, *Sports Medicine: Health Care for Young Athletes*, ed. N.G. Smith (Elk Grove Village, Ill., 1985), 142–175.

23. Ibid., 147.

24. Ibid., 156.

25. D. Costill et al., "Effects of Elevated Plasma FFA and Insulin on Muscle Glycogen Useage During Exercise," *Journal of Applied Physiology* 43 (1977): 695.

26. Ibid., 698.

27. M. Stern and W.A. Walker, "Food Allergy and Intolerance," *Pediatric Clinics of North America* 32 (1985): 471–492.

28. B. Lucas, "Diet and Hyperactivity," in *Nutrition in Infancy and Childhood*, 3rd ed., ed. P.L. Pipes (St. Louis, Mo.: Times Mirror/Mosby College, 1985), 215–228.

29. J.L. Leinhas, G.C. McCaskill, and H.A. Sampson, "Food Allergy Challenges: Guidelines and Implications," *Journal of the American Dietetic Association* 87 (1987): 604–608.

30. D. Webb, "Surprising News About Foods that Cause and Prevent Cavities," *Environmental Nutrition*, December 1985: 3.

31. P.O. Kwiterovick, "Biochemical, Clinical, Epidemiologic, Genetic and Pathologic Data in the Pediatric Age Group Relevant to the Cholesterol Hypothesis," *Pediatrics* 78 (1986): 349–362.

32. L.O. Watkins and W.B. String, "The Child: When to Begin Preventive Cardiology," *Current Problems in Pediatrics* 14 (1984): 1–71.

33. Ibid., 32.

34. NIH Consensus Development Conference, "Lowering Blood Cholesterol to Prevent Heart Disease," *Arteriosclerosis* 5 (1985): 404–412.

Part VI

The Adolescent

Chapter 15

Nutrition Assessment of the Adolescent

Carolyn McKay

OVERVIEW

Adolescents present themselves for physical examination for a variety of reasons, rarely nutritionally related. They have an acute physical complaint, they need a paper signed for participation in sports, a job, schooling, or a camp. Rarely does an adolescent ask questions about being healthy and staying healthy.

Anxiety is commonly apparent in adolescents at the beginning of an examination. They anticipate being looked at judgmentally and being asked embarrassing questions. Breast and genital exams, or just the anticipation of them, are frightening enough to make many young people avoid physical examinations.

Yet, there is in all adolescents a felt need for accurate information to enable them to judge themselves against a standard. Saying, ''Your height for a 14-year-old girl is at the 50th percentile or right in the middle of the graph, and your weight is at the 75th percentile or well above average,'' may lead a girl to verbalize her concerns about her weight. A comment on very mild acne may bring forth a flood of concern and a request for treatment of a perceived social handicap.

The reason for doing a physical examination of an adolescent varies, but the majority of such exams are of ostensibly healthy individuals. Clues to inappropriate nutrition are more likely to come from the health history than from the exam itself. To elicit such a history, a nutrition questionnaire and food and activity record are helpful (see appendixes A-1 and A-5).

Eating patterns may provide a clue to the adolescent's psychological set. Rebellion against family may be displayed by refusing to drink milk or to eat vegetables, fruits, or other foods as encouraged at home by a conscientious parent. Busy students or athletes may skip meals or miss family meals and make up by snacking. Many students work in food establishments and eat ''fast foods'' frequently. Isolated, depressed individuals may eat very little. The physical exam may reinforce impressions initiated by the history.

HEALTH HISTORY

The adolescent health history is more important than the physical examination in defining the nutritional status of an adolescent. The history leads the examiner to more detailed, focused examination. Rare problems are more likely to be identified by the history than by the examination.

Eliciting a clear and adequate history from an adolescent is a skilled task. Questionnaires can be helpful if they are followed by oral history. Young people may not know the family health history, or they may not recognize the significance of the issues revealed by the history. It is not unusual to find questionnaire answers that indicate a student lives with parents who are well, only to discover that one parent is dead and the other takes medications for a specific pathology.

Past illnesses may be important to nutritional status. Such illnesses as repaired congenital heart defects, juvenile onset diabetes, or inflammatory bowel disease may contribute to low weight, low height, or delayed onset of puberty.

A recurrent disorder may not be perceived as a disease worth mentioning in the history. However, by asking about the number of school days missed in the current or past school year, it may be discovered that dysmenorrhea occurs regularly but that it is considered ''normal'' and no help has been sought. Delayed onset of puberty may not fit a family's perception of disease and so may not have been addressed medically in a timely fashion.

The severity of the complaint needs to be judged carefully. Adolescents may have a need to either sensationalize or minimize a problem. Having adolescents compare with peers their daily ability to function in various ways may clarify the severity of an illness.

Medications taken by the adolescent or by someone else in the family may provide a clue to a disease. Is the medication taken daily? For what purpose is it taken? How long has it been taken? How long will it be taken? Who prescribed it, and who is monitoring it? Students may not consider vitamins or laxatives as medicine and may fail to report them. Taking a daily medicine for a long-established disorder may no longer be considered worth reporting.

Allergies may be reported if the adolescent is queried. However, a food dislike or intolerance may be reported as an allergy. Clarification, with a history of symptoms, may free students of needless worry and may encourage them toward a less restricted diet. Supervised challenges with foods thought to provoke allergy often demonstrate an acceptable level of tolerance.

Lack of sleep or excessive exercise may influence caloric need. Sudden weight gain may be associated with cessation of sports participation. Anorexic students may spend hours in vigorous activity. Late night hours and chronic meal skipping may cause fatigue or altered biological rhythm, leading to poor food intake and poor school performance. A well-directed history and well-focused advice can reverse this.

The data collection on a girl is not complete until a menstrual history is reviewed. Delayed onset or cessation of menses can be related to psychological, nutritional, or physical disorders. Exercise and nutrition interact with the menstrual pattern. Adolescents who are in competitive sports, ballet, or even recreational running may decrease body fat significantly. This may then lead to menstrual irregularities.

Anemia is relatively common in menstruating adolescent girls. When asked about menses, most girls assume they are "normal." It may take carefully worded queries to elicit a history of excessive bleeding. Questions about number of pads or tampons used, number of days, and "accidents" with sudden heavy bleeding may be helpful.

PHYSICAL ASSESSMENT

Physical findings are most frequently related to other than nutritional causes. However, they may also be associated with nutritional problems. Therefore, a careful differential diagnosis is essential. A finding may suggest a more careful exam of another system, more historical information, or laboratory testing to clarify it.

The physical examination is best done if the adolescent is covered enough for modesty, but accessible for inspection. A note should be made of the general quality and quantity of hair. Healthy, clean hair should resist gentle pulling, not break easily, and have pigment consistent with the genetic background of the individual. Dry, brittle, sparse, or discolored hair may be a sign of deficient diet, chemical abuse of hair, endocrine abnormality, or drug therapy for a malignancy. Any abnormality should be clarified by the history.

The condition of skin on the forehead, face, and neck, including pigmentation, should also be noted. Head lice may cause the individual to excoriate the nape of the neck. Pomade acne can occur secondary to the use of excessive hair dressing. Acne may be limited to the forehead or hairline and artfully hidden by hairstyling. Any pallor should be noted. The configuration of eyebrows and facial hair should also be noted.

Skin changes diagnostic of specific dietary deficiencies are rarely seen. However, vitamins A, B, C, E, and K and certain trace minerals are needed to keep skin healthy. Specific malabsorption syndromes, such as cystic fibrosis or bizarre eating habits, might be related to hyperkeratotic folliculitis, smooth or brown tongue, cheilosis, or changes in skin exposed to excessive sunlight. Nonspecific red, a follicular rash with loss of skin integrity, can be seen in severe alcoholism or child abuse caused by food deprivation. Both these occurrences should be rare in adolescents.

Nutrition assessment must take into account environmental factors, such as the season of the year. Wind and cold damage to the skin may resemble skin changes associated with undernutrition. Lack of personal hygiene can lead to such findings as gingivitis, which could also be associated with inadequate vitamin intake.

Postoccipital lymph nodes, as well as posterior auricular nodes, should be sought. Ear canal infection may present with postauricular nodes. Suboptimal nutritional intake predisposes the growing adolescent to increased incidence of infection.

In preadolescents, unexplained lymphadenopathy is common. By onset of puberty, lymphadenopathy should have a specific explanation. Viral infections, including Ebstein-Barr and hepatitis A, can profoundly affect appetite and weight. A hallmark of acquired immune deficiency syndrome (AIDS) (see chapter 24) is unexplained lymphadenopathy and, late in the disease, weight loss. Enlarged parotids may signal bulimia.

The eye exam should note abnormalities of eyebrows, lids, sclera, pupil, and lacrimal apparatus. Symptomatic dryness of eyes, as well as color changes in the sclera, must be explained. Keratitis (inflamed cornea) may be secondary to vitamin A deficiency. Clearness of cornea and presence of normal retinal vascularity should be documented. Pallor of conjunctiva needs further work-up.

The nose should be straight, with the ability to breathe through each nostril with the other occluded. Sports injuries can result in deviated septum with obstruction. Sinus infection should be asked for historically as well as checked for clinically. Like any other chronic infection, sinusitis can account for bad breath, fatigue, and failure to grow as expected. Allergies with respiratory manifestations can sometimes be detected by examining the nose and by findings supported by the history. Young people may say they have "sinuses" but mean infection, allergy, or sensitivity to cigarette smoke. Appetite may be markedly depressed if mouth breathing is constant or taste is impaired.

The mouth needs careful attention. This part of the exam is no substitute for a prophylactic exam once or twice yearly by the personal dentist. One should note the presence and condition of the teeth; the condition of the gums, including friability and color; hygiene; the color of the tongue and its papillae; the size of the tonsils; and the shape of the hard palate, soft palate, and uvula. Mucosal changes opposite the lower lateral teeth or anteriorly should be noted for evidence of smokeless tobacco use; leukoplakia and oral cancers are a direct result of this habit. Gums need careful examination for the presence of abscesses or pus at the base of the teeth. If the abscesses are chronic, they may be painless; but they may still be a source of anemia associated with chronic infection. If the teeth or gums are painful, food intake is likely to be impaired. Eroded enamel can signal bulimic behavior (see chapter 17).

Trauma to teeth involving broken, discolored, or dead teeth should be noted. The need for orthodontic correction of bite and other problems may be apparent.

Chronic peridontal infection is usually treated successfully; prevention is even better. A knowledgeable advocate for adolescents can sometimes identify local community resources to meet dental needs and encourage their use.

The tympano-mandibular joint should be palpated, noting any clicks. Headaches, fatigue on chewing, ear pain, and toothache can arise from temporomandibular joint malfunction and may affect food choices.

The thyroid gland should be inspected from both the front and the side. It should be palpated with two hands from the rear. Thyroiditis is common in adolescent girls with hypo-, hyper-, or normal-thyroid function present. Derangement of normal function can affect linear growth, weight gain, skin and hair quality, menstrual function, and learning ability. Occasionally, in a female athlete, the sternocleidomastoid muscles are so well-developed that the thyroid appears enlarged as well.

On inspection of the chest of females, the presence, configuration, and symmetry of the breasts and the Tanner stage of breast development should be noted. A careful examination of each breast and axilla should be completed. Depending on weight, age, and stage of development, concerns of the adolescent female about breast size will vary. This is an opportune time to review maternal family history of breast cancer, the reason for breast self-examination and awareness of masses. Some girls will believe their breasts are too small, others that their breasts are too large. In both instances, appropriate reassurance can be offered.

Early in puberty, noticeable enlargement of mammary glands occurs in approximately one-third of males. The presence of this benign phenomenon deserves a reassuring explanation.

A further inspection of the chest in both males and females should note symmetry, musculature, posture, and excursion of the ribs on breathing. Breathing should be assessed by placing hands on the thorax as well as by auscultation. Skin condition and pigmentation should be noted. Chronic pulmonary disease, such as asthma or cystic fibrosis, can markedly affect nutritional status by decreasing food intake, interfering with absorption, or increasing caloric usage. Even in adolescence, heavy cigarette smoking can cause a chronic cough or "bronchitis" with decreased caloric intake, but also with an increased need for calories to repair tissue. Scoliosis can change chest configuration and pulmonary function.

Cardiac problems may be apparent during the examination. Congenital cardiac abnormalities frequently impair growth in early childhood. Usually, by adolescence the defect has been repaired. However, catch-up growth may have occurred, or the adolescent may have ongoing problems. Any abnormalities in the cardiac examination must be completely explained or investigated.

The abdomen should be inspected before it is palpated. Striae and scars should be noted and explained. Striae suggest endocrine disorders, which can include pregnancy. Abdominal palpation for spleen and liver should be done. Chronic blood disorders can enlarge the spleen, as can severe iron deficiency. Spleen and liver enlargement can occur for infectious reasons, such as mononucleosis or hepatitis. If the history does not clarify the etiology, further investigation is in order.

A common finding on abdominal palpation is a sausage-shaped mass in the right lower quadrant. This is a descending colon full of stool and suggests chronic constipation. The history may reveal a diet low in fruits and vegetables, irregular eating habits, or a high consumption of fat and sugar. Stomach aches may be common and perceived as serious enough to justify missing school. A finding of school days lost can provide the basis for a cause-and-effect discussion of diet relevant to the adolescent at that moment and should be capitalized upon. The vocabulary of the discussion needs to be flexible enough to ensure understanding and reliable reporting.

The presence, amount, and pattern of pubic hair should be noted. For males, an evaluation of the penis and testicles is important. Here, Tanner staging can help in predicting the growth pattern and in explaining other findings. In this examination, hernias, hydrocles, and varicoceles should also be noted.

A pelvic examination should be done if pregnancy, menstrual problems, or infection are matters of concern. A chronic pelvic or urinary tract infection can affect food intake and utilization. A pregnancy may be hidden by deliberate weight restriction or it may simply be denied.

In examining the extremities, the condition of the finger and toe nails should be noted. Biting of nails may be a clue to other stress-related behaviors. Splitting, pitting, ridging, or fungal infections may also affect nails. These findings may be secondary to other serious diseases that affect growth.

The adolescent should stand, walk on the toes and heels, bend to touch the toes, squat, and then recover. This procedure allows gross assessment of muscle mass or muscle wasting, strength, and flexibility. Some judgment about fat distribution and subcutaneous fat should be made. Appendix C-1 summarizes clinical signs associated with nutritional deficiencies.

ANTHROPOMETRIC ASSESSMENT

During the years of growth, regular weight and height measurements should be recorded (see appendix D). Weighing and measuring are simple and inexpensive procedures. Careful and accurate measures of growth are essential in documenting nutritional problems. Serial measurements may be of more value than laboratory technique in defining normalcy of growth. If more objective data are not available, most adolescents can document their growth by reporting whether they wear the same jeans or shoes that they did a year ago.

Body image concerns are normal, yet disconcerting, to the rapidly growing adolescent. Confusion and misgivings about appearance peak during adolescence, due to the rapid onset and dramatic effect of hormonal changes. Most adolescents are not happy with their appearance—considering themselves as too short, too fat, too tall, or too thin. Reassurance about growth parameters can ease such worries and prevent inappropriate dieting and potential nutritional problems.

Physical Growth

Height and weight standards (see appendix D) for assessing growth in adolescence take on a particular significance. Nearly 25 percent of total adolescent growth occurs during a 24-to-36-month period; this is known as the growth spurt. The mean age of this accelerated growth is 11.5 years in females and 13.5 years in males. At the corresponding mean ages, peak height velocity is 8.3 cm/year in girls and 9.5 cm/year in boys.

See Figures 15-1 and 15-2 for graphs of height velocity for girls and boys, respectively.

Weight gain during adolescence accounts for over 40 percent of adult weight in both sexes. The peak weight velocity roughly coincides with the peak height velocity.[1,2,3] See Figures 15-3 and 15-4 for graphs of weight velocity for girls and boys, respectively.

The major difference between the sexes is reflected in the greater increase in subcutaneous fat in females and a greater increase in muscle mass in males. If there are concerns about excesses or deficits, weight gain should be compared with weight and height standards for the particular age group.

The individual growth rate among adolescents is variable. Girls can begin puberty between 8 and 14 years and complete the stage usually within 3 years of onset. Puberty in males begins about 1½ to 2 years later than in females. The development of secondary sex characteristics are the visible markers of puberty.

Sexual Maturity

While puberty varies in onset, duration, and extent in individual adolescents, there is a predictive sequence of events. Using a sexual maturity rating (SMR), known as the Tanner scale, one can assign stages from 1 (prepubescence) to 5 (adult).[4,5] Figure 15-5 shows the sequence of sexual development.

Female maturation is based on breast and pubic hair development; males are rated on genital and pubic hair development.[6,7] Table 15-1 lists the developmental stages of secondary sex characteristics.

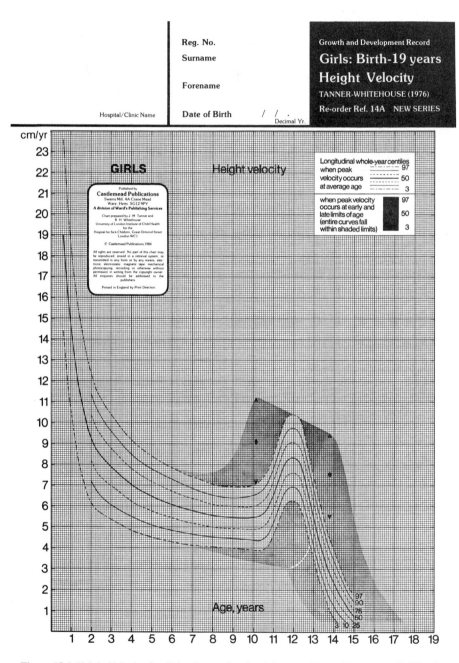

Figure 15-1 Height Velocity for Girls. *Source*: Reprinted from *Archives of Disease in Childhood*, vol. 40, pp. 454–471, with permission of Castlemead Publications, © 1965.

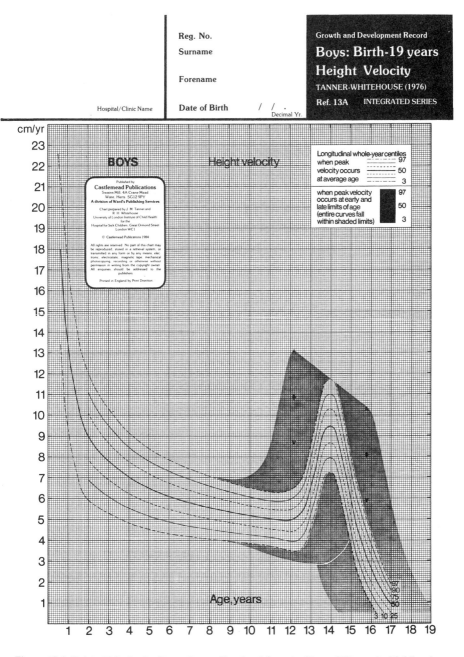

Figure 15-2 Height Velocity for Boys. *Source*: Reprinted from *Archives of Disease in Childhood*, vol. 40, pp. 454–471, with permission of Castlemead Publications, © 1965.

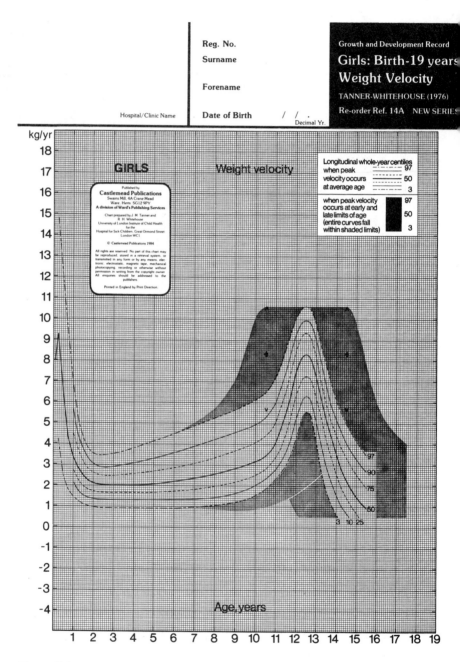

Figure 15-3 Weight Velocity for Girls. *Source*: Reprinted from *Archives of Disease in Childhood*, vol. 40, pp. 454–471, with permission of Castlemead Publications, © 1965.

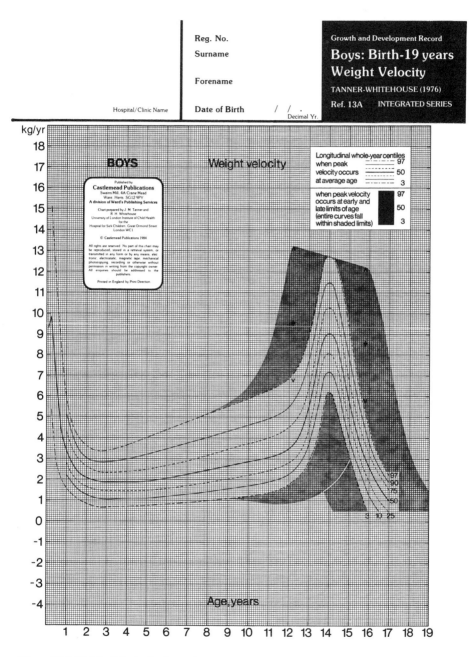

Figure 15-4 Weight Velocity for Boys. *Source*: Reprinted from *Archives of Disease in Childhood*, vol. 40, pp. 454–471, with permission of Castlemead Publications, © 1965.

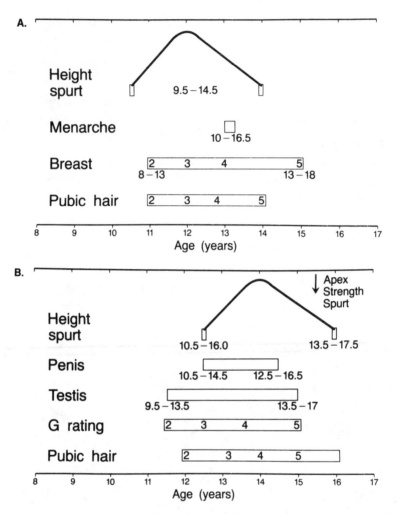

Figure 15-5 Sequence of Events at Puberty in Females (A) and Males (B). *Source*: Reprinted from *Archives of Diseases in Childhood*, Vol. 45, pp. 13–23, with permission of British Medical Association, © 1970.

The sequence of pubertal events in girls usually is in the following order: breast buds, pubic hair, peak height velocity, axillary hair, menarche, and finally ovulation. In males the usual sequence is accelerated growth of testes and scrotum, pubic hair, growth of penis, first ejaculation, peak height velocity, axillary hair, facial hair, and, finally, voice deepening.[8]

By correctly staging the sexual maturation of the adolescent, the health care practitioner can effectively assess nutritional status. Generally, between SMR 1

Table 15-1 Developmental Stages of Secondary Sex Characteristics

Stage	Female Breast Development	Male Genital Development	Male and Female Pubic Hair Development
1	Preadolescent: Elevation of papilla only.	Preadolescent: Testes, scrotum, and penis are about the same size and proportion as in early childhood.	Preadolescent: No pubic hair.
2	Breast bud stage: Elevation of breast and papilla as small mound. Enlargement of areolar diameter.	Enlargement of scrotum and testes; skin of the scrotum reddens and changes in texture; little or no enlargement of penis.	Sparse growth of long, slightly pigmented, downy hair, straight or only slightly curled, appearing at the base of the penis or along the labia.
3	Further enlargement and elevation of breast and areolae, with no separation of their contours.	Enlargement of penis, which occurs at first mainly in length; further growth of testes and scrotum.	Hair darker, coarser, and more curled; spreads sparsely over the junction of the pubes.
4	Projection to the areola and papilla to form a secondary mound above the level of the breast.	Increased size of penis with growth in breadth and development of glands; further enlargement of testes and scrotum; increasing darkening of scrotal skin.	Hair adult in type but area covered is still considerably smaller than in the adult; no spread to the medial surface of the thighs.
5	Mature stage: Projection of papilla only, due to recession of the areola to the general contour of the breast.	Genitalia adult in size and shape.	Adult in quantity and type.

Source: Reprinted from *Growth at Adolescence*, 2nd ed., by J.M. Tanner, p. 35, with permission of Blackwell Scientific Publications, © 1962.

and SMR 2 there is accelerated fat accumulation for both sexes; between SMR 2 and SMR 4, there is increased skeletal growth; increased muscle development occurs between SMR 3 and SMR 5.[9] Appropriate nutrition must take into consideration these growth parameters, which are unique to adolescence. Chapter 17 delineates the nutritional intervention strategies for the adolescent.

It is worthwhile to note that adolescents may manifest through their diet their psychological concerns regarding their body image. Adolescents who do not understand or accept the dramatic changes in their body's appearance may try to control the changes by altering their food intake. Thus, along with other nutritional counseling that may be recommended, the adolescent may benefit from a frank discussion of expected physical growth milestones and sexual maturity.

LABORATORY ASSESSMENT

Physical signs supported by the history will direct any laboratory investigation of a possible problem. Here, careful development of the differential diagnosis is critical.

Although hematocrit/hemoglobin, ferritin, and urine analyses are the most common laboratory tests, other tests may be indicated. Other laboratory test results that may be helpful include those for TSH, T4, pregnancy, liver functions, BUN and creatinine, carotene, folate, serum protein, and immunoglobulins.

Hemoglobin and/or hematocrit are indicated routinely. Frank anemia is not uncommon, since it is associated with poor iron intake, rapid growth, and, in girls, recurrent blood loss. The ferritin level allows assessment of iron stores; however, altitude norms should be kept in mind in interpreting the results of the test. Strenuous exercise may be associated with anemia: although if iron stores are sufficient, this reverses itself readily. Iron needs of a pregnant adolescent are difficult to meet with diet alone and deserve special attention (see chapter 17).

The dipstick may be a useful screening tool in examining urine for blood, protein, and nitrates. The white blood cell count and differential and the erythrocyte sedimentation rate may be useful measures with complaints of fatigue and malaise. If supported by the history, an evaluation of cholesterol and high density lipids may be needed.

SUMMARY

The history, the physical examination (including blood pressure), and good clinical judgment are more productive than any battery of screening tests. In any event, a follow-up of recommendations is important. By following up on a concern of the adolescent, the concerns can be validated. Repeated contact allows for clarification of the history and can build trust. Though adolescents may view their interest in nutrition as legitimate health-seeking behavior, the need to talk and be listened to may not be perceived as legitimate by them. Here, confidentiality and flexibility can aid in building trust. Depression, rebellion, and misinformation can be addressed best through ongoing contact.

The adolescent and family should be given as much explanation and responsibility for a problem as is individually appropriate. In this relationship, sensitive diplomacy on the part of the examiner is a welcome asset. The final goal is to help the young person achieve optimal growth and development into a capable and independent adult.

NOTES

1. J.M. Tanner, "Clinical Longitudinal Standards for Height and Weight Velocity for North American Children," *Journal of Pediatrics* 107 (1985): 317–329.

2. J.M Tanner, R.H. Whitehouse, and M. Takaishi, "Standards from Birth to Maturity for Height, Weight, Height Velocity and Weight Velocity: British Children," *Archives of Diseases in Childhood* 40 (1965): 454–471, 613–635.

3. N. Bayley, "Growth Curves of Height and Weight by Age for Boys and Girls, Scaled According to Physical Maturity," *Journal of Pediatrics* 48 (1956): 187–194.

4. W.A. Marshall and J.M. Tanner, "Variations in the Pattern of Pubertal Changes in Girls," *Archives of Diseases in Childhood* 44 (1969): 291–303.

5. W.A. Marshall and J.M. Tanner, "Variations in the Pattern of Pubertal Changes in Boys," *Archives of Diseases in Childhood* 45 (1970): 13–23.

6. J.M Tanner, *Growth at Adolescence*, 2nd ed. (Oxford: Blackwell Scientific Publications, 1962), 35.

7. G.B. Slap, "Normal Physiological Psychosocial Growth in the Adolescent," *Journal of Adolescent Health Care* 7 (1986): 135–235.

8. C.T. Torre, "Assessing the Adolescent," *Topics in Clinical Nursing* 8 (1986): 11–21.

9. Ibid., 13.

Chapter 16

Environmental Management of the Adolescent

Dorothy Hyde

OVERVIEW

Adolescence has significant implications for nutritional care. Suboptimal dietary intake and potential nutrition problems may arise as growing independence and the seeking of peer approval influence food selection outside of the home. The physical and psychosocial environment of the adolescent affects the availability of nutrients and calories and may present barriers to sound nutrition practice. These environmental barriers need to be explored in order to provide counseling, education, and management to promote, at this critical time of development, food and lifestyle habits most conducive to long-term health.

ENVIRONMENTAL ASSESSMENT

Psychosocial Development

Adolescence is a period of developing independence as the individual seeks a sense of self-identity. During this time of learning to be self-responsible, many teens are motivated to learn about their bodies and to acquire information about good nutrition for promoting health. Other adolescents, in pursuing independence, however, may become caught up in self-destructive behaviors that negatively affect their nutritional status. The resulting struggle for control over their lives must be recognized as central to nutritional counseling.

The adolescent's cognitive awareness must also be considered. Before and during early adolescence, youngsters think in concrete terms. Although capable of thinking logically, they have difficulty comprehending the future in anything but concrete terms. Yet adolescence is a time of cognitive awakening and of learning

Table 16-1 Hidden Fat and Sugar in Selected Snacks

Snack	Amount	Sugar* (teaspoons)	Fat* (teaspoons)
Apple pie	1 slice (1/8 of pie)	11.0	3.0
Brownie	1	5.0	1.0
Candy bar	2 oz.	8.0	4.5
M & Ms	1.6 oz. package	8.0	2.5
Chocolate cake, frosted	1 slice	8.5	3.0
Cereal, presweetened	1 cup	6.0	—
Chocolate milk, whole	1 cup	6.5	2.0
Donut, plain	1	3.0	1.5
Fruit, canned in heavy syrup	1/2 cup	6.0	—
Hi-C	1 cup	8.0	—
Ice cream, vanilla regular (10% fat)	1 cup	8.0	3.5
Kool-Aid	1 cup	6.0	—
Soda pop, cola type	12 oz. can	10.0	—
Pop tart	1	9.0	2.0
Twinkie	1	6.0	1.0
Potato chips	1 oz.	4.0	2.5

*4 grams of white sugar or 5 grams of fat equals one teaspoon.

Sources: From Nutrients in Food by G. Leveille et al., The Nutrition Guild, © 1983; and Food Values of Portions Commonly Used, 14th ed., by J. Pennington and H. Church, J.B. Lippincott Company, © 1985.

to think abstractly. Adolescents are only beginning to think about possible problems and outcomes and consequently are not very future-oriented.

Thus, nutrition counseling is best done in concrete terms with the support from the health care practitioner. For example, a fact sheet, such as that in Table 16-1, can be used with the adolescent to discuss fat and sugar intake. To be even more specific, one can actually measure out the relevant amounts for them to see.

The struggle for identity and a grasp on understanding the world are further complicated by a changing body image. Adolescents are very conscious of and sensitive to the perceived opinions of others, particularly those of their peers. This can readily lead to a variety of eating disorders as they conform to expectations they imagine. Likewise, it can be the source of motivation for changing or improving their diet.

As a source of behavioral standards and self-esteem, the peer group is extremely important to a teenager. At the same time, it may become a source of inaccurate health information, resulting in undesirable health and eating behaviors. Peer standards of health, diet, and nutrition thus provide valuable data for the health care practitioner in counseling adolescents.

Socioeconomics

The family environment can be an obstacle to adolescents in meeting their nutritional needs. Irregular family schedules—such as both parents working, parents away in the evening, or hectic family interactions—may interfere with the quality of the diet, family meals, and arrangements for eating together. With the large increase in single-parent families and in women employed outside the home, family structure has changed a great deal. This has had an impact on the type and frequency of family meals. In particular, it has led to an increase in snacking on foods of poor nutritional quality.[1]

Strained family relationships may cause either parent or child to avoid common mealtimes to avoid conflict. As Mahan and Rees note, "Family eating practices are among the most important influences, both positive and negative, on the food habits of adolescents. Family disorganization that leaves teens 'on their own' with respect to eating fosters poor eating habits. . . . Adolescents whose diets are the poorest are those who eat alone or with friends."[2]

Adolescents are frequently actively involved in after-school activities, athletics, or a job. This may result in skipped meals, such as dinner (because of a perceived lack of time) or breakfast (because the adolescent works late and sleeps later in the morning). Meal skipping appears in fact to be common among certain groups of adolescents, with those from minority and lower-income families and older adolescents missing more meals than other adolescents.[3] Breakfast is reported to be the most frequent meal missed.

As the adolescent becomes involved in school activities, athletic programs, and employment, snacking becomes common, with approximately one-fourth to one-third of total caloric intake consumed between meals.[4] Turning frequently to fast foods for snacks, the teenager consumes foods high in calories, sodium, fat, and sugar, often consuming 50 percent or more of the recommended allowance in one meal. It should be noted, however, that some fast-food restaurants are attempting to improve the nutritional content of their food, for example, by offering salad bars. (For a current nutrient analysis of the popular fast foods served by establishments in a particular area, one should write to the headquarters of the relevant food companies.)

Adolescents who are employed in fast-food restaurants are often provided with free soft drinks; thus they may consume a large number of empty calories during their work hours. They may also select foods of lower nutritional value on which to snack.

Research has shown that although teenagers may have an adequate knowledge of nutrition, there are barriers to improving poor dietary habits. The barriers include a lack of self-discipline and a lack of a sense of urgency.[5] It is simply easier to grab "a coke and fries" than to get involved with balanced nutrient choices; and the short-term consequences are favorable to the busy teenager—it tastes good, everyone else is eating that way, and it satisfies their hunger.

Culture

Dietary patterns have great cultural significance. Patterns based on one's culture are deeply rooted and not readily changed. In general, while reinforcing desirable dietary practices, only those cultural practices that are potentially harmful should be modified. For example, in the case of a hypertensive, Oriental, adolescent male whose family meals contain an excessive amount of sodium, counseling should focus on practicing ways to reduce the intake of sodium while maintaining some of the acceptable flavor by using low sodium soy sauce, herbs and spices. Some American blacks, Asians, native Americans, Hispanics and Middle Easterners are lactose-deficient to some degree; in such cases, the symptoms after drinking milk may include gas, intestinal pain, cramps, or diarrhea.

Compliance in cross-cultural counseling may be diminished if the client's values are inconsistent with the recommendations given or impeded by a language barrier. For example, Hmong or Laotian patients who are instructed to cut down on salt may not comply simply because they equate salt with table salt, which they rarely use, and continue to season foods with fish sauce, which is extremely high in sodium.

Behavior

Behavioral problems in adolescence stem from a number of causes, including nutrition. Poor nutrition can affect adolescents' behavior, and their behavior may in turn affect what they eat. Evidence of a number of vitamin deficiencies can be manifested by adverse behavioral changes. For example, clinical symptoms of iron-deficiency anemia include irritability, decreased attentiveness, and impaired cognitive abilities. Similarly, researchers have noted a slowing of activity and apathy in zinc-deficient individuals.[6]

Teenagers who are chronically stressed suffer some metabolic effects, depending on the frequency, intensity, and duration of the stress. Stress responses leading to the release of norepinephrine and epinephrine can result in an increase in urinary nitrogen excretion and negative nitrogen balance.[7]

Caffeine is often consumed in large amounts by teenagers in the form of cola drinks. Intake of very large doses of caffeine—for example, 600 mg/day or 48 ounces of cola—may lead to chronic insomnia, anxiety, paranoia, or depression and may produce a low calcium-phosphorus ratio. The sudden absence of caffeine for those who are daily consumers of large amounts of cola can lead to irritability and fatigue.[8]

Depression should be suspected in adolescents who appear to have bizarre eating habits, such as bingeing and purging. Depression leads to isolation and the teenager may stop eating. Depression and poor self-image are commonly seen in obese adolescents and can be a real barrier to weight loss.

Related Issues

It may be through a school nutrition education project or a sports physical examination that adolescents encounter first-hand the concept that what they eat affects their bodies. Approximately 7 million high school students participate in athletic programs. Yet, the strong emphasis placed on competitiveness can make coaches and young athletes vulnerable to the many misconceptions about the role of nutrition in physical performance. Athletic programs should be used to provide an incentive for improving the athletes' nutritional status (see chapter 17).

The percentage of adolescents who are sexually active appears to be increasing. The sexually active adolescent female is a prime target for nutrition counseling. If she is using oral contraceptives and has had a long-term, suboptimal dietary intake, she may be at risk for clinical manifestations of altered vitamin and mineral metabolism associated with the use of oral contraceptives (for example, vitamin-B_6-related depression). Marginal iron status, commonly seen in adolescent girls, may make her susceptible to iron deficiency. In any event, counseling about the avoidance of alcohol, cigarette smoking, and drug usage is appropriate (see chapter 17).

INTERVENTION

Improvement of adolescent food habits presents a challenge that may best be met by strategies that appeal to physical attractiveness or athletic performance, rather than long-term health benefits. This is especially true for young adolescents, whose level of cognitive development makes them conducive to concrete, rather than abstract, thought. However, no counseling will be successful unless the adolescent is involved in the decision making and experiences a sense of control in the process. Thus, mutual goal setting is essential.

An emphasis on the positive aspects of current dietary patterns and food preferences and suggestions for gradual, realistic changes may be particularly successful. Breakfast consumption may be encouraged by suggestions for making quickly prepared and transportable items, such as peanut butter on toast or an

English or bran muffin; cold pizza; lean meat; cheese, fish or egg sandwiches; cold (or, if available, microwave-heated) "left-overs," such as chili or casseroles; or fruit-flavored yogurts. School lunch participation may be increased by student involvement in meal planning and the selection of foods for vending machines, and the availability of self-selected items, such as salad, soup, and sandwich bars. Student participation in organizing and planning guidance for a student committee on nutrition can both improve the students' nutrition and provide the participants with an increased sense of independence.

Adolescents can be taught the skills necessary to make changes in their diet. They can learn to read labels and evaluate nutrition information and then relate this to their own needs. Strategies that can promote this type of learning could include peer teaching, the use of team projects, and training in decision making. In order to be effective, however, nutrition content and nutrition-oriented strategies need to be incorporated into the school curriculum.

SUMMARY

By providing accurate information in a manner appropriate to the developmental level of adolescents, the health care practitioner can be an important source of nutrition information and a catalyst in bringing about health-promoting behavioral changes in this age group. By individualizing nutritional assessments and interventions, the practitioner can encourage adolescent nutrition behaviors that will result in optimal health.

Access to sound, practical nutrition information is especially important to the growing adolescent. The health care practitioner needs to be recognized as the primary source of such information. Through routine health screenings and meetings with adolescents, parents, teachers, and athletic coaches, the health care practitioner can have a decisive impact in promoting food and lifestyle habits conducive to long-term health.

NOTES

1. Yankelovich, Shelly and White, Inc., *Family Health in an Era of Stress,* The General Mills American Family Report, 1978–1979 (Minneapolis, Minn.: General Mills, 1979), 1–146.

2. L.J. Mahan and J.M. Rees, *Nutrition in Adolescence* (St. Louis, Mo.: Time Mirror/Mosby College Publishing, 1984), 79–80.

3. W. Daniel, "Growth and Nutrition of Adolescents," in *Adolescent Health Care Clinical Issues,* ed. R. Blum (New York: Academic Press, 1982), 59–67.

4. A. Truswell and I. Darnton-Hill, "Food Habits of Adolescents," *Nutrition Review* 39 (1981): 73.

5. M. Story and M.D. Resnick, "Adolescent's Views on Food and Nutrition," *Journal of Nutrition Education* 18 (1986): 188–192.

6. Mahan and Rees, *Nutrition in Adolescence*, 200–204.

7. Ibid., 195.

8. Ibid., 207.

Chapter 17

Dietary Assessment and Management of the Adolescent

Irene R. Alton

- Is carbohydrate-loading recommended for the adolescent athlete?
- Should an adolescent lose weight?
- How can eating disorders be detected early?
- What are the special nutritional needs of the pregnant adolescent?

DIETARY ASSESSMENT

Overview

Nutritional requirements for adolescents correspond to growth and developmental status and activity level and thus are subject to individual variability. Established recommended nutrient intakes are based primarily on extrapolations from those for other age groups and are approximate rather than precise guidelines.

A dietary evaluation is made to determine the quality and quantity of the adolescent's current nutrient intake. All dietary methods rely on the adolescent's willingness to cooperate and ability to recall food intake, which becomes more difficult with frequent snacking in various places. Approximate estimates, rather than highly accurate intake data, are likely to be obtained. A respectful, nonjudgmental, and caring attitude on the part of the interviewer and a comfortable uninterrupted setting are also essential.

Much information can be obtained through the use of a nutrition questionnaire (see appendix A-1) that the adolescent can fill out in the clinic waiting area. The adolescent's recall may also be aided by beginning with the last food consumed on the day of the interview and working back to the previous day until a 24-hour period is covered (see appendix A-2). Here it may be necessary to use probing questions, particularly with young adolescents. A food frequency list (see appendix A-3), on which the adolescent indicates how often foods are consumed, may help to improve the reliability of other dietary information. To obtain in-depth information about actual food intake and eating behavior, the adolescent can be asked to complete a food and activity record (see appendix A-5) or food diary (see appendix A-4) and bring it to the next visit. However, keeping such a record requires a high degree of motivation and cooperation on the adolescent's part; the procedure thus is usually limited to situations where more detailed dietary information is required, as in the management of weight problems, growth deficits, or diabetes.

Diet Analysis

After obtaining the dietary intake data, possible nutritional excesses or deficiencies are determined by comparisons with recommended standards. Comparison with the daily food guide (see appendix B-1) will provide a gross estimate of the nutritional quality of the diet. The 24-hour recall and the food frequency list can pinpoint broad areas of food excesses or deficits. More specific data can be obtained by comparison of nutrient levels determined from food composition tables, such as Food Values of Portions Commonly Used,[1] with the Recommended Dietary Allowances (RDA) (see appendix B-2).

Monitoring of growth patterns based on height/weight status, as well as on the adolescent's appetite, will best indicate appropriate calorie intake. Ranges of energy intakes according to age and sex are provided by the RDA to accommodate adolescents at various stages of growth. Adolescents who engage in moderate or greater physical activity will need higher caloric intakes[2] (see appendix E-1).

Increased demands for, and consequently higher recommended intakes of, minerals occur as a result of skeletal, lean tissue, muscle, and blood volume increments during adolescent growth.[3] Of concern is the high intake of carbonated beverages, typical of some adolescents, which may compromise bone health by contributing to a low calcium/phosphorus ratio.[4] Males are more likely than females to consume sufficient food sources of calcium. In any case, the realization of a nourishing, balanced diet containing calcium-rich foods and a decrease in the intake of carbonated beverages are important goals of nutritional care for the adolescent.

Increases in muscle mass, soft tissue, and red cell mass are associated with greater iron demand. While the female experiences menstrual blood losses of 15–28 mg of iron per cycle, males have higher requirements related to greater gains in lean body mass, more extensive hemoglobin and myoglobin synthesis, and greater expansion of blood volume.

Encouraging an intake of iron-rich foods and sufficient protein and vitamin C is important in preventing iron deficiency in adolescents, as well as helpful in the management of anemia. More lean meats and citrus juices and fruits are suggested, while excessive quantities of milk, which decrease iron absorption and replace other foods, should be discouraged.

Greater demands for vitamins coincide with the increased energy metabolism, tissue synthesis, blood volume expansion, and skeletal growth associated with adolescence. In this connection, it should be noted that heavy smoking, that is, more than 20 cigarettes per day, may increase vitamin C needs as much as two-fold.[5] Generally, to improve vitamin status in adolescents, the intake of vegetables, fruit juices, and fruits should be encouraged.

After receiving counseling along the above lines, aimed at improving their nutrient intake, adolescents should be better able to appreciate the need for balanced nutritional management to meet growth requirements for their age and stature.

COMMON NUTRITIONAL PROBLEMS OF THE ADOLESCENT

Table 17-1 provides detailed information about common nutritional problems of adolescents. It also includes suggestions for further assessment, recommended actions, and steps in evaluation.

Table 17-1 Common Nutritional Problems of the Adolescent

I. OVERWEIGHT/OBESITY (also see chapter 14)

Fat deposits are normal components of adolescent growth, particularly in the female.[6]

A cycle of real or imagined rejection, followed by withdrawal, isolation, depression, boredom, inactivity, and increased eating, may also be evident.[7]

The pressure of "scare tactics" regarding health risks may be met with rebellion and negative results.

Long-term counseling and an interdisciplinary approach are essential components of adolescent obesity management.

Contributing factors to weight problems may include depression, emotional stresses, low levels of self-esteem, or family problems, such as divorce, alcoholism, or abuse.

Assessment	Action
What is the degree of overweight? (See chapter 15.)	Rigid dieting is contraindicated during early adolescence. Weight stabilization is recommended so that the adolescent may "grow out" of obesity as height increases.
	Adolescents beyond peak growth periods may lose one, or if very obese, two pounds per week (a calorie deficit of 500 to 1,000 Kcal/day).
Has the adolescent recently been on a weight reduction diet? What was the outcome?	Have the adolescent set realistic weight-loss goals, to be discussed during each visit (1–2 pounds per week weight loss).
Will family and friends support the adolescent's weight-loss program?	Make the adolescent and parents aware of the need for realistic weight loss.
	If possible, when treating an obese adolescent, involve the family or the primary adult responsible for buying and preparing the food.
What kinds of food is the adolescent consuming? What kinds of foods are served at home? What is the location of eating? Times of eating? Activities associated with eating? Speed of eating?	Have the adolescent keep an initial three-day food and activity record (see appendix A-5).
	Plan a diet with the adolescent, including three small meals and snacks. Plan an adequate intake of foods from the basic food groups (see appendix B-1). Suggest smaller portion sizes and substitutions for high-caloric foods (see appendix G-1).
	Allow limited intake of all foods, including higher-calorie popular "snacks," rather than attempt to achieve complete avoidance of any food. (See Table 16-1)

Table 17-1 continued

What is the exercise activity of the adolescent? Does the adolescent work? Engage in sports? School and social activities?	Have the adolescent agree to an ongoing activity (e.g., walk home from school three times a week).
	Develop a reward system for success, e.g., new clothes, movies, etc.
	Mutually agree to frequent follow-up visits (every 1–2 weeks) for counseling and weight monitoring. Have periodic food and activity records completed.

Evaluation

Examine the adolescent's food and activity record for positive changes in food intake, activities, and moods.

Discuss progress with the adolescent and re-evaluate weight-loss goals together.

If excess weight continues to be a serious problem, consider referring the adolescent to a behavior modification clinic or a clinic that provides weight-control sessions designed for adolescents, under the guidance of trained, experienced, and credible professionals.

II. UNDERWEIGHT

Primary causes of leanness in healthy adolescents are too few calories to support growth intake over an extended period of time, often coupled with high levels of physical activity.

Extreme leanness may be of great concern to the adolescent, especially to males who desire a muscular "athletic build."

Chemical use, food fads, emotional stress, or depression may contribute to underweight status.

Assessment	Action
What is the history and degree of underweight? Since childhood? During a growth spurt?	Set realistic goals for weight gain. These should not exceed one pound per week (an increase of 500 Kcal/day).[8]
Does underweight coincide with the growth spurt?	Reassure the adolescent that weight gain may be naturally forthcoming.
What kinds and amounts of food is the adolescent consuming?	Have the adolescent keep an initial and periodic food and activity record to evaluate the intake (see appendix A-5).
	Suggest frequent intake of basic foods of high-nutrient density, such as whole-grain breads, cereals, and pastas; nuts and peanut butter; dried fruits; and dairy products.
	Avoid excess consumption of foods containing high levels of sugar and fats, such as candy and butter. These may suppress appetite, raise blood lipids, and support fat rather than muscle gains.

Table 17-1 continued

What is the exercise activity of the adolescent?	Recommend exercise for lean tissue gain (e.g., walking).
What is the adolescent's motivation to gain weight?	Develop a reward system for success based on the adolescent's motivation.

Evaluation

Check weight at two-week or monthly intervals. Try to use the same scale at the same time of day and with the same amount of clothes. As weight gain is usually slow, frequent weight checks can be misleading and should be discouraged.

Examine the adolescent's food and activity record for a positive change in food intake.

Discuss progress with the adolescent and re-evaluate weight-gain goals. If a problem persists, refer to a registered dietitian (R.D.) for in-depth evaluation.

III. ANOREXIA NERVOSA AND BULIMIA

Eating disorders among adolescents have become so prevalent that they are regarded as a serious public health problem.[9]

Males, particularly athletes in such weight-related sports as wrestling, may also develop anorexia and bulimia.

Anorexia nervosa is a psychiatric disorder in which a disturbed body image and severe food restriction result in significant weight loss.

Induced vomiting may be used to augment weight loss.

Anorexia is found primarily in Caucasians but appears to be occurring at an increasingly younger age and among all socioeconomic and cultural groups.[10]

Bulimia involves recurrent episodes of binge-eating (rapid ingestion of a large amount of food within a short period of time).

Vomiting may be induced after eating binges to relieve discomfort and in an attempt to prevent weight gain.

Laxative or diuretic abuse and severe caloric restrictions may also be part of the binge-purge cycle.[11]

Individuals with bulimia may be obese or of normal weight, and they often experience rapid weight fluctuations.

Assessment	Action
Is weight below 15% of expected weight for height and age?	Set a weight-range goal of 90% of expected weight[12] (see appendix D).
What is the dieting history?	Have the adolescent keep a three-day food and activity record to evaluate intake.
	Review intake together with the adolescent and mutually agree to goals for eating behavior change and weight gain.

Table 17-1 continued

Does the adolescent report episodes of "binge eating"?	Plan a diet with the adolescent, with three or four meals a day, but include some "binge foods."
Does the adolescent claim to feel "too fat" even though underweight? Is there evidence of self-induced vomiting or use of laxatives? Is there an obsession with body shape and weight?	Discussion with the school psychologist and/or concurrent behavioral therapy may be indicated to facilitate a realistic perception of body image.

Evaluation

Monitor maintenance of weight gain during subsequent visits.

Review the food and activity record with the adolescent to determine if the quality and amount of intake have improved.

In females, if underweight persists, menstrual cycles are being missed, and the problem does not appear to be diminishing, refer the adolescent immediately for further evaluation and intervention, especially if weight falls below 25% for height.

IV. ADOLESCENT PREGNANCY (see also chapter 5, Pregnancy and Lactation)

Adolescents who are pregnant within two years of menarche may still be experiencing appreciable growth, and maternal-fetal competition for nutrients may occur.[13]

The adolescent who enters pregnancy with inferior nutritional habits may be at a disadvantage.

Weight gain to support pregnancy is approximately 20% above standard weight for height for normal-weight adolescents.[14]

Inadequate weight gain may occur in adolescents who have an intense desire for thinness, who may be denying or attempting to conceal their pregnancy, who have inadequate food resources, or who are abusing chemicals.

Cigarette smoking, alcohol drinking, and substance abuse during adolescent pregnancy have been associated with a decrease in infant birthweight and with other complications.[15,16]

Assessment	Action
What is the preconceptional weight history of the adolescent? Underweight? Overweight?	Weigh the adolescent at each visit and record the weight on the weight-gain grid (see Figures 3-1 and 5-1).
What is the growth status of the adolescent?	See chapter 15.
Is there sufficient weight gain? Too great a gain in weight?	See Table 5-1, Sections II, III and IV.
Is there a presence of nausea and vomiting?	See Table 5-1, Section I.
Are there food aversions, food intolerances, or a pica practice?	See Table 5-1, Section VII.

Table 17-1 continued

What is the caffeine intake of the adolescent?	See Table 5-1, Section V.
	Have the adolescent complete a nutrition questionnaire (see appendix A-1).
	Plan a diet with the adolescent that includes foods needed for pregnancy, plus food needed for adolescent growth and development (see appendix B-1).
Are protein or ketones present in the urine?	Increase quality protein foods and plan for sufficient calories and increased intake of complex carbohydrates (grains, cereals, fruits, vegetables) to achieve appropriate weight gain and prevent ketosis.
What are the hemoglobin and hematocrit levels?	A prenatal vitamin and mineral supplement containing zinc, folate, and iron may be advisable.
What support systems does the adolescent have?	Direct the adolescent to a provider of early and continuous prenatal care for pregnant adolescents, as needed. It may be advisable to try to draw on a family member such as grandmother or older sister to help the adolescent.

Evaluation

Monitor weight gain during subsequent visits.

Review the food and activity record (see appendix A-5) with the adolescent to determine if the quality of the diet is adequate for her growth and development and support of the fetus.

If the adolescent is unwilling or unable to increase intake of calcium-containing foods—especially dairy products—a calcium supplement may be indicated. Refer to a physician.

Refer the adolescent to providers of prenatal care for follow-up for such problems as edema, protein in urine, and excessive vomiting.

V. SUBSTANCE ABUSE

Extensive use of alcohol and drugs and cigarette smoking may adversely affect nutritional status and compromise adolescent growth and development.

Calorie requirements may be increased in growing adolescents who are smoking heavily.[17]

Assessment	Action
What kinds of food is the adolescent consuming? What is their nutritional quality? Quantity?	Have the adolescent keep an initial and periodic food and activity record and evaluate intake (see appendix A-5).
Is the adolescent losing weight? How much and over what period of time?	Plan a diet with the adolescent that will emphasize high-nutrient-dense foods (see Section II on underweight problems).

Table 17-1 continued

	Help the adolescent set realistic goals to increase nutrient intake.
What is the substance abuse record of the adolescent?	Refer to appropriate agencies.
Ask nonjudgmental questions, e.g., How often do you drink wine, wine coolers, beer, or liquor? How many drinks do you consume when you drink? How often do you use street drugs? What kind do you use?	

Evaluation

Examine the adolescent's food and activity record for positive changes in food intake, activities, and moods.

Discuss any progress in diet improvement with the adolescent and together re-evaluate goals to increase nutrient intake.

If weight loss and physical complaints continue, the adolescent should be referred for further follow-up.

VI. PREVENTION OF CARDIAC DISEASE (see also chapter 14)

Elevated serum cholesterol levels and hypertension have been observed among adolescents.

Atherosclerotic lesions begin in early childhood, but the process appears to be accelerated in conjunction with the rapid growth and development of the adolescent, especially the male.

Adolescence is a critical time to intervene with regard to factors that may predispose to coronary heart disease at a later age.

Efforts at dietary modifications appear to be warranted.

Normal weight patterns and physical fitness should be encouraged.[18]

Assessment	Action
If there is a family history of elevated blood lipids and/or hypertension, assess the adolescent for these problems.	Take routine blood lipids and blood pressure readings or, if necessary, refer the adolescent to a clinic for lipid readings (see Table 12-3).
Assess the current nutritional pattern with regard to high-fat dairy products and meats and high-salt and high-sodium foods, such as cured meats and salty snacks.	Have the adolescent complete a food and activity record (see appendix A-5).
	Mutually plan with the adolescent a diet with reduced salt, fat, and sugar intake (see Table 16-1).
	Suggest realistic changes, e.g., eliminate one problem food per week and replace it with a tasty substitute.
	Plan a follow-up visit to evaluate results of suggested diet changes.

Table 17-1 continued

Evaluation

Blood pressure and lipid readings should be monitored during subsequent vists to evaluate for positive change.

Review the diet with the adolescent and assess for change in food intake.

See chapter 14 for additional information on prevention of cardiac disease.

If adolescent is at risk and has elevated serum cholesterol or hypertension, refer to a physician and registered dietitian (R.D.) for in-depth follow-up.

VII. ADOLESCENT VEGETARIANISM (see also chapter 14)

Concern for life or ecology or religious reasons may motivate the adolescent to follow a vegetarian diet.

The adolescent may wish to avoid only red meats. This practice may not have a negative influence on health and may in fact be beneficial in reducing saturated fat and cholesterol intake.

Lacto or lacto-ovo-vegetarian diets, which include milk and/or milk and eggs, can be nutritionally adequate if the meals and snacks are well-planned. Eating only plant foods (vegan) can be harmful (see appendix H).

Assessment	Action
If vegetarianism is identified during the dietary assessment, follow-up questions should be asked:	Have the adolescent keep a food and activity record (see appendix A-5) for further evaluation.
Do you eat red meats? Do you eat other meats? Do you eat fish and poultry?	
Do you eat eggs and cheese and drink milk?	If the diet includes only milk and cheese (lacto) or milk and eggs (lacto-ovo), alternative iron sources should be recommended, such as iron-fortified cereals, whole-grain or enriched breads; legumes (dried beans, peas, lentils, or peanuts); and dried fruits and leafy, green vegetables.[19]
Do you not eat any of the above (vegan)?	If only plant foods are consumed (vegan), skillful combining of foods is needed. For example, legumes (low in tryptophan and methionine) can be combined with grain products (wheat, rice, corn, rye, oats, and barley) to yield a protein of higher biological value; fortified soybean milks can be used to supply calcium and vitamin B_{12}; and fortified soya meat analogs can provide protein and vitamin B_{12}. Supplemental vitamin B_{12}, D, calcium, iron, or iodine may also be required. Refer to a physician.

Table 17-1 continued

Evaluation

Review intake during subsequent visits to evaluate adequacy of the diet. Monitor growth and iron status.

Intensive dietary counseling and follow-up are recommended for adolescents following vegan diets. Refer to a registered dietitian (R.D.).

VIII. ADOLESCENT SPORTS PARTICIPATION (see also chapter 14)

Nutrient needs:

> A balanced intake of basic foods will provide nutrients for growth, maintenance, and increased physical activity.

> High-protein intakes do not improve athletic performance and may in fact result in anorexia and dehydration.

> Vitamin requirements are not significantly affected by physical activity, and vitamin supplementation is not indicated. Large doses will not increase athletic performance, and they may be toxic.

> Strenuous physical activity may be associated with iron deficiency, particularly among females, whose participation in such activity should be closely monitored.

> The achievement of standard weight for height and recommended body-fat composition requires a long-term program involving training and dietary changes initiated several months prior to the athletic season.

> Specific guidelines on nutrient needs in adolescent sports participants have been issued by the American College of Sports Medicine.[20]

Fluid and electrolyte intake during sports:

> Adequate fluid intake and the prevention of dehydration are critical for energy metabolism and maximum athletic performance.

> Dangers of water loss include cramps, fatigue, and exhaustion, while severe depletion can result in heat stroke and death.[21]

> After strenuous exercise, 16 ounces of fluid per pound of weight lost will restore water balance.

> Electrolyte replacement after an event can be easily achieved with balanced meals.

> Salt tablets may cause hypernatremia and dehydration and are contraindicated.

> Commercially available electrolyte-containing drinks are also not recommended, since their hypertonicity may depress thirst, delay gastric emptying, and reduce water absorption.

Carbohydrate-loading:

> Glycogen-loading appears to promote muscle and hepatic glycogen supercompensation.

> Simply increasing complex carbohydrate intake to approximately 75% of calories the day before an event is an effective and safe approach for the school-age athlete.

Pregame meals:

> A light meal of high complex carbohydrate content three or four hours prior to an event is recommended to ensure gastric emptying, minimum nausea and cramping, and prevention of respiratory and cardiac stress.

> Heavy meals of high protein or fat content and the consumption of carbonated beverages and foods high in fiber are not recommended.

Table 17-1 continued

Concentrated carbohydrates, such as honey or sweetened beverages, should be avoided one hour prior to athletic events because they rapidly elevate blood sugar and may result in premature exhaustion of glycogen and decreased performance.[22]

A carbohydrate source is recommended during endurance events of four hours or longer. Dilute glucose solutions or the newer beverages containing glucose polymers may be used.[23]

Food fads, myths, and ergogenic aids:

In an attempt to improve athletic performance or endurance, young athletes may resort to ineffective, costly, and potentially dangerous "ergogenic" aids.

These include supplements such as vitamin E, wheat germ oil, honey, bee pollen, or Brewer's yeast.

There are great health risks in the use of amphetamines and anabolic or androgenic steroids. All of these practices are contraindicated.[24]

Assessment	Action
Is the energy intake adequate for the adolescent's growth activity level?	Have the adolescent keep a three-day food diary to assess food intake and activity level (see appendix A-5). Review intake from the food record with the adolescent. Estimate calorie needs using appendix E.
Are the protein, fat, and carbohydrate intakes adequate?	Review intake of proteins, fat, and carbohydrates. Explain that desirable intakes for athletes can be in the range of 13–26% fat, 64–75% carbohydrate, and 10–12% protein.
Is the iron intake adequate?	Emphasize the need for adequate dietary iron and recommend sources.
What is the weight-loss and weight-gain history?	Explain to the athlete that, due to the need for growth, energy intake needs to be as high as 5,000 k/cal per day in some adolescents who participate in strenuous athletic activity.
Is the adolescent using any weight-control strategies? Are they safe? Do they provide sufficient nutritional intake?	If a fad or "quick" weight-loss diet has been followed, discuss the need for a balanced, somewhat caloric-restricted diet to maintain muscle mass and adequate growth.
Is there evidence of the presence of bulimia in the adolescent athlete who wishes to reduce weight? Is amenorrhea present?	Plan an appropriate diet with the adolescent, adapted to the adolescent's eating habits, body needs, and level of activity.
Is there adequate fluid intake during athletic performance? Is there evidence of dehydration?	Discuss fluid needs and types of fluid.

Table 17-1 continued

Is the adolescent using supplemental vitamins, minerals, or steroids in an effort to "build" the body?	Discuss the dangers of excess supplemental nutrients and steroids.
Is the athlete following harmful food fads or using ergogenic aids?	Discuss the dangers of undesirable eating practices.

Evaluation

Examine the adolescent athlete's food and activity record at regular intervals to ensure adequate food and nutrient intake.

Check weight at regular intervals.

If dehydration is suspected, check the urine for specific gravity.

If the adolescent is losing weight, check the percentage of body fat.[25]

If further intervention is needed, a registered dietitian (R.D.) specializing in sports nutrition can help in setting up an individualized program for weight loss/gain, optimal distribution of calories, fluid schedules, and other related goals.

NOTES

1. J. Pennington and H. Nichols Church, *Food Values of Portions Commonly Used*, 14th ed. (New York: Harper & Row, 1985), 1–186.

2. L. Mahan, "Physical Fitness, Athletics, and the Adolescent," in *Nutrition in Adolescence*, ed. L. Mahan and J. Rees (St. Louis, Mo.: C.V. Mosby Co., 1984), 147–148.

3. American Academy of Pediatrics, Committee on Nutrition, "Calcium Requirements in Infancy and Childhood," *Pediatrics* 62 (1978): 826.

4. R. Sandler et al., "Postmenopausal Bone Density and Milk Consumption in Childhood and Adolescence," *American Journal of Clinical Nutrition* 42 (1985): 270.

5. J.A. Olson and R. Hodges, "Recommended Dietary Intakes (RDI) of Vitamin C in Humans," *American Journal of Clinical Nutrition* 45 (1987): 693.

6. J. Brasel, "Factors that Affect Nutritional Requirements in Adolescence," in *Nutritional Disorders of American Women*, ed. M. Winick (New York: John Wiley & Sons, 1977), 60.

7. J. Mayer, "Overweight: Causes, Cost and Control," in *Obesity in Adolescence*, ed. J. Mayer (Englewood Cliffs, N.J.: Prentice-Hall, 1968), 130.

8. N. Smith, "Nutrition and Athletic Performance," *Medical Times* 109 (1981): 92.

9. J. Borgen and C. Corbin, "Eating Disorders Among Female Athletes," *Physician and Sports Medicine* 15 (1987): 80.

10. A. Anderson, "Anorexia Nervosa and Bulimia in Adolescent Males," *Pediatric Annals* 13 (1984): 901.

11. K. Halmi, "Anorexia Nervosa and Bulimia," *Psychosomatics* 24 (1983): 111.

12. D. Garner et al., "Psychoeducational Principles in the Treatment of Bulimia and Anorexia Nervosa," in *Handbook of Psychotherapy for Anorexia Nervosa and Bulimia*, ed. D. Garner (New York: Guilford Press, 1985), 543.

13. A. Frisancho, J. Matos, and L. Bolletina, "Influence of Growth Status and Placental Function in Birth Weight of Infants Born to Young, Still-Growing Teenagers," *American Journal of Clinical Nutrition* 40 (1984): 801.

14. P. Rosso, "A New Chart to Monitor Weight Gain During Pregnancy," *American Journal of Clinical Nutrition* 41 (1985): 644.

15. Z. Stein and J. Kline, "Smoking, Alcohol and Reproduction," *American Journal of Public Health* 73 (1983): 1154.

16. K. Tennes, "Effects of Marijuana in Pregnancy and Fetal Development in the Human," *National Institute on Drug Abuse Research Monograph* 44 (1984): 115.

17. J. Wack and J. Rodin, "Smoking and Its Effects on Body Weight and Systems of Calorie Regulators," *American Journal of Clinical Nutrition* 35 (1982): 373.

18. J. Dwyer, "Diets for Children and Adolescents That Meet the Dietary Goals," *American Journal of Diseases of Children* 134 (1980): 1073.

19. A. Helman and I. Darnton-Hill, "Vitamin and Iron Status in New Vegetarians," *American Journal of Clinical Nutrition* 45 (1987): 785.

20. "American College of Sports Medicine Position Stand on Weight Loss," *Wrestlers Medicine and Science in Sports* 8 (1976): 11.

21. N. Smith, "Nutrition and Athletic Performance," *Primary Care* 11 (1984): 33.

22. D. Elliot and L. Goldberg, "Nutrition and Exercise," *Medical Clinics of North America* 69 (1985): 71.

23. P. Dyment, "The Adolescent Athlete and Ergogenic Aids," *Journal of Adolescent Health Care* 8 (1987): 68.

24. Ibid., 69.

25. M.D. Simko, C. Cowell, and J. Gilbride, *Nutrition Assessment: A Comprehensive Guide for Planning Intervention* (Rockville, Md.: Aspen Publishers, Inc., 1984), 69–92.

Part VII

The Adult

Chapter 18

Nutrition Assessment
of the Adult

George Christakis

OVERVIEW

Nutrition assessment of the adult is primarily directed toward diagnosing:

- malnutrition, due either to dietary deficiencies or to specific clinical states or diseases
- nutritional determinants of chronic diseases, such as risk factors of coronary heart disease, hypertension, diabetes, or cancer, all of which relate to specific eating or lifestyle behaviors
- excess intake of total fat, including saturated fat and cholesterol, as well as sodium

In 1988, *The Surgeon General's Report on Nutrition and Health* focused national attention on nutritional determinants of chronic diseases.[1] (A discussion of these determinants appears in chapter 1.) The health care practitioner thus has clear evidence that diet has an influence on health. In particular, the continuing prevalence of inadequate intakes of vitamin C, and of iron, folic acid, and calcium in subgroups of adults in the United States has been documented.[2] In addition, there is evidence that specific protein, vitamin, and mineral deficiencies among hospitalized and clinic clients is more prevalent than had previously been recognized.[3] At the other end of the spectrum, overconsumption practices are causing dietary imbalances that contribute to the leading causes of illness and death, including coronary heart disease, hypertension, stroke, diabetes mellitus, atherosclerosis and, some types of cancer.

The primary reason for assessing nutritional status in the adult is to determine whether it is normal or abnormal. This requires the utilization of all methods of assessment: health history, physical examination, anthropometry, laboratory data, and dietary history.

HEALTH HISTORY

The individual health history provides valuable data for the overall nutrition assessment. The lifestyle of the adult is a key factor in food consumption and subsequent health status. (Chapter 19 discusses a variety of adult lifestyles and their implications for health through adequate or inadequate nutritional intake.)

In particular, the family or individual health history of disease has important implications in the evaluation of the adult's nutritional status. Table 18-1 provides guidelines for assessing cardiovascular disease, diabetes, and cancer components in the adult health history. Chapter 20 (Table 20-1) presents common nutritional problems of the adult and suggests modes of intervention for selected problems. Chapter 20 also discusses the Health Belief Model and the client's perception of vulnerability based on risk factors identified in the health history.

PHYSICAL ASSESSMENT

The physical examination is an important technique for assessing nutritional status. A well-trained health care practitioner can make this assessment; however, considerable skill and perception are needed to identify the subtle signs of malnutrition. Also, adequate time is needed to conduct a comprehensive examination, since each area of the body must be closely assessed.

The physical assessment requires a well-organized and careful inspection of the body. It begins with an evaluation of the head and the hair color and texture. The hair should be examined to see if it is dry, oily, and pluckable. The eyes and eyebrows, including any slight eversion of the lower lids of the eyes, should be examined to assess the color and presence of lesions on the mucosal tissue. The eye inspection should include examination of the bulbar conjunctivae for Bitot's spots, xerosis for dryness of the conjunctivae, and glistening for normal tear circulation.

The cornea of the eye should be inspected for xerosis and softness, which may cause a "jiggle"; this would be a clinical sign of severe vitamin A deficiency, often seen in populations of developing countries. To complete the eye assessment, a fundiscopic examination should be made to check for nutritional amblyopia and evidence of retinal artery lesions. If there is excessive straightening of the arteries, retinal hemorrhages, and exudates, these are signs of hypertension. Lesions of microaneurysms are clinical signs of diabetes. The skin around the eyes should be examined for xanthelasma, that is, raised yellow or white lesions that contain cholesterol deposits identified as Type II familial hyperlipoproteinemia. Both corners of the eyes should be inspected for swelling and redness of the lids, angular blepharitis, or palpebritis.

The physical examination moves downward to the nose and nostrils, which should be checked for excessive oil production of sebaceous glands associated with riboflavin deficiency. Also, the lips should be inspected for cheilosis and angular fissures, which are evidence of insufficient riboflavin, niacin, and iron. Using a tongue blade, the edge and surface of the protruded tongue should be inspected for ridges and color. Excessive redness, a "beefy red," is a clue to iron and folic acid deficiency, and pallor may indicate anemia. A magenta-colored or purple tongue may mean a riboflavin deficiency. The examination should include a check for swelling, as in glossitis or "baldness" or the loss of normal filiform papillae (the taste buds), since there may be atrophy and hypertrophy, which can affect the taste and flavor of food.

Using the tongue blade, the examiner should gently lift the internal aspect of the lips throughout the mouth, exposing the teeth for a check for pitting or mottling, and observe the gums for interdental hypertrophy. If these are noted, the tongue blade should be used to tap the swollen gums to determine if they are friable and bleed. For patients wearing dentures, the inspection should determine if they are fitting properly.

The examination continues down to the neck and thyroid gland. The thyroid gland should be inspected for enlargement. The carotid artery should be palpated to determine the forcefulness of pulsations bilaterally. The stethoscope should be applied to the area where the pulse is best felt in order to ascultate evidence of atherosclerotic plaque involvement.

Next, the lungs should be auscultated for evidence of congestive heart failure, which may be the result of a thiamin deficiency. The heart should be examined for heart murmurs, arrhythmias, and heart enlargement.

The physical assessment then moves to the abdomen, which should be palpated to detect liver enlargement, as has been observed in extreme form as in kwashiorkor. An abbreviated neurological examination should attempt to diagnose peripheral neuropathy and subacute combined degeneration of the spinal cord, which may result from a vitamin B_{12} deficiency. A complete neurological examination is indicated for alcoholic clients to detect evidence of thiamine deficiency, as in Wernicke's and Korsakoff's syndromes.

Finally, the physical examination moves to an evaluation of the skin and nails. Many vitamin and mineral deficiencies can be indicated by skin signs. These include deficiencies of vitamins A, D, K, and B_{12} and of folic acid, iron, and calcium. Deficiencies of protein, calcium, and iron can affect the nails. A deficiency of linoleic acid, an essential fatty acid, results in dry skin.

The physical examination in the nutrition assessment of adults provides an opportunity for the development for diagnostic skills to identify even subtle clinical signs and symptoms (see appendix C-1 for clinical signs associated with nutritional deficiencies.)

Table 18-1 Nutritional Risk Factors of Chronic Disease To Be Evaluated in the Nutrition Assessment of the Adult

Disease	Dietary and Health History	Clinical Examination	Laboratory Determination
Cardiovascular disease			
Coronary heart disease (CHD)	Family History of myocardial infarction angina elevated serum cholesterol elevated triglyceride levels diabetes mellitus Personal Practices of smoking excessive saturated fat and dietary cholesterol intake inadequate polyunsaturated fat intake inadequate dietary fiber intake	Obesity Xanthelesma, xanthomas Electrocardiographic evidence of CHD Positive stress test Type A behavioral pattern	Elevated serum cholesterol, LDL cholesterol, triglycerides, uric acid Low HDL cholesterol Positive glucose tolerance test
Hypertension	Family History of hypertension Personal Practices of excessive salt intake in salt sensitive persons inadequate calcium intake inadequate potassium and magnesium intake	Obesity Elevated blood pressure	Protein urea Elevated blood urea nitrogen (BUN)

	Family History		Elevated fasting or post-prandial blood sugar
Diabetes	Family History	Obesity	Glycosuria
Cancer (colon, breast, prostate)	Family History of Cancer Personal Practices of 　smoking 　inadequate unsaturated fat 　excessive nitrosamine 　　intake 　inadequate dietary fiber 　excessive caloric intake in 　　women (uterine cancer) 　excessive smoked foods 　excessive alcohol	Obesity	

ANTHROPOMETRIC ASSESSMENT

The anthropometric evaluation is an important part of the nutritional assessment of the adult. Together with the dietary history (see chapter 20), selected laboratory studies and the physical examination, anthropometric data can provide an indication of current, and to a certain extent, past nutritional status. There are four purposes in performing anthropometry on the adult:

1. to contribute to the overall nutritional evaluation of the adult
2. to evaluate adults who may present with any of a wide range of diseases (see Table 18-1), who have received medical and surgical treatments, or who have various degrees of protein/calorie or micronutrient deficiencies
3. to evaluate the obese adult
4. to provide baseline data for future assessments

Anthropometric examinations can be performed in outpatient clinics, during routine physical examinations or follow-up office visits, or on hospital admission. The examination is relatively easy to make, is inexpensive, and, when taken with care, contributes important data to both nutrition and clinical assessment.

Health care practitioners should be aware that anthropometric evaluations can provide a valuable means of documenting nutritional status. Furthermore, undernutrition or malnutrition may in fact be secondary to such disease states as pancreatic insufficiency or celiac disease and not due to primary food deprivation. It is thus important to combine information from the anthropometric assessment with medical and dietary histories, laboratory values and the results of the physical examination, keeping also in mind environmental factors, such as socioeconomic status, and genetic factors (for example, cystic fibrosis) that can influence growth and development.

Another important reason why the anthropometric examination should be viewed as part of a routine, overall clinical assessment is the need to detect subtle diagnostic distinctions. For example, the measurement of the parameters of subscapular skinfold thickness, as assessed in many clinical and research situations, may be falsely increased with edema or subcutaneous emphysema; further, alterations in such measurements can occur with changes in a patient's hydration. A decrease in protein stores may be matched by an increase in fluid stores because of ascites or edema and therefore result in minimal weight change. Thus, simply looking at skinfold data alone may be deceiving; other measurements are needed to verify the assessment.

Anthropometric data are especially useful in detecting undernutrition before signs of visible variations appear. However, obesity, the most frequent form of malnutrition in the United States, can also be detected as a precursor to various health hazards, such as coronary artery disease and hypertension, through the use of anthropometric data.

Body weight can be used in several ways to assess the degree of malnutrition or overweight. Body weight is usually compared with tables of ideal body weights specific for height and frame size (see Table 18-2). One way of assessing for malnutrition is to take the current weight as a percentage of ideal body weight. This percentage is calculated as current weight ÷ ideal weight × 100 = percent; 80 to 90 percent indicates mild caloric malnutrition, 70 to 79 percent indicates moderate malnutrition, and 0 to 69 percent indicates severe malnutrition.

While mid-arm muscle circumference (MAMC) is a good indicator of total body protein stores, MAMC by itself does not necessarily mean inadequate nutrition or protein malnutrition. Even with nutritional adequacy, muscle can decrease through disease atrophy, for example, in cases of hospitalized or chronically ill individuals with cardiac, pulmonary, or neuromuscular disease, arthritic damage, or central nervous system impairments. In this connection, detailed anthropometric techniques have been discussed by Robbins and Trowbridge.[4]

LABORATORY ASSESSMENT

Laboratory values are integrated with the dietary history, physical examination, and anthropometric data to provide a comprehensive basis for evaluation. For the assessment of protein/calorie nutriture, the following laboratory values are used: creatinine-height index, serum albumin, prealbumin or retinal binding protein, serum transferrin, total lymphocyte count, delayed skin hypersensitivity, and urinary urea nitrogen.

Biochemical and microbiological assay methods can detect specific hypovitaminosis, while vitamin absorption spectrophomatic data can detect mineral deficiencies. Liquid chromatographic and high pressure liquid chromatographic methods are used in other types of nutrient analysis (see appendix C-2 for selected assessment and diagnostic implications).

SUMMARY

Nutrition assessment of the adult provides an opportunity for individualized health promotion. In order to be effective, however, it must necessarily become a routine part of every health examination. The health care practitioner's role is to evaluate whether the individual has normal nutritional status as a basis for good health. The consumer looks to the health care profession for direction to this end.

Table 18-2 Height-Weight Tables for Men and Women

Metropolitan Life Insurance Company Height-Weight Data, Revised 1983

		Women Frame*					Men Frame*		
Height Ft	In	Small	Medium	Large	Height Ft	In	Small	Medium	Large
4	10	102-111	109-121	118-131	5	2	128-134	131-141	138-150
4	11	103-113	111-123	120-134	5	3	130-136	133-143	140-153
5	0	104-115	113-126	122-137	5	4	132-138	135-145	142-156
5	1	106-118	115-129	125-140	5	5	134-140	137-148	144-160
5	2	108-121	118-132	128-143	5	6	136-142	139-151	146-164
5	3	111-124	121-135	131-147	5	7	138-145	142-154	149-168
5	4	114-127	124-138	134-151	5	8	140-148	145-157	152-172
5	5	117-130	127-141	137-155	5	9	142-151	148-160	155-176
5	6	120-133	130-144	140-159	5	10	144-154	151-163	148-180
5	7	123-136	133-147	143-163	5	11	146-157	154-166	161-184
5	8	126-139	136-150	146-167	6	0	149-160	157-170	164-188
5	9	129-142	139-153	149-170	6	1	152-164	160-174	168-192
5	10	132-145	142-156	152-173	6	2	155-168	164-178	172-197
5	11	135-148	145-159	155-176	6	3	158-172	167-182	176-202
6	0	138-151	148-162	158-179	6	4	162-176	171-187	181-207

Based on a weight-height mortality study conducted by the Society of Actuaries and the Association of Life Insurance Medical Directors of America, Metropolitan Life Insurance Company, revised 1983.
*Weights at ages 25 to 59 based on lowest mortality. Height includes 1-in heel. Weight for women includes 3 lb for indoor clothing. Weight for men includes 5 lb for indoor clothing.

Source: Courtesy of Metropolitan Life Insurance Company

NOTES

1. *The Surgeon General's Report on Nutrition and Health* (Washington, D.C.: U.S. Department of Health and Human Service, Public Health Service, 1988).

2. Nutrition Monitoring in the United States—A Report from the Joint Nutrition Monitoring Evaluation Committee (Washington, D.C.: US Department of Health and Human Services and US Department of Agriculture, July, 1986).

3. G.L. Blackburn and H.B. Harvey, "Nutritional Assessment as a Routine in Clinical Medicine," *Postgraduate Medicine* 71 (1982): 46–63.

4. G.E. Robbins and F.L. Trowbridge, "Anthropometric Techniques and Their Applications," in *Nutrition Assessment: A Comprehensive Guide for Planning Intervention*, eds. M.D. Simko, C. Cowell, and J.A. Gilbride (Rockville, Md.: Aspen Publishers, Inc. 1984), 69–92.

Chapter 19

Environmental Management
of the Adult

Cheryl A. Fisher

OVERVIEW

Adult eating patterns are affected not only by economic factors but also by social and psychological factors. The environment in which the adult resides plays a major role in terms of access or barriers to good nutrition and therefore needs to be assessed by the health care practitioner. For example, the increased number of women in the work force and the increasing number of single parents may be significant factors influencing U.S. dietary habits. Similarly, men in the office setting and men in more physically demanding jobs will have different nutritional needs and different opportunities for access to good nutrition. Thus, by assessing the adults' environment, the health care practitioner can anticipate existing nutritional deficits and make recommendations to overcome dietary barriers.

ENVIRONMENTAL ASSESSMENT

Eating habits should be evaluated with regard to existing beliefs about health and the personal and environmental influences that do or do not support such beliefs. An environmental evaluation focused on nutrition is essential for identifying eating patterns, attitudes, food availability, and general nutritional health. According to Wheeler, the following information should be included in such an assessment:[1]

- a general picture of the individual's home and work environments, including personal relationships, support systems, number of persons living in the household, economic situation, and cultural or religious influences
- lifestyle habits
- social relationships

- fitness level and amount of exercise
- psychological influences on food habits, such as eating as a response to moods or emotions and special, personal meanings attached to particular foods
- attitudes, values, and beliefs about diet, health, and well-being
- exposure to hazardous materials and allergic reactions

A lifestyle or nutrition questionnaire can be used to collect most of this information (see appendix A-1).

INTERVENTIONS

Women

Working Women

The increasing trend toward women working outside the home has prompted several changes in eating behaviors among such women.[2] These changes include frequent meal skipping, an increased frequency of eating-out and an increase in the buying and consumption of convenience foods.

Several studies have indicated that the omission of breakfast or the consumption of an inadequate breakfast can contribute to dietary inadequacies. Particularly because of current concern about the overconsumption of some dietary components—for example, fat, cholesterol, sugar, and sodium—and the underconsumption of some vitamins and minerals, the eating of breakfast has been identified as an important factor in nutritional well-being. One study reported that approximately 29 percent of the women surveyed skipped the breakfast meal but that those who consumed a variety of foods—for example, bread and coffee, eggs and toast, or cereal and milk—were less likely to skip breakfast.[3] The omission of breakfast, particularly among adult females, results in significantly lower total daily intake levels of iron, calcium, pyridoxine, zinc, magnesium, and copper. It is also apparent that the consumption of ready-to-eat cereals improves the average daily intake levels of these nutrients.

Among working women, lunch is also neglected, although not as frequently as breakfast. In many work facilities, female workers hope to reduce their caloric intake through limited food selection, but in the process they sacrifice essential nutrients (see Table 20-1, Section VII). When food choices are restricted at lunch, the basic essential foods must be either included in the morning and evenings meals or remain unconsumed.

Another trend noted among working women is the increased incidence of dining out. A Gallup study has found that, of all female patrons eating lunch out, about seven in ten (69 percent) are likely to be full-time or part-time workers. For lunch in fast-food restaurants, the proportion drops to six in ten (61 percent). On the other hand, for the average on-premise company cafeteria, the proportion of working women is likely to increase to eight in ten (82 percent).[4] Another Gallup study reported that the market for take-out food has been growing rapidly, particularly among working women; for the dinner meal, women with jobs outside the home who buy take-out foods outnumber other women by a ratio of six to four.[5] All of these trends are expected to continue as more women enter the work force.

With the expanded consumption of meals away from home, consumer interest in the nutritional content of restaurant meals has increased. This has occurred in the midst of a new health and fitness awareness in the U.S. population.[6] The growing interest is reflected not only in the decision of whether to eat out, but also in decisions about where to eat and what foods to select; 75 to 85 percent of restaurant patrons who were surveyed indicated that nutrition was somewhat or very important in their deciding to eat out.[7] Here it should be noted that although restaurateurs are certainly interested in providing relevant nutrition information about their meals, the ultimate responsibility for their food choices lies with the patrons.

It is no secret that working women have greatly contributed to the success of the country's fast-food industry. Fast-food restaurants allow us to eat on the run and come as we are—all for a reasonable price, and often without even having to get out of the car. According to the U.S. Department of Agriculture, almost five out of every ten dollars we spend on restaurant food is spent at a fast-food restaurant.

Nutritionally what are the implications of this trend? Again it comes down to consumer selection. The breakfast meals available at most fast-food restaurants are not very healthful. For example, the average bacon and egg crescent sandwich provides 60 percent of its calories in the form of fat. In fact, the average fast-food item sold in such restaurants contains 40 to 50 percent fat. It also contains high calorie and sodium levels (this situation has recently been alleviated by the addition of salad-bar items by popular demand). A lunch meal consisting of a large hamburger with cheese, a chocolate shake, and fries contains all the protein and calories an average female might need in a day. It may also be deficient in dietary fiber, vitamin A, and vitamin C.[8]

Without nutrition labeling, it is impossible for consumers to know exactly what they are consuming. However, with some basic knowledge of salty, sugary, and fatty foods, it is still possible for the working woman to make wise choices (see Table 16-1).

Women at Home

Day-time meals for female homemakers with small children frequently are a day-to-day monotony of sandwiches and leftovers. This pattern is often the result of time constraints and neglect in meal planning, leading to indiscriminate snacking and malnutrition. One study revealed that 40 percent of homemakers skip at least one meal a day, putting them at equal risk for nutritional deficits with working women. They were less likely to skip breakfast because they were actively involved in getting breakfast for the family. In contrast, a factor affecting their choice of food for lunch was whether or not they would be eating alone.[9] If family members were present, they were more likely to partake of the meal with them.

Contrary to common belief, another study found that nonworking women were more likely to use convenience foods than were working women. This was especially true for canned or frozen foods.[10] Possible reasons suggested were that working women tend to have smaller families and the fact that the portion sizes for convenience foods are inconvenient for them. In such settings, the homemaker must be careful to avoid highly salty and fatty convenience items in her choice of foods.

The Single Parent

Although the total number of children living in families has been declining, the number of children who live with just one parent has been on the rise.[11] This can be attributed in part to the divorce rate and to the increase in single parenthood. Although both male- and female-headed one-parent families face the psychological and physical stresses of raising children without a spouse, it is usually the female-headed household that has the greater economic burden.[12] One might expect this additional hardship to take its toll on the nutritional adequacy of the diet in such households. Yet, from both the child's and the adult's perspective, single-parent household diets are about the same nutritionally as those in homes of lower-income working parents with children. This indicates that education may be more important than economics in the environmental management of a single parent's diet. In short, nutritionally balanced diets can be obtained economically through wise shopping and proper food combinations.

Men

The Male Office Worker

As with working women, special nutritional considerations must be taken into account in the nutrition assessment of male office workers. Like working women, working men often skip meals (especially breakfast), eat out, and consume fast foods. Also like working women, they have an increased interest in health and fitness.

In one study, 31.5 percent of the men surveyed were breakfast skippers. Again, those who chose the largest variety of breakfast foods were less likely to skip breakfast. Also, those who usually consumed breakfast were more likely to select foods at other meals that were nutrient-dense.[13] Unfortunately, as noted earlier, the choices available from most fast-food restaurants are often loaded with fat and sodium, and quick breakfast sandwiches are popular among the male population. Still, the cafeterias in places of business are now making a greater effort to identify foods with regard to their fat, sodium, cholesterol, and calorie content. Thus, employees at such worksites should be able to make better food choices when eating at the job.

Restaurant surveys have shown that men still prefer a heavier meal during the lunch hour than women do. Also, men are more likely to conduct business over lunch and to add alcoholic beverages, thereby increasing the caloric value of the meal or, in some cases, substituting alcohol for foods with essential nutrients. Again, the ultimate responsibility for food choices lies with the consumer. The properly motivated consumer will take an active role in improving nutrition by consulting with selected restaurants regarding their menu selections and food preparation.

Men in Physically Demanding Jobs

Men in physically demanding jobs have still other special needs and concerns in maintaining their nutritional well-being. Many mistakenly believe that additional amounts of protein are necessary for this group; in fact, only a small amount of additional protein is necessary, and that is usually included in the average American's diet.[14] The real need here is for additional protein-sparing calories, not for the proteins themselves. The extra caloric intake is necessary to meet the high energy needs of the men in this group.

The calories, however, must be consumed with caution. They should be chosen wisely in the form of nutrient-rich foods; this will help to generate energy and meet nutrient needs. Thus, the increased calories should be in the form of breads, cereals, fruits, vegetables, milk, and other nutritious foods.

Men in physically demanding jobs outdoors are also subject to temperature stress. Although there is no general agreement as to whether a hot environment alters metabolic rate and thus energy needs, it is suggested that, as the core temperature rises (as in the case of a fever), so does the need for calories. Further, if profuse sweating results from the hot environment, water, sodium, and nitrogen losses can result.

Often, for men in physically demanding jobs, the only available eating places are fast food restaurants, convenience stores or mobile lunch trucks. Again, the choices frequently are for foods high in fat, sodium, and calories. Yet the wisest choice could be made at home and brought to work in a brown bag or small cooler. This type of lunch could be supplemented with water and/or juices. Ultimately, such workers would make better food choices if they had proper nutrition training and motivation.

RECOMMENDATIONS

In evaluating the adult's environment with regard to access and barriers to good nutrition, a nutrition history can provide much useful information (see appendix A-1). With this tool, health care practitioners can consider the adult's food habits from a physical, social, economic, and environmental perspective. They can also evaluate the adult's existing knowledge about food and attitude regarding healthful eating.

Unfortunately, nutrition teaching is not always the best means of changing eating behaviors; increased knowledge is not always reflected in action. Thus, nutrition counseling is often necessary to take into account the individualized circumstances of the adult. Counseling may be particularly useful when assessing the nonworking adult or adults who are unable to participate in worksite nutrition programs.

In order to improve nutrition program effectiveness for mixed groups (for example, at the worksite) who vary in age, sex, and household status, the health care practitioner should look for common interests in food and nutrition. Ways should be found for the employees to share food and nutrition information with each other and with family members in order to promote new knowledge.[15] Group discussions and handouts on topics of nutrition can help in sharing the information learned and implementing the new knowledge in daily life.

The increased consumer interest in the nutritional content of restaurant meals should be encouraged and promoted. The consumer should be encouraged to take an active role in persuading restaurants to provide less fattening and more nutritious food choices. This approach has already shown some success with the addition of salad bars in fast-food restaurants. Other suggestions could be made, aimed at offering less fattening foods for breakfast in fast-food restaurants, providing nutrition information on restaurant menus, and preparing restaurant foods with unsaturated instead of saturated fats.

Favorable trends in food consumption during 1988 include evidence that cereal consumption is up. More poultry than beef is being consumed and purchase of snack foods is down. Market research indicates that the public is more interested in "foods for health," such as lower sodium containing foods and low fat beef. On the negative side, purchase of butter, margarine, ice cream, and frozen desserts has increased.[16] Being aware of food marketing trends can assist the health care practitioner to advise clients to purchase and serve more nutritious meals.

SUMMARY

In the environmental management of the adult's health and nutritional status, a positive approach that builds desirable food habits is preferable to a negative approach that merely corrects bad food habits. Despite work and family schedules, healthy food choices are still possible. To this end, health care practitioners can be effective in combating misinformation and in helping consumers in selecting a nutritious diet based on their work and home situation.[17] In this effort, it is important to start with present habits, reinforce the good aspects, and replace less desirable habits with more healthy habits. Health care practitioners must recognize that good diets do not just happen; they are planned.

NOTES

1. B. Wheeler, "Nutritional Assessment," in *Health Promotion in the Workplace*, ed. M. O'Donnell and T. Ainsworth (New York: John Wiley & Sons, 1984), 129–183.

2. For additional information on this trend, see A.T. Cross, *Nutrition for the Working Woman* (New York, NY: Simon & Schuster, 1986).

3. K. Morgan, M. Zabik, and G. Stampley, "The Role of Breakfast in Diet Adequacy of the U.S. Adult Population," *Journal of the American College of Nutrition* 5 (1986): 551–563.

4. L. Wood, "Dining Habits of Working Women Will Play Key Role in the Future," *Independent Restaurants,* January 1984: 23–24.

5. Ibid., 24.

6. B.L. Carlson and M.H. Tabacchi, "Meeting Consumer Nutrition Information Needs in Restaurants," *Journal of Nutrition Education* 18 (1986): 211–213.

7. Ibid., 212.

8. M.F. Jocobson and S. Fritschner, *The Fast-Food Guide* (New York: Workman Publishing, 1986), 132.

9. "Study of Food Habits," *Aspects of Social Nutrition,* March 1979: 15–22.

10. "What's Happening to Mealtime U.S.A.?" *Community Nutrition Institute Weekly Report,* June 1979: 4–6.

11. M.F. Epstein, "Children Living in One-Parent Families," *Family Economics Review,* Winter 1979: 21–24.

12. Ibid., 21.

13. Morgan, Zabik, and Stampley, "The Role of Breakfast," 560.

14. E. Hamilton, E. Whitney, and F. Sizer, *Nutrition Concepts and Controversies*, 3rd ed. (New York: West Publishing Co., 1982), 146.

15. A. Hertzler, J. Robbins, and S. Walton, "Assessing Nutrition Education Needs of Office Workers," *Journal of Nutrition Education* 18 (1986): 207–210.

16. A. Owen, "Health and Nutrition Trends for the 21st Century." Paper presented at the New Jersey Dietetic Association. Princeton, N.J.: November 4, 1988.

17. K. Little, "Eating for Health: Basic Nutrition Guidelines," *Caring* 3 (1984): 5–8.

Chapter 20

Dietary Assessment and Management of the Adult

Joan Howe Walsh

- How can clients be persuaded to give an honest report of what they eat?
- How does one recognize and deal with clients who do not take responsibility for complying with their dietary program?
- When should calcium supplements be recommended to clients?
- Should some degree of sodium restriction be recommended to all adult clients?

DIETARY ASSESSMENT

Overview

The eating habits of Americans have undergone significant changes in the last 25 years. With the large influx of women into the work force, there is often no one at home to shop for groceries and to plan and prepare meals. More and more, Americans rely on restaurant meals, take-out foods, microwave meals, vending machine snacks, and an array of convenience foods that did not even exist ten years ago. The distinction between meals and snacks has been blurred. The changes in food and eating habits are occurring so rapidly that it is difficult to measure their impact on health and nutritional status. With less use of home-prepared foods, it often becomes difficult for clients to adhere to dietary changes recommended for them.

Assessing the Diet of the Adult

In advising clients on improving their dietary habits, health care practitioners must be sure that they understand the clients' usual food intake. The 24-hour recall (see appendix A-2) is a valuable tool in getting the necessary information. Given today's "grazing" style of eating, it is also essential that the assessment focus not only on meal intake but on snacks as well. During the interview, it is important not to insert dietary advice and commentary; a matter-of-fact, nonjudgmental attitude is sufficient to signal the client to give candid answers.

The assessment should include an inquiry into the client's use of vitamin and mineral supplements. If possible, clients should bring in their supplement bottles so that the labels can be read to see what nutrients are present. The examiner should be particularly watchful for supplement combinations that contain more than 25,000 I.U. of vitamin A, since such amounts, combined with carotene and vitamin A in the diet, reach the toxic threshold.[1] Inquiry about the reasons for supplement use may provide useful insights into a client's health beliefs.

Food habits are very personal and very ingrained. It is important to show respect for clients' individuality by inquiring about the types of foods they like and dislike. Later, when suggesting dietary changes, one should try to emphasize the positive food habits of the client.

Traditional ethnic food patterns are usually nutritionally balanced and well-suited to the food supplies and lifestyles where they originated. Nutritional disturbances can occur when traditional foods are displaced by high-sugar, high-fat American foods or when a diet that is functional in a physically active culture is followed by a sedentary individual.

Health care practitioners should familiarize themselves with the food habits of the major ethnic groups in their client populations. One of the best ways to become familiar with ethnic foods is to eat homecooked foods in the different groups. If this is not possible, one can consult a registered dietitian (R.D.) to obtain an update on local ethnic foods.

Data Analysis

Information obtained from the initial interview with the adult client should be evaluated in terms of that client's particular nutritional needs. The client's 24-hour recall choices should be compared with those in the food group guide shown in appendix B-1.

Having clients keep a food diary is an excellent way to monitor their diet. The sample diary forms shown in appendixes A-4 and A-5 could be used, or one could create a special diary format. Food diaries have two significant advantages: (1) they save time during the office visit, eliminating the need for a diet interview, and (2) they tend to influence the client to eat more carefully. It is important that the client be instructed to write down each meal or snack as it is eaten, rather than waiting until the end of the day when some foods may have been forgotten.

Effective Client Counseling

The Health Belief Model

Research on client compliance suggests that a lack of knowledge is usually not the limiting factor in achieving diet compliance. The important thing is that the client have a set of beliefs, such as those described in the Health Belief Model.[2] This model holds that, in order for clients to participate actively in their care, they must believe:

- that they are vulnerable to a disease and its effects
- that the disease can have a serious impact on their life
- that the changes being recommended will be beneficial
- that the benefits of making the recommended changes are greater than the attendant inconveniences and obstacles

Clients who do not understand that the disease will affect their life, for example, some diabetics, may not make a serious effort to diet until they develop a complication, such as a foot ulcer. Similarly, a businessman with hypercholesterolemia may hold the first three beliefs listed above but may find that the inconvenience of ordering low-fat foods in a restaurant outweighs the perceived benefits from the prescribed diet.

A further factor in compliance is the client's perceived sense of self-efficacy. Clients who feel generally in control of their lives and their environment are good candidates for dietary programs; they feel that they will succeed with their endeavors. Clients with a low sense of self-efficacy have a more fatalistic attitude about life events and health; they are less likely to believe that they can make a difference in their health by making changes in their diet and exercise habits. Through the use of well-chosen open-ended questions, health care practitioners can often determine what their client's attitudes are on such matters and then help them to progress accordingly.

Enhancing Client Compliance

There are many reasons for dietary noncompliance. For example, among diabetic clients the major reasons are: (1) the regimen is too complex, (2) the program interferes with their usual activities, and (3) they fail to take personal responsibility in caring for the disease.[3]

Eating out and eating inappropriate food offered by others are major dietary stumbling blocks. Client counseling should address these obstacles. Dietary instructions should be streamlined so that clients do not have to track multiple categories of foods. The health care practitioner should inquire about travel plans, usual patterns in dining out, and family members who might sabotage the diet. Finally, clients should be helped to develop specific, realistic plans to deal with normal variations in their eating routines.

Multiple Diet Programs

Frequently, a client may have two or more of the following disorders: obesity, hypertension, adult-onset diabetes, hypercholesterolemia, hypertriglyceridemia, and hyperuricemia. Having more than one diet to manage for multiple disorders may cause the client to feel overwhelmed. Thus, initially, one should emphasize a treatment plan that provides the greatest benefit with the least complexity. For any combination of the diseases cited above, weight loss through a low-fat diet and an exercise program would be a solid beginning for the client care plan.

COMMON NUTRITIONAL PROBLEMS OF THE ADULT

Table 20-1 provides detailed information about common nutritional problems of the adult. It also suggests further assessment questions, recommended actions, and ways to evaluate outcomes.

Table 20-1 Common Nutritional Problems of the Adult

I. OVERWEIGHT/OBESITY

There is increasing evidence of a strong genetic component to obesity.[4,5]

Trunkal or android-type obesity, where fat is distributed around the waist, is more highly associated with adult onset diabetes, hypertension, and hyperlipidemias.[6]

Rapid weight loss is normally associated with high losses of metabolically active fat free mass (lean tissue) and a greater chance of rapid regain of the lost weight.[7]

Assessment	Action
Calculate the client's Body Mass Index (BMI),[8] using the following formula: $$\frac{\text{wt in lbs} \times 0.45}{\text{ht in (inches} \times 0.0254)^2}$$	
Is the BMI less than 25?	Reassure the client that the client is not obese. If the client is insistent that there is a weight problem, evaluate for an eating disorder.
Is the BMI between 25 and 29.9?	
Does the client have gynoid obesity (hip and thigh fat distribution) and no chronic disease (hypertension, hyperlipidemias, adult-onset diabetes)?	Reassure the client that the obesity presents no current health threat. Discourage drastic diet efforts. Advise moderate exercise and low-fat diet (see appendix G-1) to prevent further gain.
Does the client have android (upper trunk fat distribution) obesity and/or chronic disease?	Alert the client to the health risks of the obesity.
What is the client's current food intake?	Obtain a 24-hour recall (see appendix A-2). Use the information to give some basic dietary advice on reducing fat

Table 20-1 continued

	intake, sweets, and portion sizes (see Table 16-1). Teach the client how to keep a food diary (see appendixes A-4 and A-5).
Does the client have a regular exercise program?	If not, prescribe a specific, realistic exercise plan. Have the client keep an exercise log or calendar.
Does the client have a realistic weight goal?	Discuss reaching a goal of BMI <25 through losses of 1/2 to 2 pounds weekly.
Has the client successfully met the weight goal?	Encourage weight maintenance through regular exercise and moderate dietary habits.
Is the BMI between 30 and 40?	Discuss realistic weight goals with the client. A loss of 10% to 15% of body weight over 6 to 18 months is realistic.[9]
Is the client depressed?	Refer the client for counseling. Be aware that benzadiazepines frequently cause an increase in appetite.[10] Do not expect progress on a weight-control program until depression is dealt with.
Is the client motivated to lose weight?	Direct the client to a reliable source of weight-loss information: a registered dietitian (R.D.) or a hospital-based program.
Is the client asking for advice about a diet powder, pill, book, or program that is unfamiliar?	Contact a local registered dietitian (R.D.), health department, or clinician with a specialty in weight control for information. Ideally, a comprehensive weight-loss program should offer the following: (1) client record-keeping of food intake, (2) use of behavior modification to change eating behaviors and reward positive changes, (3) nutrition education, (4) the use of customary foods, and (5) exercise.[11,12]
Is the BMI greater than 40?	
Is the client seriously attempting weight loss for the first time?	Proceed as for BMI 30-40 above.[13,14] Set a weight-loss goal of 10% to 15% of present weight.
Has the client had repeated failure with conventional weight-loss methods?	Refer the client for further evaluation. Make the client aware that alternative methods require considerable adjustment by the client and that maintenance of any weight loss requires life-long vigilance.[15,16]

Table 20-1 continued

Evaluation

Review food diary or 24-hour recall at each visit to evaluate the nutritional adequacy of the diet in comparison with the table in appendix B-1.

Review client exercise log. Look for a minimum of 20 to 30 minutes of aerobic exercise three times a week, but encourage longer and more frequent workouts to promote faster weight loss.

If weight-loss goals are met, reinforce the need for continued maintenance of a good diet and exercise program.

If personal or family stresses arise that make working on weight loss difficult, advise the client to maintain the current weight range and arrange a time in the future when the client can resume the program.

For a client with an initial BMI over 30, refer for re-evaluation of blood pressure, cholesterol, and other indexes after achieving the initial 10% to 15% weight-loss goal. If these indexes are normal, determine with the client whether a further weight loss is warranted at this point; if abnormal, set a goal for another 10% to 15% weight loss during the next 6–18 months.

II. FAT/CHOLESTEROL INTAKE

The National Heart, Lung, and Blood Institute has issued very comprehensive guidelines on the interpretation of blood cholesterol levels and the use of diet and drugs for control of hypercholesterolemia.[17]

The local affiliate of the American Heart Association can provide excellent and accurate client education materials on cardiac risk reduction, including material on cholesterol-lowering diets.

Cholesterol-lowering diets are not simply diets that are low in cholesterol. They also involve weight loss and reductions in total fats, saturated fatty acids, and cholesterol.

Assessment	Action
Does the client have total cholesterol <200 mg/dl or (low density lipoprotein) LDL-cholesterol <130 mg/dl?	No dietary changes are required at this point.
Does the client have LDL-cholesterol between 130–159 mg/dl?	
Does the client have evidence of coronary heart disease (myocardial infarction [MI] or angina pectoris)?	Treat as "High-Risk LDL-Cholesterol" client (see below).
Does the client have two or more cardiac risk factors (male sex, family history of premature coronary heart disease [CHD], smoking, hypertension, [high density lipoprotein] HDL-cholesterol <35 mg/dl, diabetes, history of vascular disease, or more than 30% overweight)?	Treat as "High-Risk LDL-Cholesterol" client (see below).
Does the client have no other risk factors and no evidence of existing CHD?	Client has "Borderline High-Risk LDL-Cholesterol." Use 24-hour recall to assess current diet and instruct the client on cholesterol-lowering diet. If the client is

Table 20-1 continued

	overweight, follow steps for overweight/ obesity above. Advise on reducing intake of fatty meats, whole milk, cheeses, butter, egg yolks, chocolate, commercially baked goods and snacks, and foods containing coconut, palm, and palm kernel oil. Advise the client to reduce intake of all fried foods.
	Encourage use of fish, skinless poultry, lean meats, skim and 1% lowfat milk, fruits, vegetables, legumes, grains, and breads.
Does client have LDL-cholesterol >160 mg/dl?	Client has "High-Risk LDL-Cholesterol." Advise on the same diet as for "Borderline" client. Evaluate as described below.

Evaluation

For a client with acceptable cholesterol levels, remeasure cholesterol every five years.

For a client with borderline-high cholesterol and no other risk factors, remeasure cholesterol annually and reinforce dietary education. Aim to keep LDL-cholesterol under 160 mg/dl or total cholesterol under 240 mg/dl.

For a client with high cholesterol, aim to reduce LDL-cholesterol to <160 mg/dl, unless the client has existing CHD or two or more risk factors, in which case the goal is LDL-cholesterol <130 mg/dl. Measure cholesterol levels four to six weeks after starting the diet and again at three months. If goal is achieved, reinforce teaching and remeasure total cholesterol four times in the first year and twice annually thereafter.

If goals are not met, refer to a clinician or registered dietitian (R.D.) for more intensive education.

If diet compliance is good but cholesterol level response is inadequate, the client should be evaluated for use of lipid-lowering drugs.[18]

III. HYPERTENSION

There is still no scientific concensus on the value of population-wide sodium restriction for the prevention of hypertension.[19]

Clients vary in their responses to a sodium-restricted diet: some will experience an improvement in blood pressure, while others will have little or no change. Best results are seen in older clients, blacks, and those with more severe hypertension.[20]

Blood pressure goes up with obesity and excess alcohol intake.[21]

Hypertension may be related to inadequate intakes of calcium and potassium.[22]

Assessment	Action
Is the client overweight?	Advise the client on weight loss (see Table 20-1, Section I, Overweight/ Obesity).

Table 20-1 continued

What are the client's typical food habits?	Obtain a 24-hour recall and inquire about customary intakes of alcoholic beverages and use of salt and other sodium-rich condiments.
Does the client consume moderate-to-heavy amounts of alcohol on a regular or intermittent basis?	Advise the client on the effects of alcohol on blood pressure. Assist in developing a program to reduce or discontinue alcohol consumption.
Does the client use salt or sodium-rich condiments on a regular basis?	Advise the client on a daily sodium limit of approximately 2 grams daily. This is achieved through elimination of the use of salt and sodium-rich condiments (soy sauce, monosodium glutamate, seasoned salts) and a reduction in sodium-rich foods: processed and cured meats, canned and dried soups, sauces and gravies, canned vegetables, pickles, and salted snacks (see appendix G-2).
Does the client use polyunsaturated oils for cooking?	Advise the use of corn, sunflower, safflower or similar oils high in polyunsaturates for cooking.
Does the client have two or more servings of low-fat dairy foods daily?	If not, advise on increasing calcium intake.
Does the client have four or more servings of fruits and vegetables daily?	If not, advise on increasing potassium intake with these foods, as well as grains.

Evaluation

On return visits, monitor dietary changes. If the client seems to be having difficulty, refer to a registered dietitian (R.D.) for more intensive instruction.

To measure compliance with a sodium-restricted diet, have the client collect a 24-hour urine sample.[23] Urinary sodium of <70 mEq indicates good compliance with the diet. If urinary sodium exceeds 200 mEq, sodium intakes are so high as to overwhelm the effects of diuretic medication.

IV. CALCIUM AND OSTEOPOROSIS

An eight-ounce serving of milk or yogurt has about 300 milligrams of calcium. A one-half cup serving of cooked leafy greens has about 70 to 100 milligrams.[24]

The amount of calcium absorption from dairy products and calcium carbonate supplements is similar.[25]

Calcium cannot reverse or stop osteoporotic bone loss in postmenopausal women, but it is an important skeletal component. Elderly women tend to have poor intakes of dietary calcium, and their absorption of the mineral may not be as good as in younger women.[26]

The group that benefits most from higher calcium intakes may be adolescent girls and young women. Calcium helps build larger skeletons and thus reduces the risk of osteoporosis in later life.[27]

Table 20-1 continued

Whenever possible, the use of dairy products is recommended over calcium supplements, since dairy foods contain protein, riboflavin, vitamin D, and other valuable nutrients.

Assessment	Action
Is the client a female, white or Asian, in her 20s or 30s?	Ask the client about her usual intake of dairy foods and dark green leafy vegetables.
	Encourage an intake of 800 mg or more of calcium daily (2–3 cups of milk).
Is the client lactose-intolerant?	Advise the client of the availability of Lactaid milk (with 70 percent of lactose predigested) and Lactaid lactase tablets (for further information on these products, contact Lactaid, Inc., P.O. Box 111, Pleasantville, NJ 08232). Natural cheeses are also usually well-tolerated.
Does the client dislike most dairy products?	Encourage the use of green leafy vegetables, soybean curd (tofu), and calcium carbonate supplements.
Is the client a white or Asian female over 40?	
Is the client premenopausal or on hormone replacement therapy?	Encourage an intake of 1,500 mg of calcium daily, using a combination of foods and supplements. Use strategies discussed above if the client dislikes milk or has lactose intolerance.

Evaluation

Using the 24-hour recall, periodically check with the client on usual intake of calcium from foods and supplements.

Refer to a registered dietitian (R.D.) for further counseling if the client still has difficulty meeting daily calcium goals or has more than one diet to follow (e.g., cholesterol-lowering, sodium restriction).

V. PREMENSTRUAL SYNDROME (PMS)

There is little research evidence to suggest a major role for diet or vitamin supplements in the treatment of PMS.[28]

Dietary suggestions are aimed primarily at obtaining relief from specific symptoms.

Assessment	Action
Does the client complain of bloating or breast tenderness prior to onset of menses?	Survey the client on the use of sodium-rich foods and seasonings (see Section III, Hypertension). Advise the client to cut back on these for 10–14 days before each period to relieve water retention.

Table 20-1 continued

Does the client complain of irritability, nervousness, or sleeplessness?	Survey the client on intake of coffee, tea, colas, chocolate, and over-the-counter medications containing caffeine. Advise on reducing caffeine intake prior to onset of each period (see Table 5-1, Section V, Excess Caffeine Consumption).

Evaluation

If symptoms persist, discourage the use of megavitamin supplements and unusual diets for treatment. Encourage regular, balanced meals.

VI. TYPE II DIABETES MELLITUS

In the obese diabetic client, weight loss should be the primary focus of education. The weight loss should be achieved through a combination of exercise and moderate caloric restriction.[29]

Some foods and sweeteners promoted for use by diabetics contain fructose or sorbitol, which supply calories in amounts approximately equal to sucrose. While such foods and sweeteners may not cause hyperglycemia directly, they should be taken in limited quantities to avoid obesity. Aspartame and saccharin are essentially noncaloric and affect neither blood sugar nor weight.

Water soluble fibers, such as those found in legumes and oats, may help with controlling blood sugars and blood lipids in diabetics.[30] The use of these foods should be encouraged.

Assessment	Action
Is the client obese?	Refer to Section I, Overweight/Obesity.
Does the client have hypertriglyceridemia?	Poorly controlled blood sugars and/or obesity may be the cause. Encourage exercise, restriction of sugars, and a moderate fat reduction.
Does the client have hypercholesterolemia?	Elevated triglycerides will often raise the total cholesterol levels, due to increased very-low-density lipoprotein (VLDL) levels.
	Bring triglycerides under control and recheck blood cholesterol level before assuming the client has hypercholesterolemia.
Is diabetes poorly controlled?	Take periodic 24-hour dietary recalls or have the client keep a food diary.
Does the client frequently snack on fruit or use fruit juices or punch as a beverage?	Advise the client to take fruit with meals. Juices should be limited to four-ounce servings, also taken with meals. The use of fresh fruit instead of other juices should be encouraged.
Does the client use large portions of breakfast cereal, pasta, and other grain products?	Advise the client that carbohydrate-rich foods are essential in the diet, but that portions must be controlled. Suggest the use of scales and measuring cups to

Table 20-1 continued

	become familiar with portion sizes. One-half cup to a cup of cereal or grain per meal is standard.
Does the client use many fried or fatty foods?	Counsel the client on reduction of fats in the diet.

Evaluation

Most diabetics would benefit from at least one counseling session with a registered dietitian (R.D.). In this way, they can acquire detailed information on managing their diet for control of weight, blood glucose, and blood lipids.

Local chapters of the American Diabetes Association often offer educational programs and support groups for diabetics. Encourage the client to take advantage of these services.

VII. FOLLOWING FAD DIETS FOR WEIGHT LOSS

Many people who hope to lose weight want to do so very quickly.

There are numerous fad diets recommended for weight loss. A new one usually emerges yearly, but its popularity wanes quickly, and it is then replaced by another fad diet purported to bring about weight loss.

Many fad diets are nutritionally inadequate and could even be dangerous to health if followed rigidly for a length of time.

The only way to achieve permanent weight loss is to change eating patterns for a lifetime.

Assessment	Action
When counseling a client who claims to be following a weight-loss plan, find out:	Using a 24-hour recall (see appendix A-2), determine the type and amounts of food the client is consuming during one day. Compare with suggested food groups (see appendix B-1).
Is the client eating an adequate diet?	A weight-loss diet should include foods from all of the food groups in the amounts recommended. Calories are reduced by cutting fats, sugars, and large portions (see Table 16-1 and appendix G-1)
Is the diet safe?	
Are there too few calories?	An unsupervised diet should not be below 1,200 calories.
Is there too little of one nutrient?	For example, a diet without dairy products may be low in protein, calcium, and riboflavin.
Does the diet restrict fluid liquids and/or sodium?	Diets restricting liquids and sodium can lead to dehydration and a "false weight loss" through fluid loss.
Is there too much of one nutrient?	For example, a diet very high in fiber may reduce the intake of other important nutrients.

Table 20-1 continued

	Determine if the diet can lead to an imbalance and possible nutritional deficiency or health risk.
What does the diet promise? Is the weight-loss goal realistic?	Weight loss should average one to two pounds per week. Many diets promise too much weight loss, which may be unrealistic or even dangerous.
Is the diet available?	Foods that are difficult to obtain or prepare or are expensive will rarely be eaten routinely—even if the diet is successful.
Is the diet boring? Is there variety?	Food patterns should include a variety of foods from all of the food groups. A diet of just "grapefruit and cottage cheese" is boring, repetitive, and not nutritionally adequate. Because it is so monotonous, the client is not likely to follow it for very long.
Does the diet food taste good?	Low-calorie diets can be tasty. If a diet does not taste good, it will not be followed. Suggest the use of cookbooks featuring low-calorie foods.
Is the diet hard to prepare?	If preparing the foods causes a problem, the diet is unlikely to be followed. For example, many blenderized foods can be a bother and are boring, they also may not provide an adequate diet.
Is the diet a good one for the client to adopt to improve the eating pattern, or is it a "passing fancy"?	To be lasting, a weight-loss diet should adhere as much as possible to the eating preferences, lifestyle, and food habits of the client. Only then can it become a "way of eating for a lifetime" and bring about weight loss that is permanent.

NOTES

1. J.A. Olsen, "Recommended Dietary Intakes (RDI) of Vitamin A in Humans," *American Journal of Clinical Nutrition* 45 (1987): 704–716.

2. I.M. Rosenstock, "Understanding and Enhancing Patient Compliance with Diabetic Regimens," *Diabetes Care* 8 (1985): 610–616.

3. Ibid., 612.

4. E. Ravussin et al., "Reduced Rate of Energy Expenditure as a Risk Factor for Body-Weight Gain," *New England Journal of Medicine* 318 (1988): 467–472.

5. S.B. Roberts et al., "Energy Expenditure and Intake in Infants Born to Lean and Overweight Mothers," *New England Journal of Medicine* 318 (1988): 461–466.

6. P. Bjorntorp, "Classification of Obese Patients and Complications Related to the Distribution of Surplus Fat," *American Journal of Clinical Nutrition* 45 (1987): 1120–1125.

7. J.S. Garrow, "Energy Balance in Man—An Overview," *American Journal of Clinical Nutrition* 45 (1987): 1114–1119.

8. Ibid., 1116.

9. G.L. Blackburn and B.S. Kanders, "Medical Evaluation and Treatment of the Obese Patient with Cardiovascular Disease," *American Journal of Cardiology* 60 (1987): 55G–58G.

10. F.J. Zeman, *Clinical Nutrition and Diatetics* (Lexington, Mass.: Collamore Press, 1983), 63, 566.

11. A.J. Stunkard, "Conservative Treatments for Obesity," *American Journal of Clinical Nutrition* 45 (1987): 1142–1154.

12. C.L. Rock and A.M. Coulston, "Weight-control Approaches: A Review by the California Dietetic Association," *Journal of the American Diatetic Association* 88 (1988): 44–48.

13. G.A. Bray and R.J. Teague, "An Algorithm for the Medical Evolution of Obese Patients," in *Obesity*, ed. A.J. Stunkard (Philadelphia: W.B. Saunders Co., 1980), 240–248.

14. W.P.T. James, "Treatment of Obesity: The Constraints on Success," *Clinics in Endocrinology and Metabolism* 13 (1984): 635–659.

15. Rock and Coulston, "Weight-Control Approaches," 48.

16. M. Apfelbaum, J. Fricker, and L. Igoin-Apfelbaum, "Low- and Very-Low-Calorie Diets," *American Journal of Clinical Nutrition* 45 (1987): 1126–1134.

17. The Expert Panel, National Heart, Lung, and Blood Institute, "The Report of the National Cholesterol Education Program Expert Panel on Detection, Evaluation and Treatment of High Blood Cholesterol in Adults," *Archives of Internal Medicine* 148 (1988): 39–69.

18. Ibid., 53.

19. B. Isaksson and G.B. Brubacher, "Panel Statements: Selected Minerals," *American Journal of Clinical Nutrition* 45 (1987): 1043–1044.

20. D.E. Grobbee and A. Hofman, "Does Sodium Restriction Lower Blood Pressure?" *British Medical Journal* 293 (1986): 27–29.

21. A.S. Truswell, "Diet and Hypertension," *British Medical Journal* 291 (1985): 125–127.

22. M.H. Walczyk and D.A. McCarron, "Electrolytes and Dietary Fat in Hypertensive Cardiovascular Disease," *American Journal of Cardiology* 60 (1987): 59G–67B.

23. R.F. Gillum, R.J. Prineas, and P.J. Elmer, "Assessing Sodium and Potassium Intake in Essential Hypertension," *American Heart Journal* 107 (1984): 549–555.

24. United States Department of Agriculture, Human Nutrition Information Service, *Nutritive Value of Foods* (Washington, D.C.: USDA, 1981), 12–15, 54–59.

25. R.R. Recker et al., "Calcium Absorbability from Milk Products, an Imitation Milk, and Calcium Carbonate," *American Journal of Clinical Nutrition* 47 (1988): 93–95.

26. W.A. Peck et al., "Research Directions in Osteoporosis," *American Journal of Medicine* 84 (1988): 275–282.

27. Ibid., 280.

28. M. Miro, P.M. Stewart, and S.F. Abraham, "Vitamin and Trace Element Status in Premenstrual Syndrome," *American Journal of Clinical Nutrition* 47 (1988): 636–641.

29. American Diabetes Association, "Nutritional Recommendations and Principles for Individuals with Diabetes Mellitus: 1986," *Diabetes Care* 18 (1987): 126–132.

30. Ibid., 131.

Part VIII
The Elderly

Chapter 21

Nutrition Assessment of the Elderly

Daphne A. Roe

OVERVIEW

The aims of nutrition assessment of the elderly include collection of normative data on healthy populations, risk assessment, evaluation of current status relative to health problems, determination of unmet needs, and collection of baseline information from which to assess the effectiveness of nutrition intervention. These practical aims are linked to an overall objective of providing for the nutritional needs of the aging population.

It is important to remember that the elderly whose nutrition we assess may be either people who are healthy or people who have health problems. The nutritional needs of the healthy elderly are for health maintenance, optimal performance in cognitive and physical activities, and extended longevity. The nutritional needs of the elderly with health problems include therapeutic needs for disease management, needs for prevention or cure of deficiencies, and needs for avoidance of drug and nutrient interactions. The nutritional needs of the elderly with health problems (often referred to as the "frail elderly") may also include the need for nutrition services.

HEALTH HISTORY

For the nutrition assessment of the elderly, it is important to have accurate data collection. Depending on the client's mental status, a reliable observer, such as a relative or friend, may be necessary. Also, rushing through the interview can affect the results. Elderly clients often can speak for themselves, and they deserve courteous, patient interviewing.

The general medical history should include factors affecting the client's nutrition. Weight and appetite changes, gastrointestinal disturbances, and newly acquired food intolerances must be detected. Problems with constipation, diarrhea, and indigestion are common in this age group and require investigation. Changes in sensory abilities will affect diet. A loss of taste or decrease in smell perception may result in a decreased interest in food or excessive use of salt and sugar to compensate. Periodontal problems can lead to eating difficulties or restricted choices.

Regardless of the depth of nutritional experience of the individual assigned to carry out the nutrition assessment of the elderly client, it is recommended that an effort be made to determine all the factors that might detract from the respondent's ability to get food. Hunger in the elderly is linked to lack of food access; and the inability of the elderly to get food has been found to be strongly related to loss of mobility and to poverty.[1,2]

When the client's ability to get food has been assessed (see appendix A-1, Nutrition Questionnaire), it is necessary to obtain information about dietary adequacy. The nutritional adequacy of the diet is related to the variety of foods consumed; the greater the variety of the foods consumed, the greater is the chance that a nutrient-deficient diet will be avoided. Thus, the elderly client should be questioned about the number of different foods purchased per week. The purchase of less than 12 different foods per week indicates a significant risk that the diet will be inadequate with respect to one or more nutrients.

Information should be obtained on the number of main ("hot") meals that are consumed per week. A number less than seven is evidence of a lack of food access to an extent that may require provision of a home-delivered-meals service.

Information should also be obtained on the frequency of consumption of milk and of dark green and yellow vegetables; consumption of such foods less than three times a week indicates an unsatisfactory intake of key nutrients needed by the elderly. Low consumption of milk limits intake of calcium and riboflavin, while low consumption of dark green vegetables limits the intake of potassium and folate. Low consumption of yellow vegetables limits the intake of carotenoids, which are required for provision of a vitamin A precursor (beta carotene) and which serve as agents that may have a protective function against cancer. The elderly who have low intakes of vegetables are usually those who can no longer cook and who are without a meals service. They may also be those who are depressed and have lost interest in food (see chapter 22).

The client should also be asked for information regarding smoking and drinking habits. Smokers tend to have diets of poorer quality than those of nonsmokers, in part because smoking reduces appetite. Elderly drinkers, particularly heavy drinkers, tend to eat diets of low-nutrient density, which puts them at risk for multiple nutritional deficiencies. Among heavy drinkers, it is more informative to know about the quantity of alcohol the clients report drinking than about the diet they report eating. The elderly heavy drinker, like the younger alcoholic, commonly confabulates to indicate that the quality of the diet they report is better than the actual diet they consume.

The assessor should establish a clear record of all medications taken, including the types of doses and their frequency and timing. Medications present a potential for appetite changes as well as alteration of nutrient absorption (see Table 23-3). The daily use of vitamin and mineral supplements also merits attention, since this practice is common.

PHYSICAL ASSESSMENT

Among elderly men and women, nutritional risk is linked both to excessive thinness and to fatness. The very thin elderly are likely to be those with cancer and chronic obstructive lung disease, while the fat elderly are often those with Type II noninsulin-requiring diabetes, hypertension, or symptomatic osteoarthritis.[3] In order to use body weight or other body mass measurements as nutritional indicators of the prognosis in specific chronic diseases, it is best to express the measurements as a percentage above or below the range of normal values.

Determination of the client's mental status establishes the ability to function independently. Deficits in mental functioning may warrant investigation into alcohol abuse, anemia, or vitamin B deficiency.

The client's skin and nails should be carefully inspected. While normal aging results in loss of subcutaneous fat and elasticity, the examiner should look beyond this to evaluate the skin and nails for nutritional health. Poor healing, ecchymoses or petechiae, and dermatitis denote nutritional deficiencies. White spots on the nails may be associated with zinc deficiency, which is coupled with inadequate calorie intake.

Examination of the mouth and gums for malocclusion, thrush, and mucous membrane integrity is basic to a good nutrition assessment. The ability to chew, swallow, and enjoy food stems from good oral health. Saliva production tends to decrease with age, and the mucous membrane may appear less moist. Adequacy of hydration must also be considered.

The physical examination of the elderly client should include an attempt to gain information on the client's ability to carry out food-related tasks. The assessment of physical disability requires an evaluation of the means of ambulation, the facility with which the means of ambulation are used, and the ability to open bottles, cartons, and cans and to use simple kitchen tools. It should also include an assessment of the visual and cognitive abilities of the client with respect to use of the cooking stove.

Diagnosis of specific nutritional deficiencies may be based on clinical signs. However, in the elderly, cutaneous signs that in younger population groups may be indicative of deficiencies are often nonspecific. The signs of nutritional deficiencies are shown in appendix C-1. Differential diagnoses of the signs of deficiency in the elderly are shown in Table 21-1.

Table 21-1 Symptoms and Signs with Nutritional and Nonnutritional Etiologies in the Elderly

Signs and Symptoms	Nutritional Etiology	Nonnutritional Etiology
Night blindness	Vitamin A deficiency	Cataract
Congestive heart failure	Beriberi	Late effect of rheumatic, coronary, or alcoholic heart disease
Angular stomatitis	Ariboflavinosis	Oral candidiasis, drooling
"Phototoxic" dermatitis	Pellagra	Actinic reticuloid, thiazide photosensitivity
Peripheral neuropathy	Vitamin B_6 deficiencies (drug-induced)	Diabetic neuropathy
Purpura	Scurvy, vitamin K deficiency	Purpura, vasculitis, senile skin changes

ANTHROPOMETRIC ASSESSMENT

Physical examination of the elderly in community surveys or surveillance programs should include anthropometric measurements. The measurement data should include body weight and height (or a proxy for height, such as knee height). The normative values of body weight for height for men and women 65 years of age and over are shown in Tables 21-2 and 21-3. Assessments of body fatness and lean body mass using mid-arm circumference and triceps skinfold thickness can be completed if time permits. (For in-depth information about the anthropometric assessment of the elderly, write to Ross Laboratories, Columbus, Ohio 43216, and request nomograms for assessing the elderly.)

Constraints on obtaining useful weight measurements include the difficulty of getting the frail elderly to stand on the scale and the loss of validity of body weight as a measure of nutritional status when an amputation has been performed. Constraints on obtaining valid height measurements relate to the curvature of the spine, which is characteristic of osteoporosis in the elderly.

Height measurements cannot be obtained for elderly clients who are chair- or bed-bound. However, proxy measurements for height, including measurements of knee height or ulnar length (length of the forearm) can be used to derive an estimate of stature, using a nomogram as shown in Table 21-4. Because stature and arm span (span of the outstretched arms) are correlated, it has been recommended that arm span be used to gauge stature. However, this measure is not recommended for the frail elderly who may be incapable of stretching out their arms.

Table 21-2 Average Height-Weight Table for Men 65 Years of Age and Over

Height in Inches	Ages 65–69	Ages 70–74	Ages 75–79	Ages 80–84	Ages 85–89	Ages 90–94
61	128–156	125–153	123–151			
62	130–158	127–155	125–153	122–148		
63	181–161	129–157	127–155	122–150	120–146	
64	134–164	131–161	129–157	124–152	122–148	
65	136–166	134–164	130–160	127–155	125–153	117–143
66	139–169	137–167	133–163	130–158	128–156	120–146
67	140–172	140–170	136–166	132–162	130–160	122–150
68	143–175	142–174	139–169	135–165	133–163	126–154
69	147–179	146–178	142–174	139–169	137–167	130–158
70	150–184	148–182	146–178	143–175	140–172	134–164
71	155–189	152–186	149–183	148–180	144–176	139–169
72	159–195	156–190	154–188	153–187	148–182	
73	164–200	160–196	158–192			

Source: Adapted from *Journal of the American Medical Association,* Vol. 177, p. 658, with permission of American Medical Association. Copyright 1960, American Medical Association.

Table 21-3 Average Height-Weight Table for Women 65 Years of Age and Over

Height in Inches	Ages 65–69	Ages 70–74	Ages 75–79	Ages 80–84	Ages 85–89	Ages 90–94
58	120–146	112–138	111–135			
59	121–147	114–140	112–136	100–122	99–121	
60	122–148	116–142	113–139	106–130	102–124	
61	123–151	118–144	115–141	109–133	104–128	
62	125–153	121–147	118–144	112–136	108–132	107–131
63	127–155	123–151	121–147	115–141	112–136	107–131
64	130–158	126–154	123–151	119–145	115–141	108–132
65	132–162	130–158	126–154	122–150	120–146	112–136
66	136–166	132–162	128–157	126–154	124–152	116–142
67	140–170	136–166	131–161	130–158	128–156	
68	143–175	140–170				
69	148–180	144–176				

Source: Adapted from *Journal of the American Medical Association,* Vol. 177, p. 658, with permission of American Medical Association. Copyright 1960, American Medical Association.

Table 21-4 Formula for Calculating Stature from Knee Height

Stature for men = 64.19 − (0.04 × age) + (2.02 × knee height)
Stature for women = 84.88 − (0.24 × age) + (1.83 × knee height)

Source: Reprinted with permission of Ross Laboratories, Columbus, Ohio 43216, from *Nutritional Assessment of the Elderly through Anthropometry* by W.C. Chumlea, © 1984 Ross Laboratories.

On the other hand, mid-arm circumference is an extremely useful measure; it is easily obtained using a nylon tape measure, and community health workers who go into the homes of the elderly can easily be taught to make accurate measurements. In patients who have hemiplegia or other wasting conditions of one arm, the "good" arm should be used for the measurement.

When information is being obtained on changes in the nutritional status of the elderly over time, a continuing record of midarm circumference measurements provides a gauge to assess corresponding changes in body mass. For this purpose, the measurement of triceps skinfold thickness requires greater skill, and measurement error is common when those making the measurement are inexperienced.

LABORATORY ASSESSMENT

Decreased serum albumin, serum transferrin and lymphocyte count and a nonreactive skin may indicate protein-calorie malnutrition. A hydration deficit may be indicated by elevated hemoglobin, hematocrit, and blood urea nitrogen (BUN) levels. Decreased bone density on radiographs can be related to vitamin-D and calcium deficits. Serum, vitamin, and mineral levels may also be useful diagnostically. When inadequate nutrition is suspected as a result of a physical examination or interview, the need for laboratory values is indicated (see appendix C-2).

In elderly clients with chronic obstructive lung disease, protein-energy malnutrition (as defined by laboratory measures) has an adverse effect on pulmonary function.[4] Also, malnutrition, because of its effects on immune function, increases the risk of pneumonia in such clients.[5]

Nutritional indicators of prognostic significance have been obtained for several diseases and injuries that are common causes of hospital admission among the elderly. Serum albumin and prealbumin are useful indicators for detecting malnutrition and an associated increased risk of femoral neck fracture.[6]

SPECIAL CONCERNS

Hospitals

Nutrition assessment of the elderly in hospitals must focus on recognition of nutritional disorders that either underlie the reason for admission or are causally related to treatment received in the hospital. Neglect of routine nutrition assessment is the major reason for delays in instituting appropriate feeding strategies to prevent hospital malnutrition.

In the nutrition assessment of the hospital-based elderly, the emphasis should be on diagnostic tests for nutritional deficiencies and metabolic disorders. These tests should also provide data that may establish causal relationships between disease and nutritional status or between drugs and nutritional status.

Finally, the hospital-based nutrition assessment should provide information that will enable dietitians to design both therapeutic diets to meet the patient's needs and prognostic tools with which to assess health outcomes.

Nursing Homes

Nutrition assessment and monitoring of the elderly in nursing homes are required both to identify nutritional disorders at the time of admission and to assess the ongoing quality of their nutritional care while in the nursing home. The risk of malnutrition in nursing home patients may be linked to an inadequate diet or to diet therapies.[7] Therefore, an integral part of the nutritional assessment of nursing home patients is the documentation of change in nutritional status over time. This requires regularly planned nutrition assessments.

Most importantly, the nutrition assessment in the nursing home must include an assessment of the food available to the patient from all sources, including the dining room, snack bar, the wards, recreational areas, and relatives or other visitors. In these patients, obesity is related to overeating, a low level of activity, or the use of drugs that increase appetite. A checklist of ways to monitor the causes of weight gain or loss in nursing home patients is provided in Table 21-5.

Table 21-5 Check List for Monitoring and Recording Weight Gain or Loss Among Nursing Home Patients

1. Weight gain
   a. eating snacks _____
   b. noncompliance with diet _____
   c. congestive heart failure _____
   d. hyperphagic drug _____
   e. lack of mobility _____
   f. recovery from illness _____
   g. drug-related fluid retention _____
2. Weight loss
   a. not eating enough at mealtimes _____
   b. regurgitating food _____
   c. vomiting _____
   d. chronic diarrhea/malabsorption _____
   e. taking diuretic _____
   f. infection _____
   g. drug-induced anorexia _____
3. Weight changes
   Chart weight _____
   Weight change since last measurement _____
   Percentage of weight gain or loss since admission _____

Both overnutrition and undernutrition will have adverse impacts on a nursing home population. Weight gain not only decreases the mobility of the arthritic, it also renders nursing care more difficult. Excessive weight loss can increase the risk of infection and premature demise.

Thus, it is essential that the specific roles of the various multidisciplinary caregivers relative to nutrition assessment in the nursing home be carefully delineated and that inservice training be provided as necessary. Only in this way can overnutrition and undernutrition among the patients be accurately monitored and prevented.

NOTES

1. L. Davies, "Nutrition and the Elderly: Identifying Those at Risk," *Proceedings of the Nutrition Society* 43 (1984): 295–297.

2. D.A. Roe, D.F. Williamson, and E.A. Frongillo, *1984-85 Survey of the Elderly Recipients of the SNAP Home-Delivered Meals in New York State: Final Report* (Ithaca, N.Y.: Cornell University, 1985), 46.

3. Ibid., 18.

4. A.G. Driver, M.T. McAlevy, and L.W. Burger, "Nutritional Support of Patients with Respiratory Failure," *Nutritional Support Services* 1 (1981): 26–28.

5. M.A. Bernard and J.L. Rombeau, "Nutritional Support for the Elderly Patient," in *Nutrition, Aging and Health* (New York: Alan R. Liss, 1986), 229–258.

6. R.F. Labbe and R.L. Rettmer, "Laboratory Monitoring of Nutritional Support," *Nutritional International* 3 (1987): 1–5.

7. A. Bruyere, C.H. Rapin, and H. Dirren, "Blood Nutritional Parameters in Patients with Femoral Neck Fracture," in *Nutrition, Immunity and Illness in the Elderly*, ed. R.K. Chandra (New York: Pergamon Press, 1985), 242–246.

Chapter 22

Environmental Assessment of the Elderly

Adriana G. Austin

OVERVIEW

The environment is viewed as an open system interacting with the human system in a mutual, simultaneous, and continuous manner, leading to innovative change.[1] Those systems that are external to the human system or the environmental system participate in the change. The physical, psychosocial, and cultural aspects of daily living all participate in one's ability and desire to obtain and assimilate nutritious food in proper quantities. Assessment should thus focus on the interaction of environmental and human factors.

ACCESS AND BARRIERS TO GOOD NUTRITION

The elderly in America live in a variety of settings that require services, transportation, and security. Urban centers are more apt than rural centers to have transportation and services available. Yet many elderly in urban centers feel insecure because of crime rates, rapid traffic flow, and the impersonal attitude of the general population. In rural areas, in contrast, they may feel more secure, but they may also be inconvenienced by lack of transportation, accessibility to shopping, or services. In both settings, however, the availability of commodities is essential in maintaining adequate nutrition for the elderly population.

Indeed, food is the medium for many social events in a community. Church dinners, organizational luncheons, and going out to a restaurant are all nutritional experiences. Generally these occasions offer a variety of foods not always prepared in one's home but may provide a major portion of the individual's total nutrient intake for the day. The elderly should be encouraged to participate in such community activities.

Yet, the home is where the elderly feel most comfortable. For many, it is what is left of the past, the place where they brought up their children and entertained friends and loved ones. The permanency of the home provides a degree of security and social network relationships with one's neighbors. For many widows, the house symbolizes the deceased husband's life work and they do not feel comfortable selling his belongings. When such people move from their home to an apartment or single room out of financial necessity or as they become incapacitated, social isolation and loneliness can occur.[2]

The link between isolation and nutrition is a reciprocal one.[3] Those who are lonely and alone may not prepare adequate meals. They may develop poor eating habits. A diminished appetite and poor nutrient intake can, in turn, lead to malnutrition. This further reduces the level of energy required for maintenance of a positive spirit, healthy psyche, and physical system and for reaching out for social contacts. Such people require some affirmation of themselves from others. They need outreach programs that will locate and incorporate them into meaningful social interaction and an adequate nutrition program.

As individuals advance in years, the problems of procurement and preparation of food increase. These problems are accentuated by poor health, inadequate income, lack of transportation, and fear of going out into the community. The elderly, regardless of their income, should still be able to enjoy the activity of shopping, since it allows them personal, social, and recreational benefits that are satisfying.[4] However, when they cannot purchase the kind of food they want, food starts to lose its meaning and social value. When, because of a lack of income or accessibility or because of physical limitations, they cannot serve their friends the kinds of foods to which they are accustomed, they become discouraged and eventually drop away from their circle of friends and acquaintances. Often, their needs remain unnoticed until they are sick enough for hospitalization; then they may re-enter the system.

Housing is related to socioeconomic status. In some instances, taxes and the increased cost of maintenance will reduce the income of the elderly to near poverty levels. Nevertheless, many elderly are hesitant to leave familiar surroundings for another residence that would be more economical. Such a change in residence can in fact have an unfavorable psychological impact on an older person. When required to live with children or other relatives, the elderly may feel they are losing control over their environment. Many of their life-long food practices may be subject to change, especially if they are required to live in an institutional setting. Social interaction may become impaired as they fit into the routine of the institution. Often, in such settings, they are reluctant, or not given the opportunity, to voice their particular preferences.

It is often difficult to estimate the financial status of the elderly person, except insofar as that status is reflected in a Social Security check. Such variables as unreported income, family contributions, hidden savings, and poverty index figures that change from year to year can make estimations of financial status unreliable.[5]

In the case of the low-income or near-poor elderly, subsidized housing offers some assistance and allows a greater percentage of monthly income to be utilized for food. Still, purchasing and preparing food within budget constraints requires creative and careful planning to satisfy hunger and also obtain adequate nutrition.

In any event, proper nutrition and the general health of the elderly can be enhanced by physical exercise programs, whether they are still residing in their own home, living with their children, or living in senior residences or other congregate housing facilities. In particular, moderate exercise is prescribed for those suffering from obesity, hypertension, certain cardiac problems, and arthritis. Because the retired generally experience a considerable decrease in physical activity, planned exercise programs, such as a routine daily walk, can be helpful to both mind and body. However, such exercise needs to go hand-in-hand with an adequate nutrition program.

In one study designed to assess the factors affecting nutritional adequacy of the elderly according to residential locations, no differences were found in nutritional adequacy between the rural and urban elderly. However, significant differences were found in the suburban elderly when compared with other rural and urban residents. In particular, the suburban elderly residents were found to have higher nutritive intake. This was attributed to the fact that the elderly living in the suburbs have a higher educational and economic status compared with other rural and urban residents.[6] At the other extreme, those at poverty or near-poverty levels often face formidable barriers to good nutrition.

Table 22-1 lists some environmental factors that foster good nutrition.

RELEVANT ENVIRONMENTAL FACTORS

Socioeconomic Factors

Financial income constitutes a major environmental subsystem that exerts considerable force on the nutritional well-being of the elderly. In turn, it has been suggested that aging produces poverty.[7] In any event, for those elderly who are forced to live on a reduced income, several environmental factors must be evaluated. First, the adequacy of income seems to be more important than the objective level of income. Thus, the important question is, Does the income allow enough money to pay for necessities? Information on this point can be obtained by asking the clients to select one of the following statements that best describes their money status:

- I have enough money for everything I need.
- I have enough money for the things I need, if I am careful.
- I do not have enough money for the things I need.

Table 22-1 Environmental Factors that Foster Good Nutrition

1. Adequate income and absence of financial restraints
2. Health and absence of medical restraints
3. Independent mobility within one's environment
4. Good morale and a healthy psychosocial environment
5. Residence within outreach catchment areas
6. Incorporation into outreach programs
7. An interactive and social network
8. Social support systems and ties to a meaningful community
9. Satisfaction with one's living situation
10. Access to transportation
11. Access to supermarkets or neighborhood food stores
12. Adequate kitchens with working stoves and refrigerators and an adequate storage area for food
13. Access to community nutrition programs that provide congregate meal sites as well as meal delivery systems
14. Community assistance in procuring and preparing food for those unable to manage these tasks
15. Access to nutrition education
16. Senior citizen involvement in nutrition programs
17. An exercise program incorporated into one's lifestyle
18. A political climate and philosophy that values health promotion through adequate nutrition for the elderly, along with continued funding of current programs with commitments for expansion and outreach

A caveat here of course is that adequate income does not necessarily mean that the person is eating nutritious food.

The second factor, objective income, becomes important when it is (1) very low, (2) consistent with subsistence income, or (3) inadequate to allow the elderly person to purchase the necessities with regard to food products and other life support items. Inflation further reduces the purchasing power of the elderly. The end result may be that they buy foods that satisfy hunger rather than nutrient needs.[8] Here it should be noted that the elderly most often living in poverty are women and minorities.

Another relevant factor is socioeconomic status (SES) in relation to current income. Assessment of this factor is based on patterns of behavior relative to the SES during the major portion of the client's lifetime. The notion that the elderly are necessarily reduced to poverty by virtue of age and retirement requires careful evaluation. In many instances, poverty is an established way of life, a product of learned patterns of behavior. In other cases, eating habits and patterns and methods of planning, purchasing, and preparing food will vary as the educational level changes. Ethnicity will also influence changing food preferences and the meaning of food. Previous protein consumption in the form of meat, poultry, and seafood may become subject to drastic change due to inadequate income to purchase such foods.

The Home

The extent to which the structure and function of the home permits adequate nutrition also needs to be assessed. Is the home clean or noticeably dirty? What are the facilities for food storage and preparation? Observation of foods on the shelves and in the refrigerator can provide the health care professional with knowledge about the adequacy of the types and quantities of food. Availability of storage facilities permits the elderly to take advantage of selective shopping and bargain prices. For those living in single rooms, is there a kitchen that is shared by residents of a floor? Are the appliances clean and in working order?

What is the psychosocial climate of the home? Is there anger, conflict, or hostility present that interferes with morale and motivation?

The location of the home is also important, since aging increases one's dependency on the local environment. Is the home located in an area of age-concentrated housing where socialization is fostered and control permitted?

Food Assistance Programs

Meals-on-Wheels is a voluntary nutrition program that provides home-delivered meals to those elderly who are unable to prepare their own food. The meals usually consist of a hot noontime meal with a cold evening supper. The program is often sponsored by a civic or church organization. There may or may not be a charge to the consumer. A social agency may authorize and pay for the services, or the charges may be based on ability to pay.[9]

The Nutrition Programs of the Older Americans Act fund programs for persons 60 years of age or older. The purpose of the programs is to improve the nutrition of older citizens by providing low-cost nutritious meals, social interaction, counseling, referrals to other supporting programs/agencies, and access to transportation. Hot meals and snacks are delivered to the home-bound aged.[10]

As noted earlier, there is a link between isolation and nutrition. People who are lonely or all alone do not prepare meals for themselves that are either adequate or nutritious. Thus, congregate feeding is an important component of the above-cited federal nutrition programs. In such an environment, the general demeanor of the elderly also improves substantially.

Yet congregate feeding is not the complete answer to the nutritional problems of the elderly. Individual counseling must be provided on a continuing basis. The general well-being of the elderly will influence their nutritional status. Thus, periodic assessment of both their physical and psychosocial status should be made.

The Community

Access to Resources

The nutritional status of a community will depend on the extent to which its residents have access to its resources or service systems. Transportation to and from meal sites thus is an important feature of any nutrition program. However, such transportation may be limited due to insufficient funds. The result is that many nutrition programs have long waiting lists. Clearly, economics and physical mobility are important factors in providing access to community resources.[11]

Many communities provide senior service buses for escorting the elderly to shopping areas. Often, such services are subsidized, in part, under the Older American Act. In addition, local bus services often provide special equipment for the handicapped and offer special rates for senior citizens. Supplementing these services, many church and civic organizations provide transportation and arrange car pools with volunteers.

The home-bound aged have additional needs that may include medical and nursing services, housekeeping support, delivery of daily meals each day, or even complete home care. These elderly are at the highest risk for nutritional problems.[12]

Centers

Senior citizen centers, golden age clubs, and nutrition sites provide opportunities for social interaction by the elderly. The programs at nutrition centers may include, in addition to meals, socialization, exercise programs, health fairs, nutrition education, and individual counseling. Some senior citizen centers offer programs in arts and crafts, college courses, and vacations; a few even operate thrift and craft shops to raise monies for their activities and charities. For those unable to grocery-shop, some nutrition programs provide shopping services for the weak, handicapped, and house-bound. In some communities where crime, distance, or lack of transportation inhibit shopping, mini-mobile shopping marts have been established to provide services for the elderly.[13]

Safety

Safety problems that need identification and remediation for the elderly include crime, accidents, abuse, falls, and substandard housing. Often, thermal stressors, such as extremes in heat and cold, foster withdrawal and isolation among the elderly. Poor sanitation at senior centers and nutrition sites, combined with an unsafe neighborhood, can also create major barriers to nutrition services. Thus, security and safety are directly related to the prospects for the elderly's well-being and nutritional status.

RECOMMENDATIONS

Environmental interventions for the elderly should focus on maximizing the client's health potential and, at the same time, moving the client toward optimal functioning, even though pathology may be present.

Socioeconomic Factors

When income problems are identified as the source of poor nutrition, development of a positive relationship with the client is crucial. The goal is to motivate the client to be responsive to change by any or all of the following actions:

- Referral and follow-up for (1) a nutrition counselor regarding adequacy of diet, (2) the Social Security Administration for Supplemental Security Income (SSI), (3) social services (local) for a rent subsidy, and/or (4) a free food program
- menu planning
- counseling for economical shopping

The Home

Interventions should be targeted toward making the home safe and functional for the client. The major goal is to motivate the client to repattern and remove barriers to good nutrition. The interventions might include the following:

- if necessary, for initial clean-up, removal of filth and vermin with use of exterminator and/or industrial cleaners
- referral to an appropriate agency to facilitate repair of faulty appliances
- use of homemaker services when needed
- even if no problems exist, working with the client's strengths, providing positive reinforcement and praise for health-promoting behaviors

Food Assistance Programs

If it is determined that a client could benefit from a food assistance program for nutritional, financial, or social reasons, the following interventions may be applicable:

- provision of current program information and help with referral, allowing alternative client choices and maintaining follow-up
- obtaining the services of a willing neighbor who routinely utilizes the targeted program, to provide encouragement and escort the client to the program in initial visits
- arranging transport services
- arranging social services to enable a house-bound client to gain access to a program

The Community

Interventions in the community to facilitate access by the elderly to nutrition programs and transportation services may require mobilizing certain resources to eliminate barriers, political intervention to obtain additional funds for program expansion, and/or providing information on multiple sources of transportation. In these endeavors, community centers can be very effective. Specifically, the elderly may require the following types of support:

- education and information regarding resources and locations of centers
- facilitating referral to an agency/center
- instruction in ways to utilize the services of an agency
- mobilizing senior citizen organizations to provide car services to shopping centers, to facilitate "spending down" for foods, and to provide outings for socialization
- mobilizing nutrition programs in community-use outreach
- initiation of exercise programs for the elderly

Safety

The promotion of a safe environment should include facilitating access to good nutrition by eliminating safety hazards. Specific interventions might include the following:

- alerting individuals to the existence of unsafe environments
- motivating the elderly through education to value safety
- assisting individuals in developing plans to remove safety hazards
- encouraging the use of senior citizen groups and political action groups for community action
- using discussion groups and surveys to encourage compliance with safety regulations at congregate meal sites
- participation in neighborhood crime-watch groups

SUMMARY

In efforts to promote health through nutrition for the elderly, the primary role of the health care practitioner with respect to environmental factors is to assist with early diagnosis and treatment. To this end, the environmental needs of the elderly, based on the initial assessment, should be incorporated into an ongoing health maintenance program.

This program should include appropriate treatment interventions and monitoring as necessary. The ultimate goal is primary prevention by assisting the client, through education, to change those environmental factors that can be changed and that impact on the promotion of optimal health.[14]

NOTES

1. M.E. Rogers, *An Introduction to the Theoretical Basis of Nursing* (Philadelphia: F.A. Davis Company, 1970), 49–51.

2. J. Pelcovits, "Nutrition to Meet the Human Needs of Older Americans," *Journal of the American Dietetic Association* 60 (April 1972): 297–300.

3. Ibid., 297.

4. L. McGhee, "The Influence of Qualitative Assessments of the Social and Physical Environments on the Morale of the Rural Elderly," *American Journal of Community Psychology* 12 (1984): 709–723.

5. P. Ebersole and P. Hess, *Toward Healthy Aging* (St. Louis: C.V. Mosby Co., 1985), 423.

6. L. Norton and M.C. Wozny, "Residential Location and Nutritional Adequacy Among Elderly Adults," *Journal of Gerontology* 39 (1984): 593–595.

7. R.S. Weiss, *Loneliness: The Experience of Emotional and Social Isolation* (Cambridge, Mass.: MIT Press, 1973), 26.

8. Ebersole and Hess, *Toward Healthy Aging*, 208.

9. R. Gross, B. Gross, and S. Seidman, *The New Old: Struggling for Decent Aging* (New York: Anchor/Doubleday Press, 1978), 412.

10. D. Roe, *Geriatric Nutrition* (Englewood Cliffs, N.J.: Prentice-Hall, 1983), 5.

11. Gross, Gross, and Seidman, *The New Old*, 104.

12. D.S. Woodruff and J.E. Birren, *Aging: Scientific Perspectives and Social Issues* (New York: D. Van Nostrand Co., 1975), 83.

13. Gross, Gross, and Seidman, *The New Old*, 435.

14. S. Clemen-Stone, D.G. Eigsti, and S.L. McGuire, *Comprehensive Family and Community Health Nursing*, 2nd ed. (New York: McGraw-Hill Book Co., 1987), 688.

Chapter 23

Dietary Assessment and Management of the Elderly

Ronni Chernoff

- What changes occur in the elderly that may lead to inadequate nutritional intake?
- How do sensory changes in the elderly affect nutritional status?
- What diet is often recommended when intestinal diverticula are present?
- What are the dangers of over-the-counter nutrient supplements?

DIETARY ASSESSMENT

Overview

Chronological age is different from physiological age. It is essential to assess nutrition problems in elderly clients in the context of multiple age-related variables that include the presence of chronic or concurrent illnesses, changes in lifestyle, and economic, social, and psychological status, and then to counsel the clients with attention to their individuality. One of the difficulties encountered in providing nutritional care for the elderly is the lack of definitive recommendations about nutrient requirements in aging, healthy people. In addition, it is extremely difficult to quantitate the impact of various chronic and acute illnesses on nutrient requirements.

Assessing the Diet of the Elderly Client

Changes may occur in the diets of older individuals that will affect their overall nutritional status. It is therefore important to obtain a thorough diet history in order to assess the nutrient content of dietary intake (see appendixes A-1 and A-2, Nutrition Questionnaire and 24-Hour Recall). Short-term memory diminishes with age, and it is sometimes difficult for an older individual to recall dietary intake in the immediate past. Patience is required to elicit needed information. It is important to ask open-ended questions and allow the individual to offer information. Sometimes, if the interviewer offers too many suggestions or alternatives,

255

the elderly person will become confused or agree with the suggestions in an effort to please the interviewer or to shorten the interview.

It is also essential to be aware of cultural or religious eating patterns and foods so that the correct questions can be asked to obtain the desired information. Our society is made up of many cultures, and the elderly are likely to follow particular cultural and religious food habits. Foods that are familiar are comforting and provide a link to the past. They are associated with the habits of a lifetime, and a health care practitioner must be sensitive to their cultural and religious connotations. Attention should also be paid of course to individual food likes and dislikes.

The environment in which many older people find themselves living may be different from what they anticipated or had hoped for. They may find themselves living alone or in a situation where they have little control over their lives; choices are being made for them, choices that they might not have made for themselves. They often cannot choose their own food, leaving them only with the choice to eat it or not.

Increasing disability may restrict elderly people to their homes during periods of severe weather, impeding their ability to shop or participate in meal or social programs. Their lives may change beyond their control. Often this leads to depression, which may contribute to a lack of appetite. In all such cases, it is important to delve into the clients' lifestyles and living arrangements in order to understand thoroughly their social and economic situations.

Psychological changes that occur with advancing age are difficult to measure, but they often impact on the nutrition and health status of aging people. When elderly people experience the loss of loved ones who are their age contemporaries, they must face their own mortality. At such times, they often become increasingly isolated, lonely, and depressed.[1] Depression may lead to decreased appetite and lack of desire to cook or prepare meals. Meal planning may become a low priority, and nutritionally rich foods may be replaced by easy-to-prepare frozen or canned goods or fast foods that have high levels of commonly restricted nutrients, such as salt and fat. Elderly men who have lost their spouses or are living on fixed incomes may not be skilled in meal planning, food selection, or food preparation and may select foods that require little or no preparation or are filling and inexpensive, such as dry cereals and frozen foods, and are often accompanied by alcoholic beverages.

The impact of the emotional changes associated with feeling useless or helpless cannot be underestimated when assessing the nutritional status of elderly individuals. A clinician who is sensitive to the existence of these emotional and psychological changes will be better equipped to assess such individuals within the context of their psychological state. Environmental support groups, such as church groups or neighbors, often are better able to assess such individuals' nutrition and health status than are emotional support groups, such as family members or longtime friends, who may be geographically unavailable.[2]

Other factors that may lead to changes in the dietary intakes of elderly people include alterations in oral health and dentition status, problems with chewing and swallowing, medical restrictions, economic and social changes, and physiological changes associated with aging, such as sensory losses or decreased mobility and manual dexterity.

Data Analysis

Diet information obtained from the initial interview and records of the elderly client should be evaluated in terms of the nutritional needs of the client. Time may not permit calculation of nutrients in milligram amounts. However, the diet can be quickly assessed by comparing its content with the food groups (see appendix B-1). In this way, omissions of certain categories of foods, exceedingly high- or low-nutrient foods, and unusual diets can be noted.

The Recommended Dietary Allowances (RDA) (see appendix B-2) provide guidelines for nutritional requirements for people over 50 years of age. Since life expectancy is now approximately 72 years for males and 77 years for females and the human life span is estimated to be over 100 years, there is considerable latitude in extrapolating nutrient requirements for healthy elderly people. Yet, despite the lack of specific guidelines, allowances for nutritional demands and alterations in requirements that may be associated with episodes of acute illness or chronic conditions must still be made for older people.

Calorie needs are usually estimated by using height and weight measures, combined with a factor for activity. However, height and weight change as people age; so does body composition, which is also a factor in the estimation of energy needs. Total calories needed to maintain weight decrease as people age. Protein requirements in elderly people are generally thought to be the same as for younger adults;[3] the RDA is for 0.8 grams/kg body weight (see appendix B-2).

Carbohydrates normally provide the largest percentage of calories in a normal diet. This proportion is also appropriate for older people. Carbohydrate sources that are complex and rich in dietary fiber should be encouraged. Refined carbohydrates, for example, sweets, often have fewer vitamins and minerals.

Only small amounts of fat are required to provide essential fatty-acid and fat-soluble vitamins; these may be obtained from vegetable sources (vitamins A and K), low-fat dairy products (vitamins D and E), cereals, grains, and other food sources. If it is necessary to restrict caloric intake in order to manage obesity, limiting fat intake is a reasonable strategy (see appendix G-1).

Vitamin and mineral requirements for adults over age 50 have not been well-defined,[4] but they are assumed to be equivalent to requirements for younger adults. On the other hand, studies indicate that the elderly tend to have low intakes of calcium, iron, and magnesium.

COMMON NUTRITIONAL PROBLEMS OF THE ELDERLY

Information about common nutritional problems of the elderly is provided in Table 23-1; the table also suggests assessment questions, follow-up actions, and ways to evaluate outcomes. Table 23-2 lists types of elderly persons who are at risk of dehydration. Table 23-3 provides information on the potential drug-nutrient interactions of some commonly used drugs.

Table 23-1 Common Nutritional Problems of the Elderly

I. OBESITY/OVERWEIGHT (see also chapter 20)

As people age, calories required to maintain weight decrease.

Activity levels often decrease with the onset of chronic illnesses, cardiovascular response to exercise, loss of fitness, and lack of motivation; and this further reduces the number of calories required.

Obesity adds to the burden of the skeletal, muscular, cardiovascular, and respiratory systems and leads to a further decrease in activity.

Assessment	Action
What is the client's weight history? Does it involve a recent gain or a long-standing problem?	Discuss weight with the client. Try to determine the client's interest in a weight-loss program.
What is the food intake of the client? Quantity? Quality?	Through the nutrition questionnaire and 24-hour recall (see appendixes A-1 and A-2), determine the quantity and quality of the present diet.
Are there constraints in obtaining and preparing appropriate food? Problems with menu planning? Shopping? Food preparation?	Discuss how food is purchased and prepared. Determine if there are constraints that may be barriers to obtaining lower-calorie, nourishing food. Help the client find ways to overcome these problems.
Is the client motivated to change food habits and lose weight?	Discuss motivation with the client. Together, plan a diet that is adapted to the client's eating habits and lifestyle. Encourage the limiting of fat and refined carbohydrates (see Table 16-1).
What is the exercise activity of the client?	Encourage walking if possible. Help the client include some exercise in daily activity.
	Encourage follow-up visits (every 1-2 weeks) for further counseling and weight monitoring. If possible, have the client keep a three-day food diary (see appendix A-4).

Table 23-1 continued

Evaluation

Examine the client's food diary for positive changes in food intake.

Discuss participation in exercise activity and evaluate progress.

If excess weight continues to be a serious problem, consider referral to a support group.

II. FLUID BALANCE

Dehydration:

Fluid requirements in the elderly are frequently not met, and dehydration may occur.[5]

Adequate fluid intake in the elderly is hampered by an age-related decrease in thirst sensitivity and in the efficiency of renal and pulmonary mechanisms for fluid and electrolyte balance control.[6]

Fluid requirements increase if fever, diarrhea, vomiting, fistulous losses, exudative losses, or hemorrhage occur.

Another age-related factor is an inability to conserve water or concentrate urine effectively because of renal changes.

Individuals who have incontinence problems often limit their fluid intake in an attempt to control the problem.

Bladder training, or incontinence management, is better effected if the individual is taking enough fluid so that a regular voiding pattern can be established by routinely emptying the bladder before sphincter control is stressed.

Overhydration:

Excess fluid may also be a serious problem in elderly people.

People with chronic renal problems, congestive heart failure, or protein-energy malnutrition with severe hypoalbuminemia also are at risk of overhydration.

Assessment	Action
What is the fluid intake of the client?	By questioning, try to determine the fluid intake from the client or caregiver. Use of the 24-hour recall method may be helpful (see appendix A-2).
Is the client at risk for dehyration?	See Table 23-2 for types of elderly persons who are at risk for dehydration. Fluid requirements are approximately 1.3 quarts or about six glasses per day.[7] (Ask the client or caregiver to keep an intake record for three days to assess adequate or excess amounts of liquid intake.
Are water and other liquids readily available to the client?	Suggest to the client or caregiver to keep water in the refrigerator or on an accessible table.[8] Encourage the client to drink fluids as needed. Suggest smaller fruit and vegetable juice containers to avoid spills and waste. Encourage use of milk (skim or whole) and soups.

Table 23-1 continued

Can the client serve the liquid without help?	Suggest putting the liquid in lightweight plastic container with easy-to-open cap. Plastic glasses may be easier to handle. A set of multicolored glasses may serve to remind the elderly client how many glasses of liquid have been consumed.
Is the client at risk for overhydration?	Have the client or caregiver keep a fluid intake and output record, which should show a balance. Weight can also be used as a measure of fluid balance; either gains or losses in weight may indicate shifts in fluid balance.

Evaluation

Examine the client's fluid intake at follow-up visit and determine if adequate amounts of liquid are being taken.

Review suggestions for increasing fluids with the client and/or caregiver, and continue to encourage appropriate fluid intake.

If the problem persists and the client appears in danger of dehydration or overhydration, refer to a physician for further evaluation.

III. OSTEOPOROSIS

Osteoporosis is a common problem among elderly women.

Therapy is aimed at limiting further progression of the disease.

Once the disease process has begun, bone changes can be slowed, perhaps even stopped, but not reversed.

This is commonly done by replacement hormone therapy.

Peak bone age is reached in the mid-to-early 40s, so every effort should be made to avoid development of the disease.

For assessment, action, and evaluation in osteoporosis, see Table 20-1, Section IV.

IV. HYPERTENSION

Hypertension is a common, chronic medical problem in elderly individuals.

A low sodium diet is often recommended (see appendix G-2).

The difference between salt and sodium is sometimes confusing.

In following a modified diet, some people tend to react at the extremes and eliminate an entire class of foods or eat excessive amounts of some foods.

If a diet and drug regime is prescribed, a careful review is essential to ensure that hyponatremia or hypokalemia do not occur.

Even if a potassium-retaining diuretic is prescribed, clients may eat large amounts of potassium-rich foods.

For assessment, action, and evaluation in hypertension, see Table 20-1, Section III.

Table 23-1 continued

V. ORAL HEALTH

Loss of teeth and poor oral hygiene may contribute to diminished ability to chew fresh fruits and vegetables and whole meats. Some people eliminate these foods from their diet if eating them becomes difficult, thereby reducing the vitamin, mineral, protein, and dietary fiber content of the diet.

Pureed or blended fruits, vegetables, and meats are categorized as "baby foods" and are rejected by the elderly.

Lean body mass and bone density are reduced in elderly people, and dentures may no longer fit properly; uncomfortable, loose, or irritating dentures may not be worn.

Replacing dentures may not be a high priority for elderly people living on a fixed or limited income.

Assessment	Action
What is the food intake of the client?	With the nutrition questionnaire and 24-hour recall (see appendixes A-1 and A-2), determine the quantity and quality of the client's diet. Focus instruction on missing food groups.
Is the client able to eat fresh fruits and vegetables and whole meats?	Discuss substitutions, such as cooked fresh, canned or frozen fruits and vegetables and preparation of meats or combined dishes that will provide a softer product.
	Suggest removing fruit seeds and skin, meat sinews, and frankfurter skin.
Does the client and/or caregiver appear motivated to change food preparation?	Provide recipe suggestions for softer, easier-to-chew foods.
	Incorporate more milk, eggs, and cheese into food preparation. Increase use of fish and peanut butter.
	Demonstrations of food preparation with tasting will often increase motivation and provide an opportunity for the client to ask further questions for clarification.
Does the client report ill-fitting dentures, loss of teeth, or sore mouth?	If possible, refer the client to a dentist or dental hygienist who has been trained in geriatrics.

Evaluation

At follow-up visits, examine the client's food diary for increased intake of fruits, vegetables, and meats or of substitutions.

Discuss food preparation and continue to make suggestions for improving the diet.

Discuss home care of the mouth and determine if more regular care is needed.

Table 23-1 continued

If diet intake is very inadequate, refer to a registered dietitian (R.D.) for in-depth diet and food preparation counseling.

Encourage return visits to the dentist and dental hygienist.

VI. SENSORY CHANGES THAT AFFECT NUTRITIONAL STATUS

There is some evidence that taste sensitivity diminishes with age.

If taste sensation decreases, food will taste bland or be tasteless; tasteless food is unappetizing and will not be eaten.

Smell and taste are closely related; in lieu of taste, the smell of food is a key factor in its acceptability.

Reduced peripheral vision may affect nutritional status by restricting driving ability; making it hard to read labels, prices, recipes, and directions; and making it difficult to light pilot lights in gas stoves or to read dials on electric appliances.

Vision losses contribute to decisions to restrict social activities and may keep elderly people house-bound.

Loss of hearing may translate into an aversion to talking to grocery clerks, pharmacists, waiters, and social workers or to anyone who might otherwise provide guidance, direction, or helpful information.

Touch is also affected by aging. Loss of nerve sensitivity and manual dexterity may make food preparation difficult. Dietary intake may be limited by an inability to cut, slice, chop, or mince foods; to use can openers, mixers, blenders, or other kitchen equipment; or to hold and use a knife and fork.

Chronic problems—such as arthritis, gout, and bone pain—will contribute to these difficulties.

Assessment	Action
What is the food intake of the client? Quantity? Quality?	With the nutrition questionnaire and 24-hour recall (see appendixes A-1 and A-2), determine the quantity and quality of the present diet and compare its content with the food groups (see appendix B-1).
Is the intake inadequate because of loss of taste and/or smell?	Suggest techniques for enhancing the flavor of foods, for example, the use of strong spices, herbs, and flavorings, such as lemon dishes; lemon juice on fish, vegetables, and meats; herb bread; and coffee- or vanilla-flavored milkshakes.
Does the client have difficulties with vision that may affect food intake?	Question the client about shopping and food preparation procedures. If the client is limited by a vision handicap, refer to local support services, such as shopping buses for the elderly, Meals-on-Wheels, or visiting homemakers.

Table 23-1 continued

Does the client have dexterity problems that affect food preparation?	Make suggestions for simplified food preparation and use of special equipment to facilitate food preparation. (Refer to "Mealtime Manual for People with Disabilities and the Aging," Campbell Soup Company, Box MM56, Camden, NJ 08101.)

Evaluation

Have client keep a three-day food record (see appendix A-4) and bring it to a follow-up visit to evaluate the adequacy of the diet.

Review food purchasing and preparation problems with the client, and reinforce suggestions to facilitate obtaining and consuming adequate food.

If the diet continues to be inadequate because of an inability to obtain and/or prepare food, refer to social services for support.

VII. INADEQUATE NUTRIENT INTAKE

Due to the decline in basal metabolic rate associated with advancing age, there is often a decrease in total calorie intake to compensate for lower metabolism and to avoid weight gain.

The elderly are vulnerable to vitamin and trace-element deficiencies associated with reduction in overall intake.

It is rare to see specific vitamin or mineral deficiencies in elderly persons; if signs or symptoms of malnutrition are detected, they will reflect generalized malnutrition.

There are multiple factors, aside from voluntary calorie restriction, that interfere with elderly people having an adequate intake of nutrients.

Assessment	Action
What is the food intake of the client? Quantity? Quality?	With the nutrition questionnaire and/or 24-hour recall (see appendixes A-1 and A-2), determine the quantity and quality of the present diet by comparing its content with the food groups (see appendix B-1).
Is the intake inadequate because the client is decreasing calories in an effort to lose or maintain weight?	Cooperatively plan a diet with the client that is adapted to the client's food habits and is attainable in terms of shopping and food preparation.
Is the intake inadequate because the client is unable to eat sufficiently large amounts of food?	Make suggestions for more nutrient-dense foods.
Are there other problems that interfere with intake, such as inadequate income, physical disabilities, or oral problems?	Refer to social services or other support groups (also see Sections II, V and VI).

Table 23-1 continued

Evaluation

Have the client or caregiver bring a three-day food record (see appendix A-4) to the next visit and evaluate it for improved intake.

Reinforce information about which nutrients and food group(s) the client should increase to improve the quality of food intake.

If inadequate intake or undesirable amounts of weight loss continue, refer to a registered dietitian (R.D.) for in-depth counseling.

VIII. GASTROINTESTINAL CHANGES THAT AFFECT NUTRITIONAL STATUS

Decreased salivary secretions make mastication and the swallowing of food more difficult.

Decreased gastric secretion of hydrochloric acid, pepsin, and intrinsic factors results in impaired protein digestion, less efficient absorption of vitamin B_{12}, and a greater likelihood of bacterial contamination of gastric juice.

The increased amount of residue that results from poor digestion and absorption can cause increased flatulence.

Decreased gastrointestinal muscle tone and peristalsis make constipation a frequent problem in the elderly.

Intestinal diverticula is age-related and may result in bouts of diverticulitis. It has been suggested that increasing the amount of dietary fiber eaten will reduce the tendency to form diverticula and reduce the incidence of inflammation in existing diverticula.[9]

Assessment	Action
Does the client report problems with flatulence, constipation, or gastrointestinal discomfort?	Determine the quantity and quality of the present diet, using the 24-hour recall (see appendix A-2) and compare its content with the food groups (see appendix B-1).
What is the fluid intake? The dietary fiber content? Regularity of eating?	Plan a diet with the client that includes all food groups. Suggest dividing the food into four or five regular eating periods. If dietary fiber intake is low, suggest a moderate increase of dietary fiber, including fruits, vegetables, and some higher-fiber cereals and breads. Emphasize the need for six to eight glasses of water and other fluids each day.
What is the exercise routine of the client?	Recommend daily exercise, if possible.
What are the bowel habits of the client?	Emphasize the need to establish a regular time for bowel movement.

Table 23-1 continued

Evaluation

During follow-up visits, assess for reduction in symptoms. Have the client keep a three-day food record to use for evaluating changes in eating habits.

Evaluate for changes in lifestyle routines, such as exercise and bowel habits.

If symptoms continue, refer to a physician for in-depth evaluation.

IX. POLYPHARMACY AND ABUSE OF NUTRIENT SUPPLEMENTS

Polypharmacy is the use of multiple prescription medications.

Elderly people are likely to take many different prescription drugs and are major consumers of over-the-counter medications.[10]

Drug-nutrient interactions may have serious effects on nutritional status.

In one survey, 57 percent of the men and 61 percent of the women were taking one or more "over the counter" nutrient supplements.[11]

There is little evidence that large doses of vitamin C provide positive health benefits.[12]

There is a danger of rebound scurvy (relative vitamin C deficiency) occurring if megadoses of vitamin C are suddenly stopped.

Excessive vitamin A can be toxic and can result in general malaise, headaches, liver dysfunction, and a low white cell count.[13]

Assessment	Action
What prescription and over-the-counter medication and supplements is the client taking?	Ask the client for names of the products and the strength, amount, and frequency of dosage.
Is the client correctly following directions regarding the taking of medications and supplements?	Have the client bring in medication containers and check the dosages prescribed or recommended.
Is the client likely to be at risk for excessive intake of a medication or drug-nutrient interaction?	Check potential drug-nutrient interactions (see Table 23-3). If there is concern over combinations of medications that may cause a drug-nutrient interaction, refer to a physician for further assessment.
Is the client taking excessive amounts of supplement preparations?	Discuss the dangers of megadoses of nutrients. Review food groups (see appendix B-1) and emphasize that needed nutrients can be obtained from a balanced diet.

Evaluation

Review intake of prescription drugs and over-the-counter medications and supplements with the client at a follow-up visit.

If there is continued concern, refer the client for further assessment.

Table 23-2 Elderly Persons Who Are at Risk of Dehydration

Unconscious persons
Confused persons
Depressed persons
Disabled persons
Anorectic persons
Chair- or bed-bound persons
Laxative abusers
Diuretics users
Persons who have diarrhea, vomiting, or hemorrhage
Persons receiving tube or intravenous feeding
Persons with central nervous system impairment
Persons with renal disease
Persons with bladder control problems

Table 23-3 Potential Drug-Nutrient Interactions for Some Commonly Used Drugs

Drug	Nutrient	Potential Side Effect
Alcohol	Thiamin	Deficiency
	Vitamin B_4	Deficiency
	Folate	Deficiency
	Zinc	Deficiency
	Calcium	Deficiency
	Magnesium	Deficiency
Aluminum hydroxide	Phosphorus	Binding
	Calcium	Deficiency
Antacids	Thiamin	Decreased absorption due to
	Calcium	altered gastrointestinal pH
	Iron	
Anticoagulants	Vitamin K	Deficiency
Antihistamines		Weight gain
Amphetamines		Appetite suppression
		Weight loss
Aspirin	Iron	Anemia
Cathartics	Calcium	Impaired gastrointestinal motility
	Potassium	Impaired gastrointestinal motility
Chodestyramine	Vitamins A, D, E, K	Deficiencies
Cimetidine	Vitamin B_{12}	Deficiency

Table 23-3 continued

Drug	Nutrient	Potential Side Effect
Clofibrate	Carbohydrate	Enzyme inactivation
	Vitamin B_{12}	Decreased absorption
	Carotene	
	Iron	
Colchicine	Vitamin B_{12}	Decreased absorption due to
	Carotene	damaged intestinal mucosa
	Magnesium	
Corticosteroids	Zinc	Damage to intestinal mucosa
	Calcium	
	Potassium	Gastrointestinal loss
Ethacrynic acid	Sodium	Depletion
Furosemide	Calcium	Diuretic effect
	Potassium	Depletion
	Sodium	
Gentamicin	Potassium	Depletion
	Sodium	
Levodopa	Protein	Competition for absorption
Neomycin	Fat	Decreases pancreatic lipase,
	Protein	binds bile salts, and interferes
	Sodium	with absorption
	Potassium	
	Calcium	
	Iron	
	Vitamin B_{12}	
Penicillamine	Zinc	Altered nutrient excretion
	Vitamin B_6	
	Sodium	
Phenobarbital	Vitamin D	Impaired metabolism and
	Folate	utilization
Phenytoin	Vitamin D	Impaired metabolism and
	Folate	utilization
Tetracycline	Protein	Impaired uptake and utilization
	Iron	Impaired uptake and utilization
		General malabsorption
Tricyclic antidepressants		Weight gain due to appetite
		stimulation

Source: Reprinted from *Nutrition Today*, Vol. 22, No. 2, pp. 4–11, with permission of © by Williams & Wilkins Company, 1987.

NOTES

1. "Report of the Public Health Service Task Force on Women's Health Issues," *Public Health Reports* 100 (January/February 1985): 74–106.

2. W.A. McIntosh and P.A. Shifflet, "Influence of Social Support Systems on Dietary Intake of the Elderly," *Journal of Nutrition for the Elderly* 4 (1984): 5.

3. A. Richardson, "The Effect of Age and Aging on Protein Synthesis by Cells and Tissues from Mammals," in *Handbook of Nutrition in the Aged*, ed. R.R. Watson (Boca Raton, Fla.: CRC Press, 1985), 36.

4. E.L. Schneider, "Recommended Dietary Allowances and the Health of the Elderly," *New England Journal of Medicine* 314 (1986): 157.

5. R. Chernoff, "Aging and Nutrition," *Nutrition Today* 22 (1987): 4–11.

6. J.W. Rowe and R.W. Besdine, *Health and Disease in Old Age* (Boston: Little, Brown & Co., 1982), 172.

7. A.O. Albanese, "Nutrition and Health of the Elderly," *Nutrition News* 39 (1976): 5.

8. A. Boylan and B. Marbach, "Dehydration: Subtle Sinister . . . Preventable," *RN*, August 1979: 36–41.

9. A.B. Natow and J.A. Heslin, *Nutritional Care of the Older Adult* (New York: Macmillan Co., 1986), 96.

10. P.P. Lamy, "Drug Prescribing for the Elderly," *Bulletin of the New York Academy of Medicine* 57 (1981): 718.

11. P.J. Garry and J.S. Goodwin, "Nutritional Status in a Healthy Elderly Population: Vitamin C," *American Journal of Clinical Nutrition* 36 (1982): 319.

12. J.E. Morley, "Nutritional Status of the Elderly," *American Journal of Medicine* 81 (1986): 679.

13. Ibid., 681.

Part IX

Individuals with Special Needs

Chapter 24

Acquired Immunodeficiency Syndrome

Dena Rakower

- What food intake suggestions can help the AIDS client offset weight loss?
- Which foods may be tolerated if oral lesions are present?
- What nutritional therapies are helpful in malabsorption?
- What are the dangers of alternative nutrition therapies?

DIETARY ASSESSMENT

Overview

Acquired immunodeficiency syndrome (AIDS) is an illness caused by human immunodeficiency virus (HIV). This virus invades lymphocytes and other cells, resulting in a deficiency in cell-mediated immunity. The body is virtually defenseless against many infections.[1]

There are many nutritional problems associated with AIDS. Weight loss with protein malnutrition is probably the most devastating.[2,3,4] Protein calorie malnutrition (PCM) has an additive effect on immunosuppression, since it too results in decreased cell-mediated immunity.[5,6,7]

Some of the causes of PCM in AIDS include increased metabolic needs,[8] decreased food intake[9] secondary to anorexia, nausea, vomiting, and dysphagia (difficulty in swallowing), and diarrhea—often with malabsorption.[10] Dealing with these problems and improving clients' nutritional status can be crucial to restoring a dependent bedridden patient to self-care.[11]

Assessing the AIDS Client

Assessment of an AIDS client's nutritional status begins with an interview to evaluate:

- adequacy of recent intake
- weight history: changes from usual weight

271

- gastrointestinal problems: nausea, vomiting, diarrhea, constipation, dysphagia, odynophagia (painful swallowing), dysgeusia (taste changes), chewing problems, early satiety, and poor appetite
- use of vitamin/mineral supplements
- food intolerances (for example, milk)
- adequacy of funds to purchase food
- ability to shop and cook

Additional assessment parameters might include:

- visual assessment for cachexia with muscle wasting
- mid-arm circumference to assess somatic protein and fat stores
- intake of serum albumin and retinol-binding protein to assess visceral protein stores.

A nutrition questionnaire can be developed for assessing the AIDS client, using the generic nutrition questionnaire in appendix A-1.

COMMON NUTRITIONAL PROBLEMS OF THE AIDS CLIENT

Information about common nutritional problems of the AIDS client is provided in Table 24-1. The table also suggests further assessment questions, recommended actions, and ways to evaluate outcomes. Table 24-2 lists common drugs used for AIDS patients' drug-nutrient interactions.

ALTERNATIVE NUTRITION THERAPIES

Alternative diets are a lure for terminally ill people. These patients are often willing to try anything in hope of prolonging life, diminishing symptoms, or even finding a cure. Common alternative nutritional therapies used by AIDS clients are the macrobiotic diet, the yeast-free diet, and AL-721.

Macrobiotic Diet

The macrobiotic diet is based on the idea that eating selected foods will purify the body.[51] The diet includes certain whole grains, legumes, seeds, vegetables, fruit, and some fish. Dairy products, eggs, wheat products, and refined sugars are omitted. In some versions of the diet, liquids are restricted. There is no credible scientific evidence that the macrobiotic diet is of benefit to people with AIDS.

Table 24-1 Common Nutritional Problems of the AIDS Client

I. WEIGHT LOSS

Assessment	Action
What is the client's weight history? Has there been recent significant weight loss?	Counsel the client to follow a high-calorie, high-protein diet:
	Eat three, well-balanced meals a day, plus several snacks.
	Eat the main dish (protein food) first.
	Add calorie-dense foods, such as margarine, butter, mayonnaise, gravies, sauces, etc.
	Drink liquids at the end of the meal to avoid getting full too quickly.

Evaluation

Have the client keep a three-day food diary (see appendix A-4) and examine it for increases in food intake.

Discuss ways of incorporating additional calories into foods shown in the food diary.

Evaluate the client's weight and compare it with initial data to determine if the client is gaining or, at least, maintaining weight. An appropriate goal is an increase of one to two pounds per week.

II. ESOPHAGITIS AND ORAL LESIONS

Common etiologies of dysphagia and odynophagia include candidiasis (a fungal infection also known as "thrush"), Kaposi's sarcoma, oral herpes simplex, and cytomegalovirus.[12-15]

People with esophagitis often describe a sensation of food getting stuck in the chest when they swallow.

Assessment	Action
Is dysphagia affecting the intake of food? If so, which foods?	Counsel the client on soft, nutritious foods:
Whole meats?	High-protein, soft foods (omelettes, flaked fish, casserole dishes, cottage cheese, hot cereals made with milk and puddings).
Raw fruits and vegetables?	
Cooked fruits and vegetables?	
Can only liquids be tolerated?	Blenderized or mashed food or baby foods.
	Addition of gravies and butter to help moisten foods and add calories.
	Avoidance of rough foods, such as raw carrots and hard crackers, and sour or spicy foods, if they cause pain.
	Use of commercial, calorie-dense drinks or puddings.

Table 24-1 continued

A mixture of 10 cc, 2% viscous
lidocaine, benadryl elixer (25 mg in 5 cc
water), and 10 cc antacid (for viscosity)
can be swished in mouth before meals
for an anesthetic effect.

Evaluation

Continue to monitor food intake, weight status, and serum albumin.

If the intake continues to be inadequate, home tube feeding or parenteral nutrition can be considered.

III. DIARRHEA

Diarrhea in AIDS clients is often associated with severe weight loss.[16,17]

Although there are many possible etiologies, in over 50 percent of the clients, none is ever diagnosed.[18-20]

Diarrhea can be caused or exacerbated by infectious agents, Kaposi's sarcoma,[21-24] and protein calorie malnutrition.[25,26]

Assessment	Action
Is the diarrhea severe?	Replacement of fluids and electrolytes is essential.
Are large amounts of fluid lost because of diarrhea?	Oral rehydration is ideal. In addition to juices, caffeine-free soft drinks, water, tea, and broths, commercial fluid/electrolyte replacements are available.
	If the client is unable to take fluids by mouth, nasogastric or intravenous replacement may be necessary.
Is the diarrhea of infectious etiology?	Test stool samples for abnormal bacteria, ova, and parasites.
	If infectious etiology, refer for appropriate medication.
	If stool test is negative, give antidiarrheal medications and fluid and, if necessary, electrolyte replacement.
Is the client malabsorbing nutrients? If so, many whole foods will exacerbate the diarrhea.	Counsel on a low-fat, low-lactose, low-fiber diet. If severe diarrhea persists, consider tube feeding with elemental formula or parenteral nutrition.
Malabsorption tests:	If malabsorption tests are negative, counsel the client to increase intake of food to prevent weight loss. Stress well-balanced, high-protein intake.
Shilling test to assess absorption of Vitamin B_{12}.[27,28]	
D-xylose challenge to assess absorption of carbohydrates.[29-31]	
Sudan stain to qualitatively assess fecal fat excretion.[32-34]	

Table 24-1 continued

Evaluation

Regular monitoring of weight, fluid status, and serum electrolytes with replacement, as necessary.

IV. DRUG/NUTRIENT INTERACTIONS

Many of the medications commonly used in the treatment of AIDS have nutritional implications. Some have direct effects on nutrient utilization or availability. Others cause a variety of toxicities or GI side effects. (See Table 24-2 for a list of the nutritional interactions and interventions of certain medications.)

The macrobiotic diet is often:

- low in calories and high in fiber (fiber tends to satisfy hunger quickly and makes adequate intake of calories difficult)
- low in certain vitamins and minerals, including calcium, iron, vitamin B_{12}, niacin, riboflavin, and vitamins B_6 and D.[52]
- low in protein unless care is taken in protein complementation
- dangerous when liquids are limited, causing or exacerbating dehydration

However, when carefully planned, the macrobiotic diet can be nutritionally well-balanced. Recommended modifications of this diet include:

- increased intake of fish
- adding yogurt or other dairy foods
- use of fortified soybean milk
- increased fluids
- a one-a-day type of vitamin

Yeast-Free Diet

Advocates of the yeast-free, or candidiasis hypersensitivity, diet suggest that candida infections weaken the immune system and that certain foods stimulate yeast growth. It, therefore, stipulates the avoidance of yeast-promoting or yeast-containing foods. The list of foods to be avoided is extensive; it includes leftovers, cheeses, all sugars, breads made with yeast, all packaged and processed foods, and canned, bottled, or frozen juices.[53] However, the diet has no scientific basis. It is in fact difficult to follow and can be dangerous.[54]

Table 24-2 Common Drugs Used for AIDS Patients' Drug/Nutrient Interactions

Medication	Use	Possible Interaction/ Side Effects	Intervention
Bactrim (trimethoprim-sulfamethoxazole)[35-36]	Pneumocystis carinii pneumonia (PCP)	Nausea/vomiting Upset stomach Megaloblastic anemia (rarely) (trimethoprim inhibits dihydrofolate reductase when taken by folate deficient patient) Glossitis/stomatitis Nephrotoxicity (reversible) Hyponatremia	Antiemetics PRN Take with food or antacid If megaloblastic anemia, give folinic acid (leucovorin) Soft foods if necessary Push fluids Fluid restriction only if caused by the Syndrome of Inappropriate Anti-Diuretic Hormone (SIADM)
Pentamidine isethionate[37-40]	PCP	Taste changes (dysgeusia) Hypoglycemia Insulin-dependent diabetes (B-cell toxicity) Nausea/vomiting Azotemia (reversible) Hypocalcemia	Add strong flavors to offending food Small frequent meals Use no-concentrated sweets diet if possible Antiemetics PRN Push fluids Calcium supplementation
Dapsone[41,42]	With trimethoprim for PCP	Anorexia Nausea/vomiting	Encourage calorie-dense foods Antiemetics PRN
Pyrimethamine[43]	With sulfadiazine for toxoplasmosis	Megaloblastic anemia (inhibits dihydrofolate reductase)	Always give folinic acid
Acyclovir[44] (Zovirax)	Herpes simplex Herpes zoster	Nephrotoxicity (when given with other nephrotoxic meds) Occasional nausea/vomiting	Push fluids Antiemetics PRN

Drug	Action/Use	Side effects	Intervention
AZT (zidovudine retrovir)[45]	Inhibits HIV replication	Nausea/vomiting Reduction in serum Vit B_{12} B_{12} deficiency (rarely) Macrocytic anemia	Antiemetics PRN Monitor and replete PRN Usually nonnutritional
DHPG[46]	Cytomegalovirus (CMV)	Diarrhea (rarely) Vomiting (rarely) Gastric ulceration and GI perforation (rarely)	Antidiarrheal Antiemetics PRN Diet changes as appropriate (a medical emergency)
Amphotericin-B[47]	Cryptococcal infection Histoplasmosis Severe candidiasis	Very nephrotoxic Anorexia Vomiting Hypokalemia and hypomagnesemia	Push fluids Push calorie-dense foods Antiemetics PRN Monitor and replete
Ketoconazole[48,49]	Candidiasis Histoplasmosis	Needs acidic stomach for absorption	Avoid H_2 blockers and antacids or give ketoconazole two hours prior to above meds
Flucytosine[50]	Candidiasis Cryptococcal infections	Nausea/vomiting Diarrhea Severe enterocolitis	Antiemetics PRN Antidiarrheal Diet changes only if this occurs

AL-721

AL-721 is a lipid compound (mostly lecithin) extracted from egg yolk and taken orally mixed with fruit juice. It performs its purported antiviral activity by modification of the cell membranes' lipid composition. This is to prevent the HIV virus from attaching to receptor sites and invading cells.[55,56] As yet, no adequate clinical trials of the diet have been completed. The compound itself appears to be safe; however, people are being instructed to follow low-fat diets, especially within three hours of taking the AL-721 supplement. It should be noted that this diet can foster weight loss and can exacerbate PCM.

NOTES

1. R.C. Gallo, P.S. Farin, and E.P. Gelman, "Isolation of Human T-cell Leukemia in Acquired Immune Deficiency Syndrome," in R. Kulstad, ed., *AIDS: Papers from Science, 1982–1985*, Report May 20, 1983 (Washington, D.C.: American Association for the Advancement of Science, 1986), 44–49.

2. R.T. Chlebowski, "Significance of Altered Nutritional Status in Acquired Immune Deficiency Syndrome (AIDS)," *Nutrition and Cancer* 7 (1985): 85–91.

3. D.P. Kotler, J. Wang, and R.N. Pierson, "Body Composition Studies in Patients with the Acquired Immunodeficiency Syndrome," *American Journal of Clinical Nutrition* 42 (1985): 1255–1265.

4. D.P. Kotler et al., "Enteropathy Associated with the Acquired Immunodeficiency Syndrome," *Annals of Internal Medicine* 101 (1984): 421–428.

5. R.K. Chandra, "Nutrition, Immunity and Infection: Present Knowledge and Future Directions," *Lancet* 1 (1983): 688–691.

6. R.H. Grey, "Similarities Between AIDS and PCM," *American Journal of Public Health* 73 (1983): 1332.

7. A.R. Sherman, "Alterations in Immunity Related to Nutritional Status," *Nutrition Today* 7 (1986): 7–13.

8. Chlebowski, "Significance of Altered Nutritional Status," 88.

9. D.P. Kotler, "Why Study Nutrition in AIDS?" *Nutrition and Clinical Practice* 1 (1987): 94–95.

10. Kotler, Wang, and Pierson, "Body Composition Studies," 1259.

11. Kotler, "Why Study Nutrition in AIDS?" 94.

12. M. Andriolo, Jr., J.W. Wolf, and J.S. Rosenberg, "AIDS and AIDS-Related Complex: Oral Manifestations and Treatment," *Journal of the American Dietetic Association* 113 (1986): 586–589.

13. W.C. Santangelo and G.J. Krejs, "Southwestern Internal Medicine Conference: Gastrointestinal Manifestations of the Acquired Immunodeficiency Syndrome," *American Journal of Medical Science* 295 (1986): 328–334.

14. V.D. Rodgers and M.F. Kagnoff, "Gastrointestinal Manifestations of the Acquired Immunodeficiency Syndrome," *Western Journal of Medicine* 146 (1987): 57–67.

15. S.J. Bott, E.C. Wilson, and R.W. McCallum, "Dysphagia," *Emergency Decisions*, 1986: 6–23.

16. Kotler et al., "Enteropathy," 1265.

17. Santangelo and Krejs, "Southwestern Internal Medicine Conference," 330.

18. Kotler, "Why Study Nutrition in AIDS?" 95.

19. Rodgers and Kagnoff, "Gastrointestinal Manifestations," 61.

20. R. Modigliani et al., "Diarrhea and Malabsorption in Acquired Immune Deficiency Syndrome: A Study of Four Cases with Special Emphasis on Opportunistic Protozoan Infestations," *Gut* 26 (1985): 179–187.

21. Kotler et al., "Enteropathy," 423.

22. Rodgers and Kagnoff, "Gastrointestinal Manifestations," 63.

23. Modigliani et al., "Diarrhea and Malabsorption," 184.

24. D.M. Isrealski and J.F. Remington, "Toxoplasmic Encephalitis in Patients with AIDS," *Infectious Diseases of North America* 2 (1988): 429–445.

25. M.S. Coale, and J.R.K. Robson, "Dietary Management of Intractable Diarrhea in Malnourished Patients," *Journal of the American Dietetic Association* 76 (1980): 444–450.

26. R.R. Brinson, "Hypoalbuminemia, Diarrhea, and the Acquired Immunodeficiency Syndrome," *Annals of Internal Medicine* 103 (1985): 413.

27. Rodgers and Kagnoff, "Gastrointestinal Manifestations," 64.

28. E. Braunwald et al., eds., *Harrison's Principles of Internal Medicine*, 11th ed. (New York: McGraw-Hill Book Co., 1987), 1264–1265.

29. Kotler et al., "Enteropathy," 426.

30. Rodgers and Kagnoff, "Gastrointestinal Manifestations," 64.

31. Modigliani et al., "Diarrhea and Malabsorption," 186.

32. Kotler et al., "Enteropathy," 427.

33. Modigliani et al., "Diarrhea and Malabsorption," 186.

34. Braunwald et al., *Harrison's Principles*, 1265.

35. A.G. Goodman and L. Gilman, *The Pharmacological Basis of Therapeutics*, 7th ed. (New York: Macmillan Co., 1985), 1035–1037.

36. M.J. Wharton et al., "Trimethoprim-Sulfamethoxazole or Pentamidine for Pneumocystis Carinii Pneumonia in the Acquired Immunodeficiency Syndrome," *Annals of Internal Medicine* 105 (1986): 37–44.

37. Goodman and Gilman, *Pharmacological Basis*, 1061.

38. Wharton et al., "Trimethoprim-Sulfamethoxazole," 39.

39. P. Bouchard et al., "Diabetes Mellitus Following Pentamidine-Induced Hypoglycemia in Humans," *Diabetes* 31 (1982): 40–45.

40. R.D. Pearson and E.L. Hewlett, "Pentamidine for the Treatment of Pneumocystis Carinii Pneumonia and Other Protozoal Diseases," *Annals of Internal Medicine* 103 (1985): 782–786.

41. Goodman and Gilman, *Pharmacological Basis*, 1061.

42. G.S. Leoung et al., "Dapsone-Trimethoprim for Pneumocystis Carinii Pneumonia in the Acquired Immunodeficiency Syndrome," *Annals of Internal Medicine* 105 (1986): 45–48.

43. Goodman and Gilman, *Pharmacological Basis*, 1063.

44. Ibid., 1064.

45. D.D. Richman et al., "The Toxicity of Azidothymidine (AZT) in the Treatment of Patients with AIDS and AIDS-Related Complex," *New England Journal of Medicine* 317 (1987): 192–197.

46. D. Felsenstein et al., "Treatment of Cytomegalovirus Retinitis with 9-[2-Hydroxy-1-(Hydroxymethyl) Ethoxymethyl] Guanine," *Annals of Internal Medicine* 103 (1985): 377–380.

47. Goodman and Gilman, *Pharmacological Basis*, 1035.

48. Ibid., 1037.

49. J. Raufman, "Odynophagia/Dysphagia in AIDS," *Gasteroenterology Clinics of North America* 17 (1988): 599–614.

50. Ibid., 1264.

51. D. Erhard, "Nutrition Education for the 'Now' Generation," *Journal of Nutrition Education* 3 (1971), 135–139.

52. "Position Paper on the Vegetarian Approach to Eating," *Journal of the American Dietetic Association* 77 (1980): 61–69.

53. W.G. Crook, *The Yeast Connection: A Medical Breakthrough* (New York: N.Y.: Random House, 1986), 9–14, 81–84.

54. "Position Paper: Candidiasis Hypersensitivity Syndrome Statement," *American Academy of Allergists and Immunologists*, Summer 1985: 12–13.

55. M. Lyte and M. Shinitsky, "A Special Lipid Mixture for Membrane Fluidization," *Biochim Biophys Acta* 812 (1985): 133–138.

56. R.S. Sarin et al., "Effects of a Novel Compound (AL 721) on HTLV-III Infectivity in Vitro," *New England Journal of Medicine* 313 (1985): 1289.

Dietary Assessment Tools

Appendix A-1 Nutrition Questionnaires

GENERIC NUTRITION QUESTIONNAIRE

Instructions for Practitioner:
   The generic nutrition questionnaire has been designed so that a nutrition questionnaire can be developed for any age or category. Questions have been listed under "generic" as well as under specific groupings. To develop a nutrition questionnaire for use with your clients, select those questions from the "generic" list and the specific lists (pregnancy, infancy, young child, and elderly) that are most appropriate to your group. Other questions can be added to make each questionnaire individualized to the needs of each setting.

Name: _____Date: _____

This information will help us to give you more complete health care. It will be kept as a confidential part of your medical record. Please check answers to the following questions.

Data

*Follow-up
Required*

I. Appetite
   a. How would you describe your appetite?
       (   ) Hearty   (   ) Moderate   (   ) Poor
   b. Do you enjoy eating?
       (   ) Yes   (   ) No   (   ) Sometimes

II. Eating pattern and attitudes about food
   a. Do you eat at approximately the same time every day?
       (   ) Yes   (   ) No   (   ) Sometimes
       If yes or sometimes, which meals, and how frequently?
   b. Do you skip meals?
       (   ) Yes   (   ) No
       If yes, at what times?

   c. Are there any foods that you do not eat because you don't think they are good for you?
       (   ) Yes   (   ) No
       If yes, what?

Data	Follow-up Required

d. Do you usually eat anything between meals?

   ( ) Yes   ( ) No

   If yes, name the 2 or 3 snacks (including bedtime snacks) that you have most often.

   _____

   _____

e. During one week, where do you eat most of your food?

   Home_____   School_____
   Work_____   Restaurant_____
   Other_____ (Identify)

f. Are there any foods that you regularly eat because you think that they are good for you?

   ( ) Yes   ( ) No

   If yes, what?

   _____

III. Food choices

a. Is there any food you can't eat?
   ( ) Yes   ( ) No

   If yes, what food(s)? _____

   What happens when you eat this food?

   _____

   _____

b. Are you allergic to any foods?

   ( ) Yes   ( ) No

   If yes, what food(s)? _____

   What happens when you eat this food?

   _____

   _____

c. Are there certain foods that you do not eat because you don't like them?

   ( ) Yes   ( ) No

   If yes, what food(s)? _____

d. Are there certain foods that you avoid eating because of your religious beliefs?

   ( ) Yes   ( ) No

   If yes, what food(s)? _____

e. Are there certain foods that you eat regularly because of your ethnic/cultural background?

   ( ) Yes   ( ) No

   If yes, what food(s) and how often do you eat them?

f. Are you on a special diet?

( ) Yes   ( ) No

Specify type of diet _____

Who recommended the diet? _____

If you have been on a special diet in the past, indicate what kind and
how long _____

g. How is your food usually prepared?

( ) Baked   ( ) Broiled   ( ) Fried

Other _____

h. Do you drink milk?

( ) Yes   ( ) No

If yes:

( ) Whole milk   ( ) Skim milk

( ) Other; specify _____

i. List 5 of your favorite foods:

_____

j. List 5 of your least favorite foods:

_____

IV. Weight history

a. Have you ever had any problems with weight?

( ) Yes   ( ) No

b. If yes, what?

( ) Underweight   ( ) Overweight

( ) Other _____

c. Are you now on a diet to lose weight?

( ) Yes   ( ) No

If yes, what kind? _____

_____

How long? _____

Who recommended it? _____

d. How do you feel about your weight?

( ) Too heavy   ( ) Too thin   ( ) OK

e. Do you ever vomit to keep your weight down?

( ) Every day   ( ) 3-4 times/week

( ) Every week   ( ) Sometimes   ( ) Never

	Follow-up
Data	*Required*

V. Supplements and medications

a. Are you now taking any vitamin or mineral supplements?

( ) Yes   ( ) No

If yes, what, how often, and what brand?

_____

b. Do you regularly take any medications prescribed by your doctor?

( ) Yes   ( ) No

If yes, what? _____

c. Do you regularly take any "over-the-counter" medications?

( ) Yes   ( ) No

If yes, what? _____

VI. Smoking, alcohol, and substance use

a. Do you smoke?

( ) Yes   ( ) No

If yes, how many cigarettes per day?

_____

b. Do you drink any alcoholic beverages (liquor, wine, wine coolers, beer)?

( ) Yes   ( ) No

If yes, what do you drink and how often?

_____

_____

c. Do you smoke marijuana?

( ) Every day   ( ) Other

d. How often do you use crack, cocaine, speed, or other street drugs?

( ) Every day   ( ) 3-6 times/week

( ) Every week   ( ) Sometimes   ( ) Never

VII. Exercise

a. How often do you exercise?

( ) Every day   ( ) 3-6 times/week

( ) Once/week   ( ) Sometimes   ( ) Never

b. List kinds of exercise you do most often _____

c. How often do you get out of breath when you exercise?

( ) Often   ( ) Sometimes   ( ) Never

| | *Follow-up* |
| *Data* | *Required* |

VIII. Household information

    a. Indicate the person who does the following in your household:

       Plans the meals _____

       Buys the food _____

       Prepares the food _____

    b. How much is spent on food each week for your household?

       $_____   (   ) Don't know

       For how many people? _____

    c. Are there periods in the month when there isn't enough money for food or you run out of food?

       (   ) Yes   (   ) No

       If yes, when and how long are these periods? _____

    d. Indicate the types of kitchen equipment you have in your home.

       (   ) Refrigerator   (   ) Working stove

       (   ) Hot plate   (   ) Piped water

                                            (   ) Sink

IX. Food programs

    a. Are you receiving either of the following:

       (   ) Food stamps

       (   ) WIC vouchers

       (   ) Commodity foods

    b. Does your family use:

       (   ) Food Co-ops   (   ) Food Shelves

       (   ) Food Pantries   (   ) Soup Kitchens

       (   ) Free or reduced-price school lunch and/or breakfast

       (   ) Summer Feeding Program

    c. How many hot meals do you have each week?

       >7   7   6   <6

PREGNANCY NUTRITION QUESTIONNAIRE

Select appropriate questions from the Generic Nutrition Questionnaire and then consider inclusion of the following questions:

Data

a. What was your weight before you became pregnant?

_____lbs.   (   ) Don't know

b. During your last pregnancy, how much weight did you gain?

_____lbs.   (   ) Don't know

If known, in how many months?

_____

c. How much weight do you expect to gain during this pregnancy?

_____lbs.   (   ) Don't know

d. Has your weight changed by more than 10 lbs. within the past year prior to this pregnancy?

(   ) Yes   (   ) No   (   ) Don't know

If yes, how much? _____

If yes, why?

(   ) Dieted   (   ) Began eating more

(   ) Illness. If so, what illness? _____

(   ) Was pregnant or lactating

(   ) Change in lifestyle (for example, stress, increased exercise, or work)

(   ) Don't know   (   ) Other

e. Has your eating pattern changed since you became pregnant?

(   ) Yes   (   ) No

If yes, how? _____

_____

f. Do you think that what you eat affects your health or the health of the baby?

(   ) Yes   (   ) No

g. With this pregnancy, have you experienced either of the following?

(   ) Nausea   (   ) Vomiting

If yes, when and how frequently? _____

h. Do you have any cravings for or eat such things as:

(   ) Plaster   (   ) Laundry starch

(   ) Dirt or clay

(   ) Other nonfood items

i. How do you want to feed your baby?

(   ) Breastfeed   (   ) Formula

(   ) Undecided

INFANT NUTRITION QUESTIONNAIRE

> Select appropriate questions from the Generic Nutrition Questionnaire and then consider inclusion of the following questions:

Questions to be answered by parent or caregiver.

Data   *Follow-up Required*

a. Is the baby breastfed?

(   ) Yes   (   ) No

If yes, does the baby also receive formula?

(   ) Yes   (   ) No

If yes, what brand and kind? _____

b. Does the baby receive formula?

(   ) Yes   (   ) No

If yes:

(   ) Ready-to-feed   (   ) Concentrated liquid

(   ) Other _____

How is the formula prepared (especially dilution)?

_____

_____

Is the formula iron-fortified?

(   ) Yes   (   ) No

c. Does the baby drink milk?

(   ) Yes   (   ) No

If yes:

(   ) Whole milk   (   ) 2% milk   (   ) Skim milk

(   ) Other _____

Specify _____

_____

d. How many times does the baby eat each day, including milk or formula? _____

	Follow-up
Data	*Required*

e. If the baby drinks formula or milk, what is the usual amount in a day?

   (   ) Less than 16 oz.   (   ) 16 to 32 oz.

   (   ) More than 32 oz.

f. Does the baby usually take a bottle to bed?

   (   ) Yes   (   ) No

   If yes, what is usually in the bottle?

   _____

g. What was the infant's birthweight? _____

h. Was the infant premature?

   (   ) Yes   (   ) No

i. Do you give your infant extra fluids?

   (   ) Yes   (   ) No

   If so, what and how much? _____

   _____

j. At what age did you start cereal? _____

   Is it iron-fortified?

   (   ) Yes   (   ) No

   Vegetables? _____

   Fruit/juice? _____   Egg yolk? _____

   Meat and other protein? _____

   Table food? _____   Finger foods? _____

k. Do you make your own baby food?

   (   ) Yes   (   ) No

   Or do you use commercial foods?

   (   ) Yes   (   ) No

l. Does your infant spit up often or have loose or hard stools? _____

m. Do you think the child has a feeding problem?

   (   ) Yes   (   ) No

   If yes, describe _____

   _____

THE YOUNG CHILD NUTRITION QUESTIONNAIRE

> Select appropriate questions from the Generic Nutrition Questionnaire and then consider inclusion of the following questions:

Questions to be answered by parent or caregiver.

Data   *Follow-up Required*

(For children more than 1 year of age but less than 4 years of age)

a. Does the child drink anything from a bottle?

( ) Yes   ( ) No

If yes:

( ) Milk   ( ) Other

Specify _____

_____

b. Does the child take a bottle to bed?

( ) Yes   ( ) No

If yes, what is usually in the bottle?

_____

c. How would you describe the child's appetite?

( ) good   ( ) fair   ( ) poor

Other (specify) _____

_____

d. Does the child eat clay, paint chips, or anything else not usually considered food?

( ) Yes   ( ) No

If yes: What? _____

How often? _____

THE ELDERLY NUTRITION QUESTIONNAIRE

Select appropriate questions from the Generic Nutrition Questionnaire and then consider inclusion of the following questions:

For questions with numbered answers, circle the number beside the answer given by the respondent.

Data

Follow-up Required

a. How do you buy your food?
   1. Buy it myself.
   2. Go food shopping with a relative or friend.
   3. Have the food bought for me.
   4. Don't need to buy food at a store because I eat in a restaurant.
   5. Don't need to go food shopping because I eat with my family.

b. If you buy food at a store, which of the following foods do you buy every week?

1. Milk	8. Canned or frozen fruit
2. Eggs	9. Fresh vegetables
3. Cheese	10. Canned or frozen vegetables
4. Meat	11. Bread
5. Fruit juice	12. Crackers
6. Fresh fruit	13. Canned soup
7. Cereal	14. Canned fish

c. Do you need assistance with food shopping?

   (   ) Yes   (   ) No

   If yes, do you get the assistance you need?

   (   ) Yes   (   ) No

d. Are there days in the week when you don't eat?

   (   ) Yes   (   ) No

   If yes, which of the following reasons best describes your reason for not eating?
   1. I don't have any food in the house.
   2. I feel too sick to eat.
   3. I feel too depressed to eat.
   4. Other (give reason) _____

e. How many hot meals do you usually have each day?

    More than 3   3   2   1   Less than 1

f. How many times in a day do you usually eat?

    More than 3   3   2   1   Less than 1

g. Do you eat meals at a congregate feeding site?

    (   ) Yes   (   ) No

    If yes, how many meals do you get there per week?

    7   6   5   4   3   2   1

h. Do you get home-delivered meals?

    (   ) Yes   (   ) No

    More than 7   7   6   5   4   3   2   1

i. If you are not getting home-delivered meals, are you on a waiting list?

    (   ) Yes   (   ) No

    If yes, how long have you been on the waiting list?

    1. Less than a month

    2. 1-3 months

    3. More than 3 months

Source: Adapted from: Nutrition Questionnaire in *Nutrition During Pregnancy and Lactation* (California Department of Health, 1975); S. J. Fomon, *Nutritional Disorders of Children: Prevention, Screening, and Follow-up*, DHEW Publication No. (HSA) 77-5104 (U.S. Department of Health, Education, and Welfare, Public Health Service, Health Services Administration, reprinted 1977), 6–11; D. Wong and L.F. Whaley, *Clinical Handbook of Pediatric Nursing*, 2nd ed. (St. Louis: C.V. Mosby Co., 1986), 95; and questionnaires contributed by Irene Alton, Janet King, and Daphne Roe.

Appendix A-2 24-Hour Recall

Name _____   Date of Birth _____/_____/_____

ID# _____Sex _____   month / date / year

				For Practitioner Use	
				Code	
Time	Place	Food	Amount	Food Group	Summary

a. This is a typical day. Yes _____ No _____
b. I take a vitamin/mineral supplement. Yes _____ No _____
    If yes, name the brand _____
c. I have been on a special diet during the past three months. Yes _____ No _____
    If yes, the kind of special diet _____

INSTRUCTIONS:

1. Record time of day or night when you ate food or drank beverages (8 A.M., 9 P.M., etc.).
2. Indicate the place where you ate (home-kitchen, home-living room, restaurant, etc.).
3. Describe the specific food eaten or drunk during a 24-hour period, beginning with the first meal or snack (e.g., fried chicken, plain yogurt); use brand names.
4. Indicate the amount of food or beverage (e.g., ½ cup, 1 slice, 1 chicken leg, etc.).

Source: Adapted from *Nutrition Assessment: A Comprehensive Guide for Planning Intervention* by M.D. Simko, C. Cowell and J.A. Gilbride, pp. 123–124, Aspen Publishers, Inc., © 1984.

Appendix A-3 Food Frequency Form

Client's Name _____   Date: _____

Interviewer: _____

Food	Don't Eat	Do Eat	Serving Size	Number of Servings Per Week
I. Animal and vegetable protein foods Chicken				
Beef, hamburger, veal				
Liver, kidney, tongue, etc.				
Lamb, goat				
Cold cuts, hot dogs				
Pork, ham, sausage				
Bacon				
Fish				
Kidney beans, pinto beans, lentils				
Soybeans				
Tofu				
Eggs				
Nuts or seeds				
Peanut butter				
II. Milk and milk products Milk, fluid: type: _____				
Milk, dry				
Milk, evaporated				
Condensed milk				
Cottage cheese				
Cheese (all kinds except cottage)				
Yogurt				

Food	Don't Eat	Do Eat	Serving Size	Number of Servings Per Week
Pudding and custard/Flan				
Milkshake				
Sherbert				
Ice cream				
Ice milk				
III. Grain products Whole grain bread				
White bread				
Rolls, biscuits, muffins				
Crackers, pretzels				
Pancakes, waffles				
Cereals: Brand: ————				
White rice				
Brown rice				
Noodles, macaroni, grits, hominy				
Tortillas (flour)				
Tortillas (corn)				
Bulgar				
Popcorn				
Wheat germ				
IV. Vitamin-C-rich fruits and vegetables Tomato, tomato sauce, or tomato juice				
Orange or orange juice				
Tangerine				
Grapefruit or grapefruit juice				
Papaya, mango				

Food	Don't Eat	Do Eat	Serving Size	Number of Servings Per Week
Strawberries, cantaloupe				
White potato, yautia, yams, plantain, yucca				
Turnip				
Peppers (green, red, chili)				
V. Leafy green vegetables Dark green or red lettuce				
Asparagus				
Swiss chard				
Bok choy				
Cabbage				
Broccoli				
Brussel sprouts				
Scallions				
Spinach				
Greens (beet, collard, kale, turnip, mustard)				
VI. Other fruits and vegetables Carrots				
Artichoke				
Corn				
Sweet potato or yam				
Zucchini				
Summer squash				
Winter squash				
Green peas				
Green and yellow beans				

Food	Don't Eat	Do Eat	Serving Size	Number of Servings Per Week
Beets				
Cucumbers or celery				
Peach				
Apricot				
Apple				
Banana				
Pineapple				
Cherries				
VII. Snacks, sweets, and beverages Potato chips				
French fries				
Cakes, pies, cookies				
Sweet rolls, doughnuts				
Candy				
Sugar or honey				
Carbonated beverages (sodas)				
Coffee: Type: ————				
Tea: Type: ————				
Cocoa				
Wine, beer, cocktails				
Fruit drink				
VIII. Other foods not listed that you regularly eat				

Source: Adapted from *Nutrition During Pregnancy and Lactation*, California Department of Health, 1975.

Appendix A-4 Food Diary

Name: _____   Date: _____

Please write down everything you eat for three days before your next appointment.

To do this:

1. Write down everything you eat or drink in the order in which it was eaten.
2. Include meals and snacks as well as gum and candy.
3. Write down the amount you eat. Use standard measuring cups and spoons. Record meat portions as ounces.
4. Write down items added to food (sugar on cereal, butter on bread, salad dressing to salad, etc.).
5. Write down the time you eat.
6. Write down how you prepared it (baked, fried, broiled, etc.).
7. Include a list of any vitamin and/or mineral supplements you take. Write down the name of the supplement, the amount of vitamins or minerals it contains, and the amount taken.

Examples:

Day 1: Time	Food and Preparation	Amount
12:30 P.M.	Peanut butter sandwich	1 tablespoon peanut butter 2 slices bread, whole wheat
	Milk, 2%	6 ounces

Make a separate sheet for each day.

Source: Courtesy of Deborah Thomas-Dohersen.

Appendix A-5 Food and Activity Record

Date _____   Name _____

Time	Food (quantity-type)	Activity and Length of Time	Where/with Whom	Mood*	How Hungry
Examples:					
9:00 A.M.	Candy bar (1 large)	15 min. in hall	school friend	tired	very
3:00 P.M.	Potato chips ½ medium bag	30 min. watching TV	home, alone	bored	a little
5:30 P.M.	Cola (regular) 1 can	thirsty	work, another store clerk	"down"	thirsty
7:00 P.M.	Cookies (3 chocolate chip)	late for dinner	work, alone	upset	very

*anxious, bored, content, depressed, "down," angry, tired, happy, relaxed, "up," celebrating, other

Source: Adapted from *Food, Nutrition and the Young Child* by J. Endres and R. Rockwell, Copyright © 1985. Merrill Publishing Company, Columbus, Ohio. Used with permission. Also, courtesy of Irene Alton.

Dietary Evaluation Tools

Appendix B-1 Food Group Guide and Suggested Portions*

Food Groups	Average Size Serving	Suggested Number of Servings Daily — Age								Pregnant	Lactating
		1-3	4-6	7-10	11-14	15-18	19-22	23-50	51 and Older		
High vitamin A vegetables and fruits		½-1½	1½-2	2	2-3	2-3****	1-2	1-2	1	1-2	1-2
Broccoli, chicory, Brussel sprouts	½ cup cooked										
Greens: beets, collard, dandelion, mustard, kale, bok choy, watercress, Swiss chard, carrots, pumpkin, sweet potato and yams, winter squash	1 cup raw / ½ medium potato, yam, squash										
Apricots, cantaloupe, mango, papaya	½ small cantaloupe, mango or papaya										
Vitamin C rich fruits and vegetables		1	1	1	1	1	1-1½	1½-2	1	1	1-2
Orange and orange juice, grapefruit and grapefruit juice, tomato and tomato juice, tangerines, papaya, cantaloupe, strawberries, acerola cherry, mango, green and red peppers, cauliflower, raw cabbage	1 medium fruit / ½ cup fruit juice / 1 cup tomato juice / ¾ cup strawberries / ½-1 cup raw vegetables										

Suggested Number of Servings Daily

Food Groups	Average Size Serving	Age								Pregnant	Lactating
		1-3	4-6	7-10	11-14	15-18	19-22	23-50	51 and Older		
Other fruits and vegetables											
Asparagus, artichokes, beets, corn, green peas, celery, lettuce, potatoes, stringbeans, summer squash, turnips, ñame, plantain, cucumbers, zucchini, chili pepper	½ cup cooked 1 cup raw	2-2½	2-3	2-3	4-5	4-5****	2-3	2-3	2-3	2-3	2-3
Apple, banana, cherries, pineapple, watermelon	1 medium fruit 1 cup pineapple or watermelon										
Protein foods											
Animal—Fish, chicken, turkey, duck, lean meat (beef, pork, lamb, goat, rabbit), liver, kidney, tongue	1-2 ounces cooked	1½-2	2-2½	2½-3	3	4-5****	2-3	2-3	2	2-3	2-3
Vegetables—Legumes: dried peas and beans, soybeans, tofu, peanut butter, nuts and seeds	½ cup cooked legumes 2 tablespoons peanut butter 3 ounces tofu 1 medium egg	3-4/wk	3-4/wk	2-3/wk	2-3/wk	2-3/wk	2-3/wk	2-3/wk	2-3/wk	2-3/wk	2-3/wk

*Also see Chapter 2.
**Use low fat milk.
***Amount suggested should support adequate weight gain.
****Lower number servings for females.

Suggested Number of Servings Daily

Food Groups	Average Size Serving	Age								Pregnant	Lactating
		1-3	4-6	7-10	11-14	15-18	19-22	23-50	51 and Older		
Milk and milk products											
Milk, fluid: whole, low fat, skim	1 cup fluid milk	2-3	3	4**	4**	4**	2-3**	2**	2**	3-4	3-4
	½ cup evaporated milk										
Milk, dry: whole, skim											
Milk, evaporated											
Yogurt—plain, flavored	1 cup										
Cheese—cottage, pot, farmer, American, cheddar	1 ounce hard cheese										
Pudding/custard/flan	½ cup										
Ice cream											
Ice milk											
Sherbert											
Grains: cereals, breads, grain products		3-4	7-8	8-10	8-10	9	6-8	5-6	3-4	6-8***	6-8
Bread: whole wheat, white, rolls	1 slice										
Biscuits, muffins (made with whole grain or enriched white flour)	1 medium										
Pancakes, waffles	2 small										
Cereals: kind _____	½ cup cooked										
brand _____	¾ cup ready-to-eat										
Rice: white, brown, wild											
Pasta: noodles, macaroni, spaghetti	½ cup cooked										
Cornmeal, grits, bulgar, hominy											
Tortillas: flour, corn	6 inches										
Pizza	⅛ slice of 14" pizza										

Suggested Number of Servings Daily

Food Groups	Average Size Serving	Age									
		1-3	4-6	7-10	11-14	15-18	19-22	23-50	51 and Older	Pregnant	Lactating
Fats											
Salad oil, cooking oil Margarine Mayonnaise	1 teaspoon	2	3	3-5	4-5	4	3-4	4-5	4	3-4***	3-4

*Also see Chapter 2.
**Use low fat milk.
***Amount suggested should support adequate weight gain.
****Lower number servings for females.

Appendix B-2 Recommended Dietary Allowances, Revised 1980.* Designed for the maintenance of good nutrition of practically all healthy people in the U.S.A. Food and Nutrition Board, National Academy of Sciences-National Research Council

age and sex group	weight kg	weight lb	height cm	height in	protein g	fat-soluble vitamins			water-soluble vitamins							minerals					
						vitamin A μg R.E.†	vitamin D μg‡	vitamin E mgα T.E.#	vitamin C mg	thiamin mg	riboflavin mg	niacin mg N.E.¶	vitamin B$_6$ mg	folacin|| μg	vitamin B$_{12}$ μg	calcium mg	phosphorus mg	magnesium mg	iron mg	zinc mg	iodine mg
infants																					
0.0-0.5 yr.	6	13	60	24	kg.×2.2	420	10	3	35	0.3	0.4	6	0.3	30	0.5**	360	240	50	10	3	40
0.5-1.0 yr.	9	20	71	28	kg.×2.0	400	10	4	35	0.5	0.6	8	0.6	45	1.5	540	360	70	15	5	50
children																					
1-3 yr.	13	29	90	35	23	400	10	5	45	0.7	0.8	9	0.9	100	2.0	800	800	150	15	10	70
4-6 yr.	20	44	112	44	30	500	10	6	45	0.9	1.0	11	1.3	200	2.5	800	800	200	10	10	90
7-10 yr.	28	62	132	52	34	700	10	7	45	1.2	1.4	16	1.6	300	3.0	800	800	250	10	10	120
males																					
11-14 yr.	45	99	157	62	45	1,000	10	8	50	1.4	1.6	18	1.8	400	3.0	1,200	1,200	350	18	15	150
15-18 yr.	66	145	176	69	56	1,000	10	10	60	1.4	1.7	18	2.0	400	3.0	1,200	1,200	400	18	15	150
19-22 yr.	70	154	177	70	56	1,000	7.5	10	60	1.5	1.7	19	2.2	400	3.0	800	800	350	10	15	150
23-50 yr.	70	154	178	70	56	1,000	5	10	60	1.4	1.6	18	2.2	400	3.0	800	800	350	10	15	150
51+ yr.	70	154	178	70	56	1,000	5	10	60	1.2	1.4	16	2.2	400	3.0	800	800	350	10	15	150
females																					
11-14 yr.	45	101	157	62	46	800	10	8	50	1.1	1.3	15	1.8	400	3.0	1,200	1,200	300	18	15	150
15-18 yr.	55	120	163	64	46	800	10	8	60	1.1	1.3	14	2.0	400	3.0	1,200	1,200	300	18	15	150
19-22 yr.	55	120	163	64	44	800	7.5	8	60	1.1	1.3	14	2.0	400	3.0	800	800	300	18	15	150
23-50 yr.	55	120	163	64	44	800	5	8	60	1.0	1.2	13	2.0	400	3.0	800	800	300	18	15	150
51+ yr.	55	120	163	64	44	800	5	8	60	1.0	1.2	13	2.0	400	3.0	800	800	300	10	15	150
pregnancy					+30	+200	+5	+2	+20	+0.4	+0.3	+2	+0.6	+400	+1.0	+400	+400	+150	††	+5	+25
lactation					+20	+400	+5	+3	+40	+0.5	+0.5	+5	+0.5	+100	+1.0	+400	+150	††	+10	+10	+50

*The allowances are intended to provide for individual variations among most normal persons as they live in the United States under usual environmental stresses. Diets should be based on a variety of common foods in order to provide other nutrients for which human requirements have been less well defined. See text for detailed discussion of allowances and of nutrients not tabulated. See preceding table for weights and heights by individual year of age and for suggested average energy intakes.

†Retinol equivalents: 1 retinol equivalent = 1μg retinol or 6μg β-carotene. See text for calculation of vitamin activity of diets as retinol equivalents.

‡As cholecalciferol: 10 μg cholecalciferol = 400 I.U. vitamin D.

#α tocopherol equivalents: 1 mg d-α-tocopherol = 1αT.E. See text for variation in allowances and calculation of vitamin E activity of the diet as α tocopherol equivalents.

¶1 N.E. (niacin equivalent) = 1 mg niacin or 60 mg dietary tryptophan.

‖The folacin allowances refer to dietary sources as determined by *Lactobacillus casei* assay after treatment with enzymes ("conjugases") to make polyglutamyl forms of the vitamin available to the test organism.

**The RDA for vitamin B_{12} in infants is based on average concentration of the vitamin in human milk. The allowances after weaning are based on energy intake (as recommended by the American Academy of Pediatrics) and consideration of other factors, such as intestinal absorption; see text.

††The increased requirement during pregnancy cannot be met by the iron content of habitual American diets or by the existing iron stores of many women; therefore, the use of 30 to 60 mg supplemental iron is recommended. Iron needs during lactation are not substantially different from those of non-pregnant women, but continued supplementation of the mother for two to three months after parturition is advisable in order to replenish stores depleted by pregnancy.

Note: Revised Recommended Dietary Allowances are expected to be published by late 1989 or early 1990.

Source: Reprinted with permission from *Recommended Dietary Allowance*, Revised 1979. Food and Nutrition Board, National Academy of Sciences-National Research Council, Washington, D.C.

Appendix C
Clinical Tools

Appendix C-1 Clinical Signs Associated with Nutritional Deficiencies

Body Area	Normal Appearance	Clinical Sign(s)	Nutritional Deficiency Indicated
Hair	Shiny, firm, not easily plucked	Hair dull and dry, lack of shine, thinness and sparseness, depigmentation (flag sign), straightness of previously curly hair, easy pluckability	Kwashiorkor; less commonly, marasmus protein-calorie
Face	Uniform skin color, smooth, healthy appearance, not swollen	Depigmentation: skin dark over cheeks and eyes, moon face	Protein-calorie, protein
		Scaling of skin around nostrils, nasolabial seborrhea	Riboflavin or niacin pyrodoxine
Eyes	Bright, clear, shiny, healthy pink moist membranes, no prominent blood vessels	Pale conjunctiva	Anemia: iron, folate, or B_{12}
		Bitot's spots, night blindness, conjunctiva and corneal xerosis (drying), keratomalacia	Vitamin A
		Redness and fissuring of eyelid corners (angular palpebritis)	Riboflavin, pyridoxine, niacin
Lips	Smooth, not chapped	Redness and swelling of mouth or lips, especially at corners of mouth (cheilosis) and angular stomatitis, angular scars	Riboflavin, niacin, iron pyrodoxine
Mouth		Ageusia, dysgeusia	Zinc
Tongue	Deep red in appearance, not smooth or swollen	Glossitis	Niacin, folate, riboflavin, iron, vitamin B_{12}
		Scarlet and raw	Nicotinic acid
		Magenta tongue	Riboflavin
Teeth	Bright, no cavities, no pain	Pitted, grooved teeth	Vitamin D
		Missing or erupting abnormally, gray or black spots (fluorosis) mottled	Fluoride
		Cavities	Poor hygiene and fluoride
		Mottled enamel	Excess fluoride
Gums	Healthy red, do not bleed, not swollen	Spongy, bleeding gums, swollen	Ascorbic acid (vitamin C)
Glands	Face not swollen	Thyroid enlargement	Iodine
		Parotid enlargement	Starvation (protein-calorie)

Body Area	Normal Appearance	Clinical Sign(s)	Nutritional Deficiency Indicated
Skin	No signs of rashes, swelling, dark or light spots	Dryness of the skin (xerosis), sandpaper feel of skin (follicular hyperkeratosis)	Vitamin A or essential fatty acid
		Petechiae ecchymoses	Ascorbic acid and vitamin D
		Red, swollen pigmentation of exposed areas (pellagrous dermatosis)	Nicotinic acid and tryptophan
		Flakiness of the skin, lack of fat under skin	Kwashiorkor, essential fatty acid
		Increased fat	Obesity
		Scrotal and vulvar dermatosis	Riboflavin
Nails	Firm, pink	Nails spoon shaped (koilonychia)	Iron
Muscles and skeletal system	Good muscle tone, some fat under skin, can walk or run without pain	Muscle wasting	Starvation, Kwashiorkor marasmus
		Knock knees or bow legs	Vitamin D
		Thoracic rosary	Vitamin D, ascorbic acid
		Musculo-skeletal hemorrhage	Ascorbic acid
Organ Systems:			
Gastro-intestinal	No palpable organs or masses	Hepatomegaly (fatty infiltration)	Protein
Cardio-vascular	Normal heart rhythm, no murmur, normal blood pressure for age	Cardiac enlargement, tachycardia	Thiamin
Nervous system	Psychological stability, normal reflexes	Psychomotor changes, mental confusion	Kwashiorkor protein, thiamin , nicotinic acid
		Sensory loss, motor weakness, loss of vibration, loss of ankle movement, knee jerks, calf tenderness	Thiamin , vitamin B_{12} deficiency

Note: Data for this table contributed by George Christakis, Kathleen Mammel, Susan Rosenthal, and Celia Padron.

Source: Adapted from McLaren and Burman, *Textbook of Pediatric Nutrition*, 2nd ed. (London: Churchill Livingstone, 1982), 95; Walker and Hendricks, *Manual of Pediatric Nutrition* (Philadelphia: W.B. Saunders Co., 1985), 30; R.M. Suskind and R.J. Varma, "Assessment of Nutritional Status of Children," *Pediatrics in Review* 5 (1984): 199–200; and H.M. Sandstead and W.N. Pearson, "Clinical Evaluation of Nutritional Status," in *Modern Nutrition in Health and Disease*, eds. R.S. Goodhart and M.E. Shils (Philadelphia: Lea and Febiger, 1973).

Appendix C-2 Selected Laboratory Assessment and Diagnostic Implications

Laboratory Test	Diagnostic Implication	Comment
Hemoglobin and hematocrit	Used to screen for anemia; if present, further evaluation done to determine cause	Common nutritional anemias include iron, folate, or vitamin B_{12} deficiency Because of the increase in blood volume, iron requirements go up in growth; pubescence is a common time for anemia to be present
Lead	Measured in the serum; if present, further evaluation done to determine source Need careful investigation for practice of pica	Can occur in children from eating lead-based paint chips or unglazed pottery or from cigarette butts, batteries in mouth, inhaling gasoline fumes, or drinking water containing lead Found in old houses in paint
Total lymphocyte count	Used to screen for immune dysfunction Can occur secondary to severe malnutrition	Diminished cell-mediated immunity and diminished complement protein and hemolytic complement may indicate risk for recurrent and/or significant infection
Glucose	Measured in urine and blood; urine glucose will be positive only if the plasma glucose is markedly abnormal	Elevated in shock, burns, dehydration, and acidosis
Vitamins and minerals	Levels measured directly or by enzyme assay Important for normal cellular composition and function	Laboratory assessment suggested if clinical signs are demonstrated (see appendix C-1) Water soluble vitamins can be measured in the urine
Cholesterol	Elevated serum cholesterol in adults is a major risk factor for coronary heart disease; the incidence of coronary heart disease in adult populations correlates with the cholesterol levels of children in these populations; lower dietary cholesterol and saturated fat in populations correlates with lower plasma cholesterol levels and less coronary heart disease	200 mg/dl desirable blood cholesterol 200-239 mg/dl borderline high blood cholesterol 240 mg/dl high blood cholesterol For children aged 2-19, see Table 12-3

Laboratory Test	Diagnostic Implication	Comment
Lipoproteins	Low-density lipoprotein (LDL) and very low-density lipoproteins (VLDL) are highly correlated with total cholesterol and, like total cholesterol, are atherogenic High-density lipoproteins (HDL) are inversely correlated to total cholesterol and to the occurrence of arteriosclerotic vascular lesions	<130 mg/dl desirable LDL-cholesterol 130-159 mg/dl borderline high risk LDL-cholesterol >160 mg/dl high risk LDL cholesterol For children aged 2-19, see Table 12-3
24-hour urine creatinine excretion	Proportionally reflects amount of muscle mass Creatinine-height index calculated from mg creatinine/24 hour ÷ normal mg creatinine/24 hour × 100 = percentile	Careful collection of specimen is essential Elevation may reflect high-protein diet or exercise Creatinine-height index of less than 90 percent reflects muscle protein store depletion
Urinary urea nitrogen	Will drop with a deficiency of protein intake	Nitrogenous constituent of urine; mean daily excretion of 7-18 g
Delayed hypersensitivity skin antigen testing	Delayed response in malnourished patients	A risk factor for infection, sepsis, and mortality in debilitated patients
Plasma proteins: Albumin	Low plasma levels reflect malnutrition, liver disease, kidney disease, or inflammation of the gut	Due to endogenous albumin synthesis, serum level stays up until very late in protein malnutrition
Transferrin	Decreased levels occur in protein-losing enteropathies, liver disease, and chronic infection; increased levels indicate severe iron deficiency	Transports circulating iron; measurement of transferrin alone is not a reliable index to assess protein nutriture
Thyroxine-binding prealbumin (PA) Retinol-binding protein (RBP)	PA-RBP complex is the most sensitive predictor to assess dietary protein deprivation	The serum levels of PA and RBP in children are approximately half those of adults

Source: Adapted from F.X. Pi-Sunyer and R. Woo, "Laboratory Assessment of Nutritional Status," in *Nutrition Assessment: A Comprehensive Guide for Planning and Intervention*, ed. M.D. Simko, C. Cowell, and J.A. Gilbride (Rockville, Md.: Aspen Publishers, Inc., 1984), 130–174; "The 1988 Report of the Joint National Committee on Detection, Evaluation and Treatment of High Blood Pressure in Adults," *Archives of Internal Medicine*, Vol. 148, May 1988, p. 1017–1188. T.C. Jensen, D.M. Englert, and S.J. Dudrick, *Nutritional Assessment: A Manual for Practitioners* (Norwalk, Conn.: Appleton-Century-Crofts, 1983), 171–190; and J.E. Rhoads, "The History and Development of Nutritional Assessment of the Hospitalized Patients," in *Nutritional Assessment*, ed. R.A. Wright and S. Heymsfield (Boston, Oxford, and London: Blackwell Scientific Publications, Inc., 1984), 1–10.

Appendix D

Anthropometric Tools

Appendix D-1 Weight for Stature: Boys 2 to 18 Years

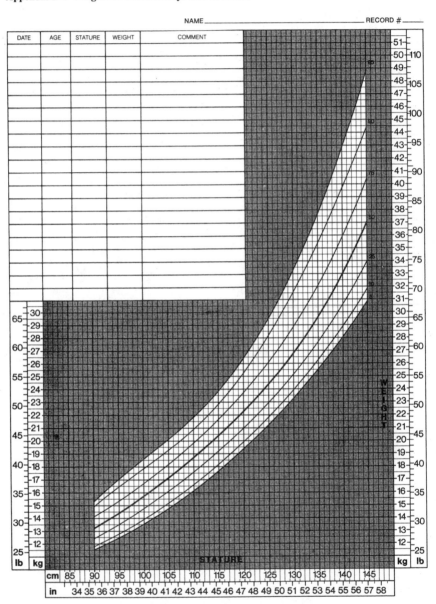

Source: Adapted from: Hamill PVV, Drizd TA, Johnson CL, Reed RB, Roche AF, Moore WM: Physical growth: National Center for Health Statistics percentiles AM J CLIN NUTR 32:607-629, 1979. Data from the National Center for Health Statistics (NCHS), Hyattsville, Maryland. Copyright © 1982 Ross Laboratories.

Appendix D-2 Weight for Age: Boys 2 to 18 Years

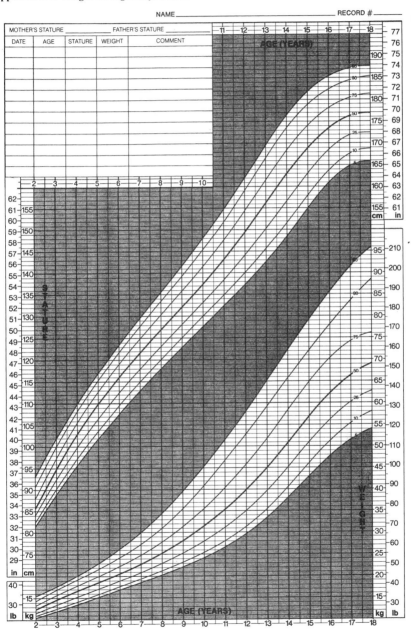

Source: Adapted from: Hamill PVV, Drizd TA, Johnson CL, Reed RB, Roche AF, Moore WM: Physical growth: National Center for Health Statistics percentiles AM J CLIN NUTR 32:607-629, 1979. Data from the National Center for Health Statistics (NCHS), Hyattsville, Maryland. Copyright © 1982 Ross Laboratories.

Appendix D-3 Weight for Stature: Girls 2 to 18 Years

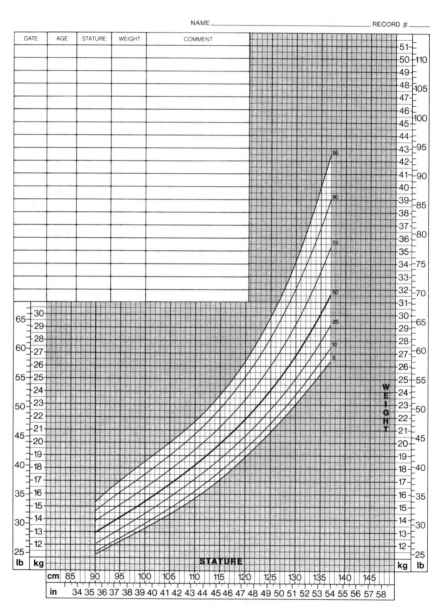

Source: Adapted from: Hamill PVV, Drizd TA, Johnson CL, Reed RB, Roche AF, Moore WM: Physical growth: National Center for Health Statistics percentiles AM J CLIN NUTR 32:607-629, 1979. Data from the National Center for Health Statistics (NCHS), Hyattsville, Maryland. Copyright © 1982 Ross Laboratories.

Appendix D-4 Weight for Age: Girls 2 to 18 Years

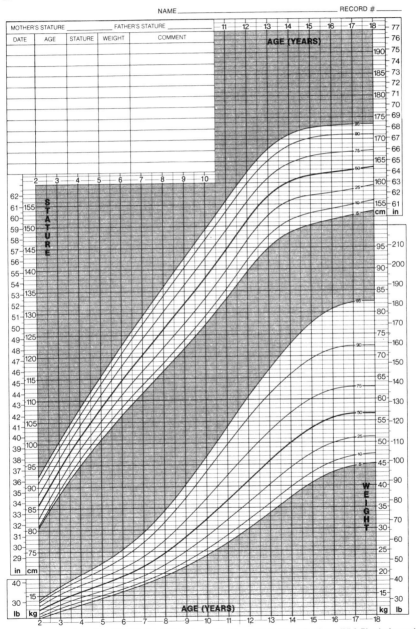

Source: Adapted from: Hamill PVV, Drizd TA, Johnson CL, Reed RB, Roche AF, Moore WM: Physical growth: National Center for Health Statistics percentiles AM J CLIN NUTR 32:607-629, 1979. Data from the National Center for Health Statistics (NCHS), Hyattsville, Maryland. Copyright © 1982 Ross Laboratories.

Energy Information

Appendix E-1 Recommended Energy Intake for Various Age Groups (RDA)

**Food and Nutrition Board, National Academy of Sciences—
National Research Council Recommended Daily Dietary Allowances,[a] Revised 1979
Designed for the Maintenance of Good Nutrition of Practically
All Healthy People in the U.S.A.
Mean Heights and Weights and Recommended Energy Intake**

Category	Age (Years)	Weight (kg)	Weight (lb)	Height (cm)	Height (in)	Energy Needs (with range) (kcal)	(MJ)
Infants	0.0 – 0.5	6	13	60	24	kg × 115 (95 – 145)	kg × .48
	0.5 – 1.0	9	20	71	28	kg × 105 (80 – 135)	kg × .44
Children	1 – 3	13	29	90	35	1300 (900–1800)	5.5
	4 – 6	20	44	112	44	1700 (1300–2300)	7.1
	7 – 10	28	62	132	52	2400 (1650–3300)	10.1
Males	11 – 14	45	99	157	62	2700 (2000–3700)	11.3
	15 – 18	66	145	176	69	2800 (2100–3900)	11.8
	19 – 22	70	154	177	70	2900 (2500–3300)	12.2
	23 – 50	70	154	178	70	2700 (2300–3100)	11.3
	51 – 75	70	154	178	70	2400 (2000–2800)	10.1
	76+	70	154	178	70	2050 (1650–2450)	8.6
Females	11 – 14	46	101	157	62	2200 (1500–3000)	9.2
	15 – 18	55	120	163	64	2100 (1200–3000)	8.8
	19 – 22	55	120	163	64	2100 (1700–2500)	8.8
	23 – 50	55	120	163	64	2000 (1600–2400)	8.4
	51 – 75	55	120	163	64	1800 (1400–2200)	7.6
	76+	55	120	163	64	1600 (1200–2000)	6.7
Pregnancy						+300	
Lactation						+500	

The data in this table have been assembled from the observed median heights and weights of children . . . together with desirable weights for adults . . . for the mean heights of men (178 cm) and women (163 cm) between the ages of 18 and 34 years as surveyed in the U.S. population (HEW/NCHS data).

The energy allowances for the young adults are for men and women doing light work. The allowances for the two older age groups represent mean energy needs over these age spans, allowing for a 2% decrease in basal (resting) metabolic rate per decade and a reduction in activity of 200 kcal/day for men and women between 51 and 75 years, 500 kcal for men over 75 years and 400 kcal for women over 75 (see original text). The customary range of daily energy output is shown for adults in parentheses, and is based on a variation in energy needs of ±400 kcal at any one age (see original text and Garrow, 1978), emphasizing the range of energy intakes appropriate for any group of people.

Energy allowances for children through age 18 are based on median energy intakes of children these ages followed in longitudinal growth studies. The values in parentheses are 10th and 90th percentiles of energy intake, to indicate the range of energy consumption among children of these ages (see original text).

Source: Reprinted with permission from *Recommended Dietary Allowances,* Revised 1979. Food and Nutrition Board, National Academy of Sciences—National Research Council, Washington, D.C.

Appendix E-2 Calorie Expenditure for Various Activities

Activity	Calories Per Hour	Activity	Calories Per Hour
At 300		*At 400*	
Vacuuming	300	Kayaking (2–4 mph)	400–500
Light calisthenics	360	Gardening (digging, bending)	400–600
Dance, slow fox-trot	360	Bicycling	420–660
Basketball	360–660	Stationary cycling (10–13 mph)	420–660
Scrubbing	300–360	Mowing lawn (hand mower)	450
Light carpentry	380	Tennis (singles)	480
Golf, carrying clubs	360	Brisk walking (4 mph)	480
Tennis, doubles	360		
Horseback riding (trot)	360		
At 500		*At 600*	
Mountain climbing	550	Sawing hardwood	600
Cross-country skiing (2½–8 mph)	560–1020	Aerobic dance	600–750
Square dancing	560	Stair climbing	600–1080
		Swimming (50 yards per min.)	
		crawl	750
		backstroke	750
		butterfly	840

Note: Calories expended are for a 150–pound person. There is a 10 percent increase in calories burned for each 15 pounds over 150 and a 10 percent decrease for each 15 pounds under 150.

Source: Reprinted from *The Book of Health* by E.L. Wynder, p. 292, with permission of *The American Health Foundation*, © 1981.

Appendix E-3 The Energy Balance Equation

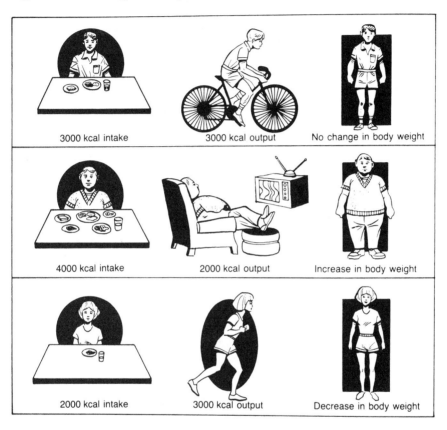

3000 kcal intake	3000 kcal output	No change in body weight
4000 kcal intake	2000 kcal output	Increase in body weight
2000 kcal intake	3000 kcal output	Decrease in body weight

Source: Reprinted from *Nutrition, Weight Control, and Exercise*, 2nd ed., by F.I. Katch and W.D. McArdle, p. 160, with permission of Lea & Febiger, © 1983.

Selected Nutrients and Major Food Sources

Nutrient	Function	Food Sources
Protein	Builds and repairs all body tissues—skin, bone, hair, blood, muscle, etc. Helps form antibodies to fight infection. Is a part of hormones and enzymes that are responsible for regulating body functions, such as digestion and growth. May be used to furnish energy (calories).	Meat, fish, poultry, eggs, dried peas and beans (especially soybeans), milk and milk products, peanut butter, and nuts
Fat	Supplies of a large amount of energy in a small amount of food. Some fats carry vitamins A, D, E, and K. Needed for a healthy skin. Helps delay hunger feelings. Many medical authorities recommend that no more than 30 percent of the calories eaten in a day come from fat.	Oil, shortening, butter, margarine, bacon, visible fat on meat, chocolate, and nuts
Carbohydrates	Supplies food energy. Helps the body make the best use of other nutrients.	Cereal grains, rice, pastas, selected fruits like bananas and dried fruits, and selected vegetables like potatoes, corn, lima beans, and sugar and sweets
Minerals Calcium	Helps build strong bones and teeth. Helps blood clot. Helps muscles and nerves function normally. Needed to activate certain enzymes that help change food into energy.	Milk and milk products, such as cheese; sardines and shellfish; and green leafy vegetables, such as turnips, spinach, and mustard greens
Phosphorus	Helps build strong bones and teeth. Needed by certain enzymes that help change food into energy.	Meat, fish, poultry, dried peas and beans, milk and milk products, egg yolk, and whole grain bread and cereal
Iron	Combines with protein to make hemoglobin, the red substance in the blood that carries oxygen from lungs to cells, and myoglobin, which stores oxygen in muscles. Needed to prevent iron-deficiency anemia.	Liver; red meats; shellfish; egg yolk; dark green leafy vegetables; dried peas and beans; dried prunes, raisins, and apricots; molasses; and whole grain and enriched bread and cereal
Iodine	Necessary for proper functioning of thyroid gland. Prevents some forms of goiter.	Seafoods and iodized table salt

Nutrient	Function	Food Sources
Vitamins		
Thiamin	Promotes normal appetite and digestion. Necessary for a healthy nervous system. Needed in certain enzymes that help change food into energy.	Liver, meat (especially pork), dried peas and beans, wheat germ, and whole grain and enriched bread and cereal
Riboflavin	Helps cells use oxygen. Helps maintain good vision. Needed for smooth skin. Helps prevent scaling or cracking of skin around mouth and nose. Needed in certain enzymes that help change food into energy.	Liver, milk and milk products like cheese, green leafy vegetables, meat, eggs, whole grain and enriched bread and cereal
Niacin	Promotes normal appetite and digestion. Necessary for a healthy nervous system. Needed in certain enzymes that help change food into energy.	Liver, meat, fish, poultry, green vegetables, nuts (especially peanuts), whole grain bread and cereal (except corn), and enriched bread and cereal
Vitamin C	Ascorbic acid. Helps bind cells together and strengthens walls of blood vessels. Needed for healthy gums. Helps body resist infection. Promotes healing of wounds and cuts.	Fruits and vegetables like citrus fruits and juices, broccoli, strawberries, mangos, papaya, tomatoes, cauliflower, cabbage, melons, green leafy vegetables, and potatoes
Vitamin A	Helps keep the skin healthy. Protects against night blindness. Needed for normal vision. Promotes growth and development. Helps build resistance to infection.	Liver, fish liver oils, dark green leafy vegetables, deep yellow fruits and vegetables, egg yolk, butter, fortified margarine, whole milk, and vitamin-A-fortified skim milk
Vitamin D	Helps the body absorb calcium and phosphorus, which build strong bones and teeth.	Vitamin-D-fortified milk, liver, fish liver oils, and egg yolk
Other		
Dietary fiber	Helps keep digestion running smoothly by pushing food through the intestines more quickly. Provides bulk the intestines need to function well.	Whole grain breads, oat cereals and cereal products (wheat germ, bran), fresh fruits with skins, dried fruits, raw vegetables, legumes, nuts

Source: Adapted from U.S. Department of Agriculture, Food and Nutrition Service, 1979.

Food Preparation Tips

Appendix G-1 Ten Tips to Trim Fat from the Diet

Planning Menus

1. Choose low-fat or skim milk products; read all labels.
2. Select fresh fruits for dessert to avoid high-fat bakery products and snack foods.
3. Use more fish and poultry and only lean cuts of meat.

Food preparation

4. Broil, steam, bake, or roast instead of frying.
5. Use tomato juice, vinegar with herbs, or low-fat yogurt instead of oily dressings.
6. Remove the skin from poultry and trim all visible fat from the meat before cooking.

Eating away from home

7. Order salad dressing on the side; use sparingly.
8. Request butter, sauces, and toppings be withheld on entrees and desserts.
9. When possible, choose from a salad bar and avoid oily and high fat dressings.
10. Order foods like:

    Appetizers: fruit or tomato juice, clear soup
    Sandwiches: chicken, fish, or peanut butter
    Salad platter: fish or seafood, chicken, or cottage cheese and fruit
    Entrees: broiled, baked, roasted, or steamed fish, seafood, poultry, or meat
    Vegetables: steamed, baked, or broiled
    Desserts: fresh or canned fruit, unfrosted angel food cake, sherbert or ices
    Beverages: coffee or tea, low-fat or skim milk, fruit juice

Appendix G-2 Low-Sodium Flavor Tips

NO SALTS! NO SUBSTITUTES!
All is not lost! Be adventurous!
Try herbs, spices, and other seasonings.
Go lightly—a little goes a long way.

Using Herbs

With dried herbs, start with ¼ teaspoon in a dish for four.
If you use fresh herbs, use 3 to 4 times the quantity specified for dried herbs. Cutting, crushing, or mincing fresh herbs brings out the volatile oils and true flavors.

Vegetable Juices

For foods that are not to be cooked, such as vegetable juices, add herbs well in advance of serving time—even overnight—so that the full flavor will be developed. The herbs may be tied in a small piece of clean muslin and removed from the juice just before serving.

Salads and Cooked Dishes

For a cooked dish or a salad, the full flavor of the herbs is realized if the herbs are first moistened with a little milk, vegetable oil, or lemon juice and allowed to stand for half an hour before using.

Soups and Stews

For best flavor of soups and stews, add herbs during the last hour of cookery.

Tips on Flavors

Asparagus	lemon, caraway
Beans, green or wax	dill seed, lemon juice, marjoram, nutmeg, rosemary, sugar,* unsalted French dressing*
Beef	bay leaf, dry mustard, green pepper, grape jelly,* marjoram, mustard, nutmeg, onion, pepper, sage, thyme
Broccoli	lemon juice, oregano, tarragon
Chicken	cranberries, ginger, mushrooms, paprika, parsley, sage, tarragon, thyme
Corn	chives, green pepper, tomato
Eggs	curry, dry mustard, green pepper, jelly,* mushrooms, onions, oregano, paprika, parsley, tomato, tumeric
Fish	basil, bay leaf, chervil, curry, dry mustard, dill, green pepper, lemon juice, mushrooms
Lamb	basil, curry, garlic, mint, pineapple,* rosemary
Peas	chives, green pepper, mint, mushrooms, onion, parsley
Pork	apples,* applesauce,* garlic, onion, sage
Potatoes	green pepper, mace, onion, parsley, rosemary
Squash	basil, ginger, mace, oregano
Sweet potatoes	apples,* cinnamon, nutmeg, brown or white sugar*
Tomatoes	basil, onion, oregano, sage, sugar*
Veal	bay leaf, currant jelly,* curry, ginger, marjoram, spiced peaches or apricots*

*May be used if calories are not restricted.

Experiment with caution. Combine with imagination and a bit of common sense.

Source: The New Jersey Heart Association in cooperation with New Jersey State Department of Health and Corinne Robinson, Former Head, Department of Food and Nutrition, Drexel Institute of Technology.

Appendix H

Nutritional Hazards of Vegetarian Diets

Diet Classification	Animal Protein Consumed	Possible Nutritional Problem
Lacto-ovo vegetarian	eggs, milk, dairy products	Low energy
Lacto vegetarian	milk, dairy products	Low energy and iron
Vegan	none	Low energy, B_{12}, iron, protein, calcium, vitamin D, riboflavin

Source: Adapted from *Pediatric Clinics of North America*, Vol. 32, No. 2, p. 431, with permission of W.B. Saunders Company, © 1985. Contributed by Deborah Thomas-Dobersen.

Appendix I

Selected Resource Listings

The government agencies and professional organizations listed often provide nutrition information and/or materials.

GOVERNMENT

Congress

Select Committee on Aging, Subcommittee on Health and Long-Term Care	(202) 226-3381
Select Committee on Hunger	(202) 226-5470

Department of Health and Human Services

General Information	(202) 245-6296
Administration on Aging	(202) 245-0641
Food and Drug Administration	(301) 443-3170
Health Resources and Services Administration	(301) 443-2086
National Center for Health Statistics	(301) 436-8500
National Institutes of Health	
Main number	(301) 496-4000
National Library of Medicine	(301) 496-6095
National Center for Education and Maternal Child Health	(301) 496-1752
National Institutes on Aging	(301) 443-4515
National Institutes of Mental Health	(301) 443-4515
Office of Disease Prevention and	
Health Promotion	(202) 245-7611
Health Information Center	(800) 336-4797
Office of Human Development Services	(202) 472-7257
Institute of Medicine	(202) 233-2180
Veterans Administration	(202) 233-2180

U.S. Department of Agriculture

Food and Nutrition Information Center	(301) 344-3719

PROFESSIONAL ASSOCIATIONS AND PRIVATE RESEARCH GROUPS

American Anorexia/Bulimia Association .... (201) 836-1800
American Association of Family Physicians .... (816) 333-9700
American College of Sports Medicine .... (317) 637-9200
American Dental Association .... (800) 621-8099
American Diabetes Association .... (800) ADA-DISC
   Virginia and District of Columbia .... (703) 549-1500
American Dietetic Association .... (312) 899-0040
American Heart Association .... (800) 527-6941
American Home Economics Association .... (202) 862-8379
American Medical Association .... (312) 654-5000
American Nurses Association .... (800) 444-5720
La Leche League International .... (312) 455-7730
National Academy of Science .... (202) 334-2000
National Cancer Institute
   Cancer Information Service .... (800) 4-CANCER
Nutrition Foundation .... (202) 659-0074
Society for Nutrition Education .... (303) 831-6338

Index

A

Abdomen, examination of
  in adolescents, 167–68
  in adults, 205
Acquired immunodeficiency syndrome,
  271–78. *See also* AIDS; AIDS client
Acyclovir, nutrient interactions with, *276*
Adolescent(s). *See* Child(ren),
  adolescent
Adult(s)
  anthropometric assessment of, *206–7*,
    208–9, *210*
  cholesterol levels in, *226–27*
  diabetes mellitus in, *230–31*
  dietary assessment of, 221–24
  dietary noncompliance by, 223
  environmental assessment of, 213–14
  ethnic food patterns of, 222
  fad diets for weight loss and, *231–32*
  fat intake by, *226–27*
  food diary for, 222
  food habits of, 222
  health history of, 204, *206–7*
  hypertension in, *227–28*
  laboratory assessment of, 209
  nutritional counseling for, 222–24
  nutritional deficiencies in, 203

nutritional problems of, 224, *224–32*
nutritional risk factors of chronic
  disease in, *206–7*
nutrition assessment of, 203–10
nutrition interventions for, 214–17
obesity in, *224–26*
osteoporosis in, *228–29*
physical assessment of, 204–5
premenstrual syndrome in, *229–30*
supplements used by, 222
AIDS, 271–78
  drug-nutrient interactions in treatment
    of, *275, 276–77*
  protein calorie malnutrition in, 271
AIDS client
  alternative nutritional therapies used
    by, 272, 275, 278
  diarrhea in, *274–75*
  dietary assessment of, 271–72
  esophagitis in, *273–74*
  nutritional problems of, 272, *273–75*
  oral lesions in, *273–74*
  weight loss in, *273*
AL-721, 278
Alcohol
  consumption
    by elderly persons, 238
    during pregnancy, *22*